THE MARXIST CONCEPTION OF IDEOLOGY

A *CRITICAL ESSAY*

MARTIN SELIGER

Professor of Political Science
The Hebrew University of Jerusale

CAMBRIDGE UNIVERSITY PRESS

CAMBRIDGE

LONDON · NEW YORK · MELBOURNE

Published by the Syndics of the Cambridge University Press
The Pitt Building, Trumpington Street, Cambridge CB2 1RP
Bentley House, 200 Euston Road, London NW1 2DB
32 East 57th Street, New York, N.Y.10022, U.S.A.
296 Beaconsfield Parade, Middle Park, Melbourne 3206, Australia

First published 1977

Printed in Great Britain by
Western Printing Services Ltd, Bristol

Library of Congress Cataloguing in Publication Data
Seliger, M
The Marxist conception of ideology.
(International studies)
Bibliography: p.
Includes index.
1. Communism – History. 2. Ideology. I. Title.
HX44.S394   335'.43'8'145   76–11092
ISBN 0 521 21229 4

To R

CONTENTS

Contents

A PREFATORY NOTE AND
ACKNOWLEDGMENTS

For almost two decades now we have witnessed a remarkable resurgence in the West of a concern with Marx and Marxism both scholarly and ideological. Although in the proliferating studies of aspects of Marx's work, it is Marxist and pro-Marxist authors who have taken the lead, they have actually engaged in some criticism, even if on the whole they present, or elaborate on, a Marxian Marxism often more or less removed from Engels. They tend to play down those elements which are regarded as intellectually obsolete and those, above all, which furnish too obvious a foundation for the least engaging traits of communist rule and Marxist revolutionism.

In connection with this trend in Marx scholarship, fundamental tenets of Marxist ideology have regained in the West an ascendancy which in the 1950s nobody could have foreseen, as distinct from having desired. As in the 1920s and 1930s, the political echo nowadays raised by (neo-)Marxist ideology is out of proportion to the number of those actually committed to it. On the one hand, social democrats and progressive moderates in general have been caught napping ideologically on the laurels of post-war recovery and its corollary, the relative ideological quiet of the 1950s, characteristically misconceived as 'the end of the age of ideologies'. On the other hand, they have become increasingly handicapped in their opposition to Marxism by clinging to the belief in the end of the Cold War and all that it meant. Social democrats and progressive liberals have become embarrassed as much by having their policies denounced from the Right as Marxist as by having them disparaged by the extreme Left(s) as anti-Marxist and hence unsocialist and non-progressive. This situation seems to have built up in conjunction with the scare of a nuclear Armageddon attendant upon the competition and confrontation between the super powers in the nuclear arms race, and conducted by proxy, though not always in accordance with their own scenario, in the wars in Korea, Vietnam and the Middle East. To this must be added the adverse economic developments which have set in lately, and which, exploited rather than created by oil-producing countries, have increased anxieties and perplexity. In the pursuit of *détente* and economic self-interest, Western governments, supported by large sections of public opinion, tend to apply double standards by supporting, more than their ideological orientation and long-range national interest would warrant, acts and aspirations of communist states and movements and those which are otherwise undemocratic and by self-definition anti-(neo)colonialist and anti-imperialist.

Now, although these postures are adopted for the purpose of appeasing such forces, and thereby to contain the hold on them by the two communist super powers – that is to say, although these postures do in no way emanate from a pro-Marxist orientation – they nevertheless benefit Marxists at home, because concessions to communist, even more to 'anti-imperialist' regimes (for the most part those opposing the West or imposing on it in order to extract economic and other support), and particularly to revolutionary movements of such persuasions, is a matter of principle for Marxists and pro-Marxists. Thus, even though Marxist ideas are, as always and everywhere upheld by minority groups only, and the largest and best organized in the West, the Italian and French Communist Parties, now endeavour to join coalitions, various tendencies like those intimated have combined in focusing once more an extraordinary amount of attention on Marxism.

This study does not deal with this phenomenon and its manifestations, but it inevitably bears on them in so far as a critical analysis of the Marxist theory of ideology implies a critique of Marxist ideology itself. The assumption of the interdependence between social theory and philosophy on the one hand and ideology on the other is basic to Marxism, and the denial that Marxism itself reflects this interdependence did not survive its founders. Conclusions as to the tenability of Marxist propositions therefore raise the question of the tenability of well known and still widely held Marxist ideological tenets. This fact has not, to the best of my belief, influenced my critical presentation of the Marxist theory of ideology – nor is such an influence inescapably bound up with the interdependence of ideology and social theory.

Academic propriety apart, the plausibility of the claim that my ideological preferences, which I have made no effort either to hide or to elaborate, have in no way affected my judgment as to the validity of Marxian and Marxist propositions and postulates, lies precisely in my ideological preferences. The denial in principle inherent in any authentic version of Marxism of both the desirability and the necessity (except for tactical purposes) of pluralist political democracy and ideological diversity, is the unsurmountable barrier to my becoming a Marxist; and this leaves me free to accept as valid any number of Marxist theoretical assumptions. Conversely, and by the same token, adherents of the fundamental aims and political methods of Marxism need not, and do not, shun admission of the untenability of certain original Marxist propositions. There have been Marxists who in the wake of Lenin defy orthodox premises, but unlike him, are ready to acknowledge this. Neither persisting on this basis in the belief in the possibility and desirability of the classless or even stateless society, nor rejecting this belief on the grounds of upholding public political competition and the tolerance of ideological diversity as the preconditions of advancing and maintaining a society, renders the corrective function of the critical analysis of ideologies irrelevant. From that function ideological change largely derives, for whether acknowledged or not, ideological change is designed to secure the survival of the central tenets of an ideology by adapting it to new insights and requirements. Yet the disproof by argument and by experience of the presuppositions and predictions of an ideology which lay claim to representing its scientific basis, i.e. its verified or verifiable propositions, can also assist in the rejection of that ideology and its cutting down to size in the political struggle over claims and votes.

Thus, because Marxists and non-Marxists remain divided over final goals and fundamental principles, including the methods required for their realization, the critique or invalidation of certain Marxist sociological and philosophical presuppositions need not divide Marxist and non-Marxist scholarship, just as its results cannot remain irrelevant for ideological controversy and reorientation. For obvious reasons, by themselves rather significant, this is more readily evident and applicable where the political outlook of masses and elites is in principle recognized to be a matter of free choice – however weird in itself or socially or otherwise conditioned such a choice might appear to be.

In recording now my acknowledgments of indebtedness, I must first of all mention my friend Professor Leonard Schapiro, who has allowed me to benefit from his erudition and insight, often conveyed through his raising points and questions which also drew my attention to matters so far not sufficiently treated. I owe him a quite special debt of gratitude for his unflagging interest in the progress of this study, which he was the first to read in its penultimate draft, commenting on it perceptively and indeed suggesting the separate publication of what was then intended to form part of another book. It was on his initiative, supported by Professor Geoffrey Goodwin, the director of The Centre for International Studies of the London School of Economics and Political Science, that the Centre invited me to be a visiting fellow for six months, thus enabling me to extend a sabbatical leave for the entire academic year 1970–1. I am also grateful to Professor Goodwin for having given me the opportunity to address his graduate seminar and to benefit from his comments and those of its participants. A similar expression of thanks goes to Professor Bernard Crick whose graduate-staff seminar I addressed three years later. I owe an apology to other friends and colleagues in England whose invitations to speak on the subject I was unable to accept.

In its original form the manuscript was completed in 1971 when I still thought that it would form part of my *Ideology and Politics*. Ultimately, it was not just the question of size but the distinctive nature of the subject matter which made separate publication incumbent. I revised the manuscript for this purpose in London during a term's leave of absence and cast it in its present form during the remainder of the academic year 1974–5, expanding also on the substantive basis and taking into account some more recent publications. As on previous occasions, the participation of talented students in graduate seminars which I conducted was most helpful and induced me to reformulate some arguments. Thanks are due also to my research students and assistants, Mr Yigal Donyetz and Mr Gershon Seyman, for technical help. I am grateful to Mrs Rigbi who checked the English of the first complete draft and to the two friends who have already helped me once in this respect. My colleague Dr David Ricci subjected the argument of the penultimate draft to perceptive scrutiny and Dr Phyllis Gaba of our English Department applied again her sensitivity and resourcefulness to the style and syntax of the final draft.

Of course, I alone am responsible for the imperfections that remain, as well as for the views and arguments presented.

I am indebted to Mrs Regina Alcalay for dealing patiently once more with the intricacies of the various drafts until she could proceed to the production of the final typescript. The Research Fund of The Eliezer Kaplan School of Economic and Social Sciences, The Hebrew University, deserves my gratitude for having provided me with most of the funds needed for editing and typing, and so does the London School of Economics and Political Science for a supplementary grant to this effect.

Lastly, I have myself translated all quotations from works written in languages other than English, except when the bibliographical reference is explicitly to the English translation of such a work.

Jerusalem   M.S.
April 1976

INTRODUCTION

For some decades now the term 'Ideology' has been used in a variety of senses. Recently, some on the whole cursory discussion of the meaning of the term has flared up, especially in conjunction with the post-war evaluation of totalitarianism and the correlative debate about the end of ideology. Yet the problem of an adequate definition and uniform usage of the term is still with us. The definitions which are in use and which, if defended at all, are defended rather by assertion than demonstration, can be divided into two main categories. One may be called the restrictive conception, because it confines the concept to specific political belief systems. The other category of definitions may, I suggest, be designated the inclusive conception, since according to it 'ideology' is applied to all political doctrines. In the context of social and political theory and science, this usage means that the concept covers sets of factual and moral propositions which serve to posit, explain and justify ends and means of organized social action, especially political action, irrespective of whether such action aims to preserve, amend, destroy or rebuild any given order. According to this conception, ideology is as inseparable from politics as politics from ideology.

In my book *Ideology and Politics*[1] I have tried to make out a case for the inclusive conception, by showing that all political belief systems exhibit a basically similar structure of 'formal content', in so far as in each such system descriptive and analytical statements intermingle with prescriptive statements. All political belief systems also fare and function alike in the political process, which is to say that they affect and are affected by it in the same fashion. On the other hand, I have attempted to demonstrate that the employment by modern political scientists and theorists of a conception which does not regard all politics as ideological entails

---

[1] George Allen & Unwin (London, 1976) and Free Press (New York, 1976). References to page numbers apply equally to both editions.

self-contradiction, and is based on criteria which also apply to doctrines, parties and regimes other than those which these criteria are held alone to characterize. These two shortcomings may be noted already in the first and most influential theory of ideology which is based on a restrictive conception of ideology, that of Marx and Engels. With the critical analysis of their theory and with its fate at the hands of the immediate successors of the two founders of Marxism, the present study is concerned.

The tenability of a restrictive conception of ideology obviously does not depend upon the success or failure of Marx and Engels in maintaining such a conception consistently. At the same time, it is significant and symptomatic that Marx, and Engels, too, could not uphold a restrictive conception, and that their most important immediate successors did not abide by the founders' conception. Nevertheless, the two intertwined theses which characterize Marx and Engels's theory of ideology have not ceased to exercise social theorists. The theses are that all socially relevant thought is conditioned by reality (until the disappearance of the division of labour) and that because ideology is so conditioned, it distorts reality. To establish affinities and differences in these respects between Marxist notions and those espoused and applied in modern social theory and research, plainly calls in the first place for a detailed critical account of Marx and Engels's theory of ideology. Surprisingly enough, such an account is as yet lacking.

Both pro- and anti-Marxist bias have played a role in the creation of one-sided versions of the founders' theory. Unprejudiced critical treatments have not been wanting and some have delineated appositely the fundamental problems,[2] but these too are not sufficiently comprehensive. Unbiased analysis certainly has not 'become increasingly impossible'.[3] In academic life in the West, neo-Marxists and survivors of the old radical Left, as well as most orthodox Marxists, have for quite some time now ceased to be an harassed minority. Their convictions, rather than outside pressure, have caused them to be unduly selective in their choice of textual evidence, and to take as bias any criticism by non-Marxist scholars. For the most part, they have either been at pains to

[2] See, for example, the treatments of Barth, Merton and Bendix cited in Chapter 1, note 4.
[3] Without specifying what precisely he had in mind, K. Lenk, *Ideologie, Ideologiekritik und Wissenssoziologie* (Neuwied and Berlin, 1961, repr. 1967), p. 33, made this allegation, which is as out of place today as when it was first made.

present the founders' theory of ideology as essentially self-consistent, or they have tried to explain away contradictions as logical (dialectical) necessities, laying the blame for dogmatism (and vulgarization) at the door of their *bêtes noires*, Kautsky and Bernstein.[4] It is rather ironical, though quite characteristic, that insufficient note is taken by the various schools of Marxists and sympathizers with Marxism of the stance of the two men whom Lenin followed (without acknowledging it in respect of Bernstein) in his attitude towards what by any standards of responsible textual analysis must be appraised as Marx and Engels's dogmatic view of ideological thought.

Thus, despite innumerable comments, especially on various aspects of the founders' theory of ideology, neither this nor its immediate post-Marxian developments have received the attention they deserve in their own right. One reason might be that neither topic has been systematically approached with the question in mind whether a restrictive and pejorative (truth-excluding) conception of ideology can be consistently maintained. At any rate, to view the Marxist conception of ideology from this vantage-point reveals clearly that the founders have been unable, and their most influential successors unwilling, to maintain such a conception. Part of this approach and of the critical and explanatory examination undertaken here represents a distinction basic to the theory of ideology developed in Chapter vi of *Ideology and Politics*. This distinction which I wish to recapitulate briefly at the outset, bears on a phenomenon noted in Marxist theory itself and in the latter's self-justification. Indeed it is as helpful for the interpretation of some of the vacillations of Marxism as for those to be found in any other political and social ideology or philosophy.

[4] Lenk, pp. 33–8, for instance, does most of this quite skilfully in his brief account of the Marxian theory. His account is all the more persuasive since it is not only largely unburdened by references to the sources, but also makes cogent points which could be useful for an amended Marxist theory of ideology. Except for presenting it as the original version, I have nothing against extracting a tenable theory from Marx and Engels's pronouncements. Indeed, this is what my own critical analysis leads towards. For other recent examples of explaining away a fundamental contradiction by disregarding the major aspect of the problem of ideology, see below, pp. 26–7, 55, 69, 73–4. Lukács, as we shall see in some detail, provided an outstanding example for the complete disregard of any inner conflict in Marx's theory of ideology. Lenk's misjudgment of the contribution of Kautsky and Bernstein is noted below, p. 109.

Whatever weight one attributes to the role of political belief systems in guiding, aside from justifying, political action, observation of their use in actual politics reveals that not only are they employed to deal with change, whether advocated or opposed, but that in the process the proponents of a doctrine must also face the challenge of changing the doctrine itself. Party ideologies, and also the more abstract political philosophies (when they refer to matters of immediate political significance), must relate to circumstances which demand compromise over, and even contradiction of, some of their basic tenets. Since in the course of such deviations fundamental principles are not necessarily renounced or altered, all political argumentation normally bifurcates into two interacting and intersecting dimensions: the dimensions of fundamental and of operative ideology, as I call them. To the first dimension belong the principles which determine the evaluation of an existing order, and hence the final goals of the movement or party. These principles also include the broadly conceived ways and means in and by which the goals will be realized. The principles which actually underlie the politics and policy recommendations of parties or, as in political and social philosophies in particular, simply reflect more than do other principles the concern with practical and pressing exigencies, constitute the operative dimension. It is likewise characteristic of all political argumentation that ideologists and political philosophers try to relate the operative to the fundamental dimension. Sometimes this is a straightforward matter, in the main because operative principles may and do reflect fundamental principles quite faithfully. Yet relating the two dimensions to each other frequently serves the purpose of evading the admission of a change in fundamental principles. Then contradictions between fundamental and operative principles are ignored and deviations blurred. These phenomena are not suspended by identifying Marxism as 'a relational philosophy', that is, by actually precluding the possibility of contradictoriness. Such an approach to Marx and Engels's Marxism fails at least in respect of the issue most crucial for the Marxist theory of causation, economic determination, quite apart from issuing generally in inconclusiveness.[5]

---

[5] B. Ollman, *Alienation: Marx's Concept of Man in Capitalist Society* (Cambridge, 1971). On the first point, see below, pp. 44–5. Ollman bases his interpretation on what he presents as Marx and Engels's own 'philosophy of internal relations'. Briefly, such a philosophy involves a conception of social factors as 'tied facets' (pp. 14, 205), intelligible

Awareness of two-dimensional argumentation is thus indispensable in the analysis not only of politics, but of systems of social and political thought in general. These are never far removed from practical and topical issues, and the tensions pervading party ideologies therefore also intrude into political and social philosophies, though normally to a lesser degree. Recognition of the inevitability of the bifurcation of political belief systems, and its more immediate causes, makes it easier to understand the tensions between the strands of argumentation which permeate the Marxian theory of ideology, and the abandonment, or evasion, of the theory's dogmatic hard core by the immediate successors of Marx and Engels. Although they neither called the phenomenon

in terms of their organic conjunction ('inneraction' rather than interaction [p. 17]) and related, therefore, to their own past and future forms, as well as to those of the surrounding factors (p. 18). 'Through its internal ties to everything else, each factor is everything else, . . . and what applies to them necessarily applies to it', i.e. 'has – in theory – the potential to take the names of others . . . when it functions as they do' (p. 23). In the relational conception facts and values are not segregated (pp. 48, 51); apparently opposite qualities are not logically independent of one another; what was identical can become different, and cause become effect, just as North becomes South (pp. 55–6).

Contradictoriness is thus in effect preempted because 'it must be possible' to interpret Marx's theoretical claims 'in a manner . . . compatible' with the divergent principles underlying his description of 'real events', for 'this is how Marx uses his theories in practice' (pp. 8–9; see also pp. 24, 37–8, 41, etc.). This use must not be taken at its face value. In the first place, when 'a thinker [of stature] is shown, practically at every turn, to have strayed from his general conception, there is every likelihood that it is we who have misinterpreted him' (p. 10). Second, 'an ordinary language interpretation' must not be applied to Marx's key terms such as 'primary', 'basic' or 'determining', since he used them ambiguously. His using 'the same words as we do' does not signify that he uses the same concepts (p. 24), and, moreover, he attached different meanings to the same expression (pp. 69–70). Nevertheless in the light of Marx's relational presupposition, 'totality' as the ties of the parts (pp. 32–5), we can infer 'what he could be saying', so that we can understand 'what he is in fact saying' (p. 11).

Ollman admits that his interpretation stands or falls according to whether or not its presuppositions are accepted. Quite apart from the nature of his assumptions and a few explicit objections made in the course of this study, non-acceptance of Ollman's presuppositions is indicated by the fact that, like those who have treated Marx's apparent contradictions as real and significant ones, Ollman himself finally insists that Marx should have given more short definitions and abided by them, or else should have made explicit any changes. Nevertheless, Ollman asserts, perhaps somewhat immodestly, that he 'has . . . provided Marx's terms with the only kind of dictionary they could have' (p. 237).

of two-dimensional argumentation by that name, nor made its substance part of their theory of ideology, the members of the second generation applied the substance of the notion more plainly and self-consciously than other theoreticians. In point of fact, we might well regard the principle of two-dimensional ideological argumentation as an elaboration of the Marxist distinction between 'final goal' and activity in the here and now (Kautsky), or between 'general fundamental aims' and 'the aims of direct and immediate action' (Lenin).[6]

The analysis in Part One of the orthodox Marxist theory of ideology and in Part Two of its unorthodox development in the Marxist camp is thus intended to fill a *lacuna* and to set the historical record straight. Being critical in aim, however, the analysis must transgress the confines set by these purposes, since problems are involved which still occupy students and practitioners of politics. That Lenin's inclusive and hence unorthodox use of 'ideology' squares with Bernstein's critique or orthodox doctrine is indicative not just of affinities that seem strange at first sight, but also of the continued relevance of Bernstein's arguments. Their gist underlies a good deal more in the recent 'humanist' and other reinterpretations of Marx's Marxism than is there acknowledged. In addition, Marxist hypotheses inspire directly modern behavioural views, or reverberate in them. Yet in the context of the latter, basic Marxian tenets more often than not are inverted, although they are intimately connected with the Marxian hypotheses that are made use of in modern behavioural theories.

If Marx's view that all politics so far known are ideological stands in no need of correction, this view, and whatever else in his conception contributes to a pertinent theory of ideology, must be retrieved from his reductionism, which of necessity inheres in what is the latest of the time-honoured attempts to reveal the preponderant cause and ultimate goal of human development. As a consistent and self-contained edifice, Marx's ultimately monocausal system is philosophically much less impressive than

---

[6] K. Kautsky, *Die proletarische Revolution und ihr Programm* (Stuttgart and Berlin, 1922), pp. vi, 2, and 'Die Revision des Programmes der Sozialdemokratischen Partei in Österreich', *Die Neue Zeit*, xx, i, 3 (1901–2), 69; and V. I. Lenin, 'Certain Features in the Historical Development of Marxism', *Zvezda*, 5 January 1911/23 December 1910, in *Selected Works* (2 vols., Moscow, 1946) – subsequently cited as SW – i, 481.

Hegel's, but it has been the most persuasive of all, particularly in politics, but also in its impact on social science. Apart from the vigour with which Marx's main theses were asserted, their influence was perhaps largely due to the appearance of scientific rigour that coated his dogmatic, though fortunately not consistent, treatment of both economic causation and ideology. Modern social empirical researches and theories, which are preoccupied with emulating the more exact sciences, when dealing with the relationship between political orientation and the pursuit of group interests take their cue from Marxian presuppositions. Yet they tend to reverse the significance Marx attached to the dependence of political postures on material group interests. They contrast political allegiance based on group or class identification with ideological politics, whereas Marx maintained that ideology and politics are the corollary of particularist class interests. Similarly, the proponents of the idea of the end of ideology proceeded according to Marxist causality in their explanation of the phenomena which attested in effect the changes rather than the end of ideologies. They regarded the putative evanescence of the divisiveness of the political doctrines prevalent in the West, that is of liberalism and democratic socialism, as the corollary of the economic development and corresponding social consciousness of advanced industrial civilization in the West. At the same time, they inverted Marx's use of the term 'ideology'. Although they used it in a restrictive sense, as he did, they applied it in contrast to Marx, to political belief systems conceived and propagated for the realization of radical structural change, and therefore classified Marxism above all as an 'ideology'.

The two modern reversals of the Marxian tenets just mentioned are rooted in a common ground provided by two Marxian assumptions: first, that socio-economic facts condition the behaviour and destiny of social classes and account for the prevailing superstructure of specifically political ideas and institutions; second, that that which is ideological does not reflect the true nature of the facts. According to Marxism, the superstructure of bourgeois society is ideological inasmuch as it is designed to preserve the *status quo*. Hence bourgeois ideas must do violence to facts just as the bourgeoisie must do violence to the proletariat. Today non-Marxist adherents of a restrictive definition of ideology regard an ideological orientation as reality-transcending and, therefore, as doing violence to facts and justifying the use of violence not in order to maintain, as Marx argued, but to destroy the existing order. Those Marxist and non-Marxist adherents of a restrictive definition who do not evaluate ideology pejoratively also ascribe to it, as Marx did not, the function of justifying radical structural change.

The use of 'ideology' for extremism can be traced back to Mannheim in the sense that this usage represents an inversion of the meaning which Mannheim normally attached to the term. Although generally treating all political doctrines as ideologies, in his abortive attempt to distinguish 'ideology' from 'utopia' Mannheim fell back on the Marxian restrictive connotation of 'ideology' when he opposed it to 'utopia' and defined the latter as the genuinely radical, that is, transformative, genre of doctrines.[7] The modern restrictive use of 'ideology', therefore, reflects by inversion Mannheim's use of 'ideology' in the Marxian sense. 'Ideological' is substituted for what Mannheim called 'utopian' thinking. Indeed, it is on similar grounds that we can trace back to Marx the present-day distinction between the ideological and the matter-of-fact approach – a distinction today applied by many researchers and empirical theorists differently from that which acquired not only notoriety through Marx and Engels's identification of ideology with the falsifying presentation of reality, but also a good deal of bewildering complexity.

In view of these brief indications concerning the relationship between the original Marxist conception of ideology and present-day non-Marxist conceptions, it hardly needs saying that the thematic connection and substantive similarities between them are far from overshadowing their intrinsic difference. Some remarks may be in order, however, to explain why, *mutatis mutandis*, the same applies to the relationship between the critical study of the Marxist conception of ideology and its development in the present book and my attempt in *Ideology and Politics* to arrive by way of eliminating logically and empirically untenable propositions at a generally acceptable conception of ideology, and to elaborate on this basis the foundations of a general theory of ideology.

The thematic connection of the two studies has caused some overlapping, but the difference expressed in the different headings of sections touching on similar (or identical) subjects does not consist merely in the fact that an issue treated *in extenso* in one

[7] See my *Ideology and Politics*, pp. 80–6.

book is summarized in the other. Even where this seems to be the case, apart from the explanation of analytical tools, such as the distinction between fundamental and operative ideology, the approaches to similar, or identical, themes and their treatment vary according to the different subject matter and objectives of the two studies. Thus, the issue of the equation of ideological with distorted thought, and the related question of the partial or complete divorce of ideology from factual or truth content, have been analysed in *Ideology and Politics* in connection with the nature and consistency of the conception of ideology which emerged in the aftermath of World War Two. Only those points of that analysis have been reproduced in the present study which are necessary to demonstrate the general significance and applicability of the criteria used here in the assessment of the self-consistency of Marx and Engels's views on the relationship between factuality and ideology, of the avowed or unavowed changes made by their successors in the Marxist camp, and finally of the solution suggested by Mannheim. Conversely, yet by the same token, ideological pluralism is treated extensively here in Part Three and provides the ground for the conclusion of this book. The phenomenon is of decisive importance in the present study in so far as the demonstration of both its existence and its recognition in original Marxism is concerned, particularly with respect to the significance of these two facts for the tenability of Marxism's most fundamental assumptions. What is summarily reproduced in *Ideology and Politics* serves to underpin the argument against the attempt to set one kind of political belief system, ideology, apart from others, to strengthen the evidence against the tenability in general of a truth-excluding conception of ideology, and to enlarge on the manifestation of ideological pluralism as the concomitant of the inevitable interplay between political doctrines and politics.

The fact that what is ancillary and illustrative in one book assumes not only different proportions but a distinct complexion in the other, and *vice versa*, reflects itself in respect of the two remaining identical issues which are treated in both books. The reificatory implications in the general use of 'class' are demonstrated here in special reference to Marx, whereas in the other study the conclusion reached here is merely mentioned. Concerning the comparative analysis of behavioural and Marxist assumptions about the separability of ideology from class consciousness, diversity beyond thematic identity is clearly evident, inasmuch as the nature of Marxist assumptions and their roots in Marx and Engels are our main concern here and determine the angle from which the difference (and analogy) is assessed, while in *Ideology and Politics* it is the other way about.

The dogmatic association by Marx and Engels of ideology with falseness (and therefore also the belief of latter-day scholars in the mutual exclusiveness of pragmatic and ideological politics) is a continuation of the pejorative meaning the term 'ideology' received almost simultaneously with its appearance in philosophy. There it designated a further attempt at explaining the formation of ideas. The new word did not strike root in philosophy and might not have been heard of any more, except in textbooks, had it not become immediately linked with politics. As a result, the characterization of ideological thought was from the outset clogged and prejudiced by overstatements with derogatory intent.

PART ONE

THE SIN OF OVERSTATEMENT

1

THE PROBLEM AND THE BASIC
CONTRADICTION

i. Birth and Fall

The *Encyclopédie*, the work mainly of men whose political convictions the *idéologues* adopted and extended, does not, as is well known, contain the word *idéologie*. Even doctrine is not dealt with as a separate item, but only *doctrine chrétienne*. It is described as the aim of a religious congregation founded in Cavaillon, Provence,[1] to teach the people in imitation of the apostles the mysteries of the Christian faith. *Idée* we find equated with logic, including sensation and *idée proprement dite*. The latter can assume the form of abstract ideas – *idées générales ou universelles*.[2] These reflect a manner of thinking in relation to universals whose existence is ideal only but which are founded in the nature of things or in the resemblance to particulars. The separate definition of *idéal* severs the bond with reality and already has that pejorative tinge which was to recur in the political connotation possessed almost from the outset by the term *idéologie*. 'On dit c'est un homme idéal, pour déligner le caractère chimérique de son esprit.'[3] The equation of ideal and chimerical precludes the attribution of a corrective function to an ideal since no concession to its realizability is intimated here. In this spirit Napoleon gave the newly coined word *idéologie* his unimaginative but alas effective twist.

The *idéologues* were men who, inspired by Maine de Biran and building on the foundations laid by Locke and developed by Condillac, elaborated theories about the formation of ideas as a science connected ultimately with zoology.[4] The papers Destutt

---

[1] *Encyclopédie ou Dictionnaire raisonné des sciences, des arts et des métiers*, v (Neufchâtel, 1765), 9.

[2] *Encyclopédie*, viii, 489 and 491–2.

[3] *Encyclopédie*, viii, 489.

[4] F. C. Picavet, *Les Idéologues: Essai sur l'histoire des idées et des théories scientifiques, philosophiques, religieuses* etc., *en France depuis 1789* (Paris, 1891). Brief surveys have by now become quite numerous. The one contained in H. Barth, *Wahrheit und Ideologie* (Zürich, 1945), and the critical discussion of Marx and Mannheim and

de Tracy delivered at the *Institut* on this science of ideas, and the papers and discussion which followed, had already given currency to the designations of their subject matter as *idéologie* before the word appeared in 1801 in the title of Destutt's *Traité de l'idéologie*.[5] The philosophical enterprise of establishing a science of ideals in close contact with the natural sciences had a short-lived success. Yet the attempt to link philosophy with the natural sciences was characteristic of a persisting tendency: the breaking loose from metaphysics and theology. Nobody could have been more painfully aware than the theocrats of this elaboration of the anti-metaphysical and anti-theological orientation bequeathed by the eighteenth-century *philosophes*. Thus, the theocrat de Bonald, who used the term at about the same time as Destutt de Tracy, though apparently independently of him, in effect concurred with *l'idéologie*'s major exponent that *idéologie* had replaced metaphysics in becoming man-centred. Bonald's verdict that ideology would, therefore, eventually kill philosophy[6] was in fact taken up by Marx, precisely because the theocrat was far from bemoaning the demise of rationalist philosophy turned ideology. In words which Marx could have used, de Bonald characterized such philosophy as 'a sterile study, the working of thought upon itself, incapable of being creative'.[7]

There was therefore already in existence a negative use of the term 'ideology' which Napoleon could have relied upon when he turned against the *idéologues* and denigrated them for their stubborn adherence to the liberal ideals of the Enlightenment. He closed the section of moral and political sciences at the *Institut* to which almost all the *idéologues* belonged. He also forced them to dissolve *la société d'Auteuil*, a circle that met in the house of Mme de Helvétius, and was regularly attended by Cabanis, Volney, Garat, Chénier, Ginguené, Thurot, Daunou and Tracy,

of the literature of the sociology of knowledge by R. K. Merton, *Social Theory and Social Structure*, rev. edn (New York, 1957), Chapters xii and xiii, still merit special mention, as does R. Bendix on Marx in his succinct account 'The Age of Ideology: Persistent and Changing', in D. E. Apter (ed.), *Ideology and Discontent* (London and New York, 1964), pp. 306–10.

[5] F. Mignet, *Portraits et notes historiques et littéraires*, 2nd edn (2 vols., Paris, 1852), i, 336–8.

[6] A. Naess *et al.*, *Democracy, Ideology and Objectivity* (Oslo and Oxford, 1956), p. 151.

[7] Quoted in Larousse, *Grand Dictionnaire universel du XIXe siècle*, ix (Paris, 1873), under the item '*idéologie*'.

with Siéyès as an occasional visitor. As Mignet said, they culti-
vated philosophy and literature but did not dissimulate their
'philosophical opposition' to the Emperor, who had become increasingly impatient with critics and called 'the last opponents,
disdainfully, *idéologues*'.[8] The disappointment was mutual. These
liberals had pinned their hopes on Bonaparte's assumption of
power, expecting him eventually to bring in constitutional government. Throughout his reign they could neither forgive him his
failure to live up to their expectations nor altogether give up hope.
Even when all was over they did not condemn him indiscriminately.[9]

Napoleon confused what the Encyclopedists had clearly distinguished and what in the retrospective appraisal of Mignet, a
political disciple of the *idéologues*, were not much more than two
simultaneous preoccupations: their philosophical theory concerning the formation of *ideas*, and the defence of their political
ideals. The conceptual confusion that presumably underlay
Bonaparte's use of the new word and the equally loose pejorative
connotation he gave it survived the Emperor. Possessing quite
definite ideas about what a political order should be, that is to
say, entertaining ideals of his own, he in fact reserved for the
ideals of his liberal critics the epithet *chimérique*, which the
Encyclopédie had indiscriminately applied to all ideals. This
simple-minded tendency to consider only one's own ideas and
ideals as realistic also underlay the approach to ideology of a great
thinker like Marx. In the twentieth century, similarly, Bonaparte's
way of hitting at a critically minded minority was perpetuated in
the attitude of the Nazi and other totalitarian regimes or movements towards 'uprooted' or 'cosmopolitan' intellectuals, and in
the attitude to 'eggheads' in America during the 1950s.[10] The
critical detachment of which intellectuals – Max Nordau's *Luft-
menschen* – are thought capable is valued as an asset only in
societies which permit freedom of inquiry and dissent. Such
detachment is the cognitive vantage-point from which falsifica-
tions, delusions and the one-sided pursuit of interests can be

8 Mignet, *Portraits et notes*, pp. 338–9.
9 See M. Seliger, 'Napoleonic Authoritarianism in French Liberal
   Thought', in A. Fuks and I. Halpern (eds.), *Studies in History, Scripta
   Hierosolymitana*, vɪɪ (1961), esp. pp. 256–69.
10 T. B. Bottomore, *Critics of Society: Radical Thought in America*
   (London, 1967), p. 12, and L. Broomfield's definition of an 'egghead'
   quoted here.

revealed, as Mill and Mannheim held in their different ways. The *idéologues* themselves hoped to provide such a vantage-point in their new science of ideas.

Under Napoleon, and after his downfall, Destutt de Tracy's neutral use of the term 'ideology' persisted for some time in the literature. It meant the totality of ideas of mankind (or other zoological species), and a general doctrine about these ideas; it also meant the emotional and volitional elements of convictions: the neutral substratum of Napoleon's specifically political pejorative usage. However, in a dictionary published in 1827,[11] neither this neutral substratum nor the Napoleonic pejorative use is mentioned. The words *idéologie* and *idéologues* make their appearance but they are defined only generally, as, respectively, the science and treatment of ideas and the intellectual faculties of man and the men who occupy themselves with that science. Besides the repetition under *doctrinaire* and *doctrinal* of the definition given in the *Encyclopédie* of *doctrine chrétienne*, the word *doctrine* now occupies a place by itself and is also defined in a general sense: 'connaissances acquises, savoir, érudition, sentiments, maximes, systèmes que l'on enseigne'. Two other significant changes occur in the item *idée*. Firstly, apart from the general definition which subsumes opinions, beliefs, thought and so on under ideas, the disparagement attached to *idéal* in the *Encyclopédie* is now tacitly abandoned, or at least toned down. This would seem to follow from the characterization of *idée*: 'The philosopher forms a system in his idea, the ambitious politician has in his mind projects of elevation.' We may infer that in the wake of the Revolution and the Empire the positive connotation of *idéal* had re-emerged and come to stay. Secondly, and most importantly, the authors quote Buffon's words: 'Our ideas, very far from being capable of being the causes of things [*choses*], are only their effect.' Point is followed by counterpoint and the stage is set for new variations on an age-old theme.

The first elaborate theory known to us of the determination of ideas and ideals is embedded in Plato's political philosophy. I find myself in agreement with Popper's critical evaluation of the nature of Plato's political aims and methods. At the same time, it seems to me that in its general thrust Plato's theory of determina-

---

[11] *Dictionnaire classique de la langue française avec des exemples tirés des meilleurs auteurs français et des notes puisées dans les manuscrits de Rivarol*, par quatre professeurs de l'université (Paris, 1827).

tion has not been much improved upon by subsequent thought. I would call it the theory of the determinability (or manipulation), within limits, of socio-economic determination. The reasons Plato gave for his well known plan of organizing the life of the guardians amply attest his awareness of the decisive impact of socio-economic factors on man's consciousness and social behaviour. Inborn qualities and deliberate selection for rationalized breeding are paramount, but not sufficient. To fulfil their functions properly, the guardians must not become involved in the main forms of conventional socialization, and must therefore abstain from any economic pursuit. Thus, underlying his rules of conduct and education of the guardians is Plato's acknowledgment of the determining power of socio-economic conditions, but the idea includes the assumption that in virtue of his superior knowledge the philosopher-king can devise and create the specific conditions which have the determining effects reason permits us to envisage.

Hence Plato's belief in the possibility of building the best state rests on the premise that most men must remain subject to the undesirable effects of socio-economic determination, which can be obviated only with respect to a specific group of men and women. On the strength of what Plato considered to be the objectively correct idea of the order that corresponds with the division of men according to their different inborn capacities, he believed that through political *fiat* it is possible to create a social environment in which the precisely planned and rigorously controlled education and way of life of a specifically endowed class of men and women will ensure the political consciousness and behaviour of an elite on whose shoulders philosophers can become kings, or kings philosophers. Even the tacit assent of the majority, Plato thought, can be assured with the help of appropriate, though not particularly elaborate or refined, indoctrination.

The Platonic determinability of determination was not only applied in Harrington's *Oceana* but remained a fundamental tenet of eighteenth-century political philosophy. Montesquieu stated, and Rousseau quoted him approvingly, that 'at the birth of societies it is the leaders of states who make the institution[s] and afterwards it is the institution[s] which shape the leaders of states'.[12]

[12] C. L. de Secondat de Montesquieu, *Grandeur et décadence des Romains*, in *Grandeur et décadence des Romains, Lettres persanes, Politique des Romains*, ed. and introd. by E. Faguet (Paris, 1946),

In quoting Buffon's words, the Dictionary of 1827 recalled a later manifestation of a different theory of determination, one, that is, which rejected the Platonic view that ideas were the prime determinant and regarded them as being conditioned by other factors. Destutt de Tracy himself, who in his studies had first turned to Buffon and then to Lavoisier, finally enlarged upon Locke's and Condillac's derivation of ideas from sensory experience. Mignet had made his *début* during the Restoration with a memorable concise history of the French Revolution. Like Mme de Staël before him and other members of his generation, such as Guizot and Thiers, who adopted the liberalism of the *idéologues*, he was far from neglecting social determination and considering history as a fortuitous concatenation of the whims of men.[13] However, he felt that de Tracy's theory of ideas must needs raise the query what 'active principle' that theory leaves to man 'to reflect upon sensation, to produce judgment, to engender will, to practise virtue and love his fellow men'? For if the science of ideas is part of zoology and intelligence is determined by man's physical constitution, 'man is determined in his actions by his desires and his desires by his sensation'. This signifies that there can be nothing but servitude for man, inasmuch as he is only matter.[14] Mignet thought that the assumption of such physiological determination must lead to an egotistic interpretation of life, but he absolved Destutt de Tracy of any such intention.

Like de Bonald's critique of *idéologie*, Mignet's critique anticipated Marx, who strove hard to steer clear of any kind of psychophysiological materialism, although one might ask whether the latter is entirely separable from the socio-psychological conse-

Chapter I, pp. 334–5. J.-J. Rousseau, *Du contrat social*, in *Oeuvres choisies*, Classiques Garnier (Paris, 1954), Book II, Chapter 7. Under the impact of the Napoleonic experience, the Platonic view merged into the conception of the great man's role in history. See my essay mentioned in note 9.

[13] The facts and conclusions indicated here and in the following passage are based on my doctoral dissertation, 'The Conception of History of the French Historians of the Restoration (1815–1830) in their Treatment of French History', unpubl. doctoral thesis (in Hebrew), The Hebrew University of Jerusalem, 1956.

[14] Mignet, *Portraits et notes*, pp. 334, 323–3, 334–5. In his not sufficiently substantiated claim that for its proponents, *l'idéologie* eventually extended also to their political conceptions, H. M. Drucker, *The Political Uses of Ideology* (London, 1974), pp. xii, 5–9, ignores that the determinist implication of *idéologie* proper constitutes the crucial link between the conceptions of ideology of the *idéologues* and of Marx and those who came after him.

quences Marx attributed to extreme socio-economic polarization, leaving capitalist society eventually with a dehumanized proletarian. Such a creature is surely inconceivable except as a bundle of predictable sensory reflexes. Some questions therefore arise concerning the self-liberation *qua* self-rehumanization of the proletariat. Tilting the balance struck in the writings of the French historians of the Restoration between the influence of social conditions and of ideal forces in favour of the former, Marx added to the problem of determination his variation of a likewise old theme. He maintained in principle that in societies as we know them, the dependence of ideas on the relation between economic and social conditions affects adversely the truth-value of ideas. He thus incorporated in his conception of socio-economic conditioning that line of thought on the fact and consequences of imperfect cognition which extends from Plato's denial to those imprisoned in the cave of more than shadows of knowledge (hence their susceptibility to 'noble' lies), through Bacon's 'idols' (especially *idolon specus*), up to Montesquieu's *honneur faux*.[15] In this lineage of thought the correctness of ideas is in various ways not evaluated as the necessary condition of their efficacy as action-oriented ideals. Indeed, neither Marx, the founder of the modern theory of ideology, nor Mannheim, who initiated the modern sociology of knowledge – the science of ideology or, more specifically, of the determination and distortion of social thought by social conditions – was, like Napoleon, guilty of an inadvertent confusion of ideals and ideas. They perpetuated it as a matter of principle on the basis of Marx and Engels's views of the interaction between socio-economic and ideational factors.

II. The tree of knowledge: Elusive and exclusive

It is perhaps rather to those who claim to be following Marx than to non-Marxists that ideology still means, above all, 'false consciousness'. However, there are Marxists and non-Marxists who believe that such consciousness attaches to some, or even to all, socially relevant thought. Since theories about the total or partial 'falseness' of socio-political doctrines have spread beyond the Marxist camp, it seems advisable to begin with some general observations about what has been perceived fairly often to be the vulnerable core of such theories.

[15] See below, p. 20.

Pareto's 'theory of doctrines', for instance, is in fundamental aspects similar to that of Marx, although he tried to put a distance between himself and Marx.[16] Pareto lifted economic interests above all other social motivations and proclaimed economic relations to be a suitable subject matter for scientific thought.[17] He retained the possibility of objective knowledge in one sphere of social activity at the cost of stamping it as non-social. One reason why he remained Marxist against his intention was that he considered economic relations to be the immediately and hence objectively perceptible reality – the non-epiphenomenal matrix. The other reason was that, according to him, all social thought proper consists of 'derivations' whose social utility is anything but an indication of their truth.[18]

This particular variation of 'false consciousness' is not new. It is implicit in Plato's 'noble lie' and Bacon's 'idols'. Or, as Montesquieu said:

> It is true that, philosophically speaking, it is a false honour which guides all the parts of the [monarchic] state; but this false honour is as useful to the public as the true [notion of honour] would be to individuals who could perceive it.

Pushing the point still further, Nietzsche said:

> We are inclined to assert as a matter of principle that the falsest judgments . . . are for us the most indispensable, that . . . without a constant falsification of the world . . . man could not live . . . that to renounce false judgments would be a renunciation of life, a negation of life.[19]

---

[16] Barth, *Wahrheit und Ideologie*, pp. 296, 345; T. Geiger, *Ideologie und Wahrheit, Eine soziologische Kritik des Denkens* (Stuttgart and Wien, 1953), p. 69; and esp. S. E. Finer in his introduction to his selection *Vilfredo Pareto – Sociological Writings*, trans. D. Mirfin (London, 1966), pp. 77f, 84ff; Pareto's text, pp. 166ff, 173f, 183f, 188ff, 201, etc. See also Finer's 'Pareto and Pluto-Democracy: The Retreat to Galapagos', *American Political Science Review*, LXII, 2 (1968), 440–5, esp. 445f.

[17] See Finer's Introduction, p. 44, and Pareto's text, pp. 184ff, 196, 212, 213, for criticism of, and agreement with, 'economic determinism'.

[18] Pareto, pp. 189, 194ff. For the extended and systematic treatment of 'residues', which are the forces of non-logical action and are given logical appearance in 'derivations', see pp. 216ff. M. Ginsberg, 'The Sociology of Pareto', in *Reason and Unreason in Society* (London, 1947), offers an extensive critique of Pareto's conception of 'residues'.

[19] C. L. de Secondat de Montesquieu, *De l'esprit des lois*, ed. G. Turc, Classiques Garnier (Paris, 1949), Book III, Chapter VII; and F. Nietzsche, *Jenseits von Gut und Böse, Werke, Taschenausgabe* (10 vols., Leipzig, 1906), VIII, 12–13.

Pareto also followed his predecessors in thinking that for some people truth about social and political relations was attainable and useful. He quite cogently made the perfection of the art of rulership dependent upon the premise that 'the man who can escape the blind domination of his own sentiments is in a position to make use of the sentiments of other people for his own ends'.[20] But for Pareto to assume such a possibility contradicts his thesis that in their social relations men act according to doctrines which are rationalizations of 'non-logical behaviour'. He settled this contradiction of, or exception to, the rule of falsifying determination as little as he reconciled with it his claim to a scientific 'theory of doctrines'. This theory, like Marx's theory about the prevalence of illusory conceptions of reality, implies what has come to be known as 'the Mannheim paradox', although Mannheim himself was not guilty of it:[21] it is to assume that the unexceptional conditioning of our ideas precludes their objectivity while at the same time claiming objectivity for this proposition and the social analysis resting on it.

Pareto's view that social thought is a rationalization of 'non-logical behaviour' is as distant from, or as contradictorily related to, the assumption of a true theory of social doctrines, as Marx and Engels's most quoted pronouncements on the inevitable clash between the prevalent consciousness and socio-economic reality. Taking into consideration the dogmatic assertions in this respect of both thinkers, as well as those of Mannheim, it is a matter of fundamental truth that our cognitive ideas, to say nothing of our values, consist of thought dictated to us by the situation in which we live, and that we cannot appraise the significance of the situation correctly. To be conditioned is to be barred from comprehensive objective knowledge.

This opinion and the unquestioned exemption of their own theory from this rule exemplify the irreconcilable poles in Marx and Engels's teachings.[22] Marx, Engels, Pareto and Mannheim

20 Pareto, in Finer, p. 244.
21 See below, pp. 133–6.
22 H. B. Acton, *The Illusion of the Epoch: Marxism–Leninism as a Philosophical Creed* (London, 1955), p. 173, contests the validity of the objection. He does little to prove his view but simply reproduces the dichotomous strands of argumentation. On the one hand Acton admits that, according to Marx and Engels, ideologies comprise ideas and consciousness as such (p. 126) and hence also 'systems of thought, outlooks and theories' (p. 174), and all these 'reproduce a false consciousness of things' (p. 126) which goes back to the 'the division

contradicted themselves and even admitted exceptions to both conditioning and distortion; but Mannheim alone was moved thereby to revise the burden of the argument. Marx and Pareto self-contradictorily proceeded on the assumption that everybody but themselves was barking up the wrong tree of knowledge. They generally failed to bring the shifts in their argumentation to bear upon what in the light of these shifts must be considered as over-statements about the case they were trying to make out in principle. The shifts and twists in Marx and Engels's utterances connected with the issue of ideology attest that it is untenable to identify ideology with distorted consciousness and to ascribe it to the belief system of a certain class alone. To demonstrate these specific points, I propose first to turn to Marx and Engels's writings and then to supplement their analysis by Lukács's treatment of their conception of ideology.

of labour between material and mental work'. On the other hand, he accepts as justified that Marx and Engels contrasted their 'positive science of man' with 'ideological reflexes', actually on no other grounds than that they said so. Surely, not to consider whether they were logically at liberty to do so is no foundation for rejecting the argument of those who show the irreconcilability of Marx and Engel's standpoints. Connected with the assertion under discussion here is Acton's attempt to attribute to Marx a distinction within the superstructure of a more and a less distorted dimension. See below, p. 37, note 33.

2

THE FACETS OF ORTHODOX
MARXIST DOCTRINE

i. Exegesis and evidence

In order to buttress the analysis of Marx and Engels's conception of ideology, I turn to Lukács and not to the founders' immediate successors, because he produced an entirely uncritical (and none too polished) synthesis of Marx and Engels's scattered pronouncements on the subject. He did not regard the lack of a concentrated treatment of ideology in their works as a reason for correcting Marxist theory. While Lukács would not condone any 'deviation, improvement or correction' of Marx himself, he was prepared to engage in polemics with Engels over some of the latter's utterances and thereby even to defend orthodox Marxism against Engels, though on the issues connected with ideology he expressed only agreement. But since for many recent interpreters of Marx the relinkage of Marx to Hegel is accompanied by moving Marx away from Engels, it is also of interest to note that in the book often taken to reflect Lukács's most Hegelian phase, the general accusation he levels against Engels is that he sometimes followed 'the false example of Hegel'.[1]

For our purpose it is of particular importance that in his retrospective criticism of *History and Class Consciousness* Lukács should have excluded from his account of the errors of the book not only its definition of orthodox Marxism as a method ('dialectical Marxism is the road to truth'), but also what that method implies, the explanation of 'all ideological phenomena by reference to their basis in economics'.[2] He thus reconfirmed the

---

[1] G. Lukács, *Geschichte und Klassenbewusstsein, Studien über Marxistische Dialektik* (Berlin, 1923), pp. 7, 17, note 1, respectively. He also commented on 'the Hegelian Engels's almost incomprehensible terminological inexactness' in his judgment of the Kantian *Ding an sich* as the barrier to our extension of knowledge (p. 145).

[2] Preface (1967) to the German re-issue in 1968 of *Geschichte und Klassenbewusstsein*, repr. in G. Lukács, *History and Class Consciousness, Studies in Marxist Dialectics*, trans. R. Livingstone (London, 1971), pp. xxv–vii, xvi. Only references to the Preface are to the English translation, while all other references are to the German original cited in note 1.

correctness of Marx and Engels's theory of ideology and the adequacy of his presentation of that theory. In one point alone the young Lukács was unfaithful to both masters. In a few instances he did not use 'ideological' in a pejorative, truth-excluding sense. This mainly terminological *faux pas* was a faint echo of the far-reaching reassessment in the Marxist camp of the relationship between economic base and class consciousness. There seems to be little warranty to disregard these developments, in which Kautsky, Lenin and Bernstein took part, when it is argued that *History and Class Consciousness* recaptures the Hegelian dimensions of Marx's thought, whether or not the book is evaluated as the work most inspired by Hegelianism.[3] For what goes beyond

---

[3] His retrospective criticism of *History and Class Consciousness*, in the Preface of 1967, quite clearly adds up to the conclusion that Lukács regarded the book as the most Hegelian contribution to social theory in his attempt to reinterpret Marxism. True, he confessed his failure to subject the Hegelian heritage, 'a source of confusion' (pp. xxi–xxii), to a thorough-going reinterpretation which might transcend and preserve that heritage (p. xx). He declared that what seemed to him the great merit of the book, i.e. 'to have reinstated the category of totality in the central position' it had in Marx's work, was actually marred by his succumbing to 'Hegelian distortion', since the central position ought to have been accorded to economics. Lukács also said that, while the return to revolutionary Marxism required the revival of the Hegelian tradition (p. xxi), the attempt to do so led him 'to out-Hegel Hegel' (p. xxxiii). All this hardly testifies to underplaying, as distinct from criticizing, the fact that Lukács thought that Hegelianism was central to *History and Class Consciousness*. P. Ludz, 'Der Begriff der "demokratischen Diktatur" in der politischen Philosophie von Georg Lukács', in Ludz (ed.), *Georg Lukács: Schriften zur Ideologie und Politik*, Sociologische Texte, vol. LI (Neuwied and Berlin, 1967), p. xxxviii, finds that in comparison with earlier writings, Lukács's interpretation of 'objective possibility' and hence of class consciousness reflects an increase in *History and Class Consciousness* of Hegelian influence. While M. Watnik, 'Relativism and Class Consciousness: Georg Lukács', in L. Labedz, *Revisionism: Essays in the History of Marxist Ideas* (London, 1962), p. 152, and G. Lichtheim, *Lukács* (London, 1970), p. 55, in fact agree with Lukács's own assessment that he re-revealed the Hegelian cast of Marx's thought, it is in apparent contrast to the views so far cited that R. N. Berki, 'Georg Lukács in Retrospect', *Problems of Communism*, XXI (Nov.–Dec. 1972), 55, regards *History and Class Consciousness* as being, by comparison with Lukács's later writings, 'a profoundly un-Hegelian work'. Unfortunately Berki does not prove his contention and by and large he in fact follows Lukács's self-criticism. Thus he speaks of the latter's attempt 'to infuse Hegelian dialectical categories with the messianic activist spirit' deriving, according to Berki, 'from Feuerbach and the young Marx', although Lukács himself ascribed it to his 'purely ethical preoccupations' (Preface, p. x), which expressed themselves in the 'passion for revolutionary messianism', or 'messianic

the merely terminological reverberation of the explicit loosening in the Marxist camp of the determinist bond between economic base and ideology stems above all in Lukács's presentation and defence of the original Marxist theory of ideology from his faithful reproduction of Marx and Engels's dogmatic propositions about ideology, as well as of their deviations from these propositions, without, of course, appraising the deviations as such. Much as Lukács indulged retrospectively in pointing out his earlier 'internal contradiction' or even 'mental confusion', he never connected these with any shortcomings in Marx's theory.

His uncritical faithfulness to the founders, therefore, would seem to have been the real object of Zinoviev's denunciation of Lukács's 'extreme left tendency'. If it is fair to accuse Lukács of attributing a role to human consciousness well beyond the 'transcript' doctrine of Lenin's *Materialism and Empirio-Criticism*,[4] it is not less true that he did not go half as far beyond the founders as Lenin did in *What Is to Be Done?*. When it was through the medium of an interpretation of Marxism that Lukács's book created 'an idealized portrait of the revolutionary movement',[5] on the basis that is to say of pre-Leninist orthodoxy, then that interpretation must have proved an embarrassment to the Russian leadership and caused the book's condemnation.[6] After all, it did not take Moscow long to accuse people of doing and saying the opposite of what they were really doing and saying, if this was apt to raise doubts about the doctrinal faithfulness of the reigning potentate(s).

One of the greatest difficulties in the exegesis of even the most important issues in Marx's theoretical endeavours consists in the fact that his published work breaks off at the point where everything seems to indicate that the clarification of the nature of classes was to be taken up systematically.[7] The break-off could

utopianism' (pp. xiv, xxiv), attendant upon his bourgeois provenance and issuing in (idealist) 'sectarianism' – both clearly pointing to the 'confusing' Hegelian heritage.

4 M. Watnick, 'Relativism and Class Consciousness: Georg Lukács', in Labedz, *Revisionism*, pp. 146 n.10, 154.

5 T. B. Bottomore, 'Class Structure and Social Consciousness', in I. Mészáros (ed.), *Aspects of History and Class Consciousness* (London, 1971), p. 56.

6 Given the orthodoxy of Lukács's interpretation, to be demonstrated in this and the following chapter, I therefore find, unlike Bottomore, p. 62 n.1, and others, that Moscow's attitude is easy to understand.

7 Lukács, *Geschichte und Klassenbewusstsein*, p. 57. W. Sombart, *Der proletarische Sozialismus* ('Marxismus'), 10th enlarged edn (2 vols.,

explain why we can discern at least six ways in which Marx and Engels conceived the capitalist class structure. Even admitted that these are in some way reconcilable,[8] the grounds of equivocation remain. Both thinkers were wont to make categorical pronouncements on the central issues of their social theory. These are all connected with the notion of class and are thus likely to vary in accordance with at least some of the six conceptions of the capitalist class structure.[9] Given the intimate relationship between issues of class and ideology, the absence of a systematic treatment of the nature of class might easily account for the other important exegetical obstacle: the absence of a systematic treatment of the nature of ideology.

Marx did not use 'ideology' according to a uniform definition, and the term itself did not occupy a central position in his work. He used interchangeably *Ideologie, Ideen, Anschauungen* and *Doktrinen*.[10] But here again he and Engels made categorical assertions which in principle identified these and similar terms with thought that was distorted, because all socially relevant thought was dependent on economic and social conditions. In so far as Marx did make a distinction between distorted thought and thought conditioned by class and time but reflecting reality faithfully, he did so neither clearly nor consistently, as Max Weber was to do.

Mannheim imputed such a distinction to Marx, but, like Lichtheim, he produced no evidence to bear out his assertion.[11] Indeed,

Jena, 1924), I, 370, thought that the break-off was not accidental because the various and contradictory pronouncements on class could not lead to the uniform definition Marx was aiming at.

[8] S. Ossowski, *Class Structure in the Social Consciousness* (London, 1963), p. 83. According to G. Lichtheim, *Marxism, An Historical and Critical Study* (London, 1961), pp. 380ff, Marx's class theory is restricted to historical change with social conflict as its mechanism.

[9] For a typical semantic inconsistency, see below, pp. 152–3.

[10] Naess, *Democracy, Ideology and Objectivity*, p. 154. Marx also used *Einbildung, Vorstellung* and *Illusion*. As P. Stadler, *Karl Marx, Ideologie und Politik* (Göttingen, Frankfurt and Zürich, 1966), pp. 66–7, observes, Marx neither used *Bourgeois* and *Bourgeoisie* uniformly, nor did he proceed according to a uniform definition of *Proletariat*. Hence also his misconceptions or contradictions as to the confrontation of only two classes (pp. 133–4).

[11] G. Lichtheim, 'The Concept of Ideology', *History and Theory*, IV, 2 (1965), 184. K. Mannheim, *Ideology and Utopia – An Introduction to the Sociology of Knowledge*, trans. L. Wirth and E. A. Shils, Harvest Book (New York, n.d.), pp. 139–40. J. Plamenatz, *Ideology* (London, 1970), pp. 23f, ascribed the distinction to Marx with some qualification ('presumably he meant'), but unfortunately he for the most part made

scholars who reveal a sympathetic approach to Marx, but are not professed Marxists, continue Marxists' attempts to attenuate Marx and Engels's combative and dogmatic pronouncements either by textually unfounded assertions or by the attribution of a modifying intention to the founders' self-contradictions; or else, like some of their Marxist colleagues, they enlarge on some premises and implications of the original doctrine in order to construe a theory that is inspired by Marxian tenets but actually goes beyond the original doctrine, or for that matter, falls short of it.

I propose to show that Marx and Engels's utterances on the problem of ideology exhibit aspects not so much 'related', as different, and that their deviations from positivist combative thought certainly do not create internal conflict at one point alone.[12] Marx's view that in so far as bourgeois society leads to the new society it provides the basis for facing man's real condition, perhaps spells admiration, but certainly not approval, for certain elements of bourgeois society and ideology.[13] To assume his approval is to hold that Marx evaluated as inherently positive that in bourgeois conditions and ideology which he considered to be presuppositions and antecedents of the understanding and historical development supposed to issue in the post-bourgeois stage. Berki, in fact, turns into a positive evaluation of certain traits of bourgeois society the function Marx ascribed to bourgeois society in the historical process,[14] a function which Marx of course evaluated positively inasmuch as it was bound to bring about the classless society. An attitude of 'accommodation' alongside one of

> his claims without reference to anybody's text. He could not expect to be taken on trust, since together with perceptive comments and critique, he made assertions which ran straight counter to the text on which he commented. See, for instance, below, note 21 and Chapter 4, note 21.
>
> [12] As Drucker, *The Political Uses of Ideology*, p. 15, and R. N. Berki, 'The Marxian Conception of Bourgeois Ideology: Some Aspects and Perspectives', in R. Benewick, R. N. Berki and B. Parekh (eds.), *Knowledge and Belief in Politics: The Problem of Ideology* (London, 1973), p. 89, respectively maintain.
>
> [13] Berki, pp. 95, 98–100.
>
> [14] Whether this confusion can be attributed to Marx or not, Berki has not so far proved, and I doubt whether it can be done. He favours in this connection the view of H. Lefebvre, *The Sociology of Marx*, trans. N. Guterman (London, 1968), p. 85, that truth and falsity are dialectically related to each other, the first emerging from the second. Berki concludes, however, that the two are generally blended in ideas 'in a hopelessly conceptual tangle' (pp. 92–3; see also pp. 101–2, 106–7).

'conflict' towards bourgeois society and thought is again not indicated by Marx's admission that bourgeois achievements will be carried over into the post-capitalist stage, for these achievements are to be perfected, and thus transformed, as part of an entirely new socio-economic setting.

The different aspects which, according to Drucker, are implicit in Marx and Engels's statements concerning the problem of ideology are certainly not those referring on the one hand to 'false consciousness' and on the other to the function of a theory in serving the theorist's class interests and in influencing people to act. On both Marxian and logical grounds it is untenable to maintain that bourgeois ideology at different stages presents either 'false consciousness' or 'apology' (inconsistent and incoherent views or deliberate distortion designed to advance partisan interests).[15] An incomplete and incoherent view issues in distortion, just as an opinion misleading intentionally or otherwise does, and this, as will be shown, is what Marx's notion of the illusory or falsifying consciousness of the bourgeoisie amounts to. Such misunderstanding and misrepresentation of reality is, in his view, the corollary of the predetermined pursuit of bourgeois interests. True, he also said that bourgeois thought can be more or less scientific – or rather more or less unscientific – or even correct in certain points. This is indeed one of the 'autonomous positions'.[16] It must be understood, however, that these positions remain unreconciled in Marx and Engels's theory of ideology.

To appraise correctly that theory and its inner difficulties, or conflicting aspects, it is inappropriate to relegate into the background Marx and Engels's direct statements on the problem of ideology and the issues intimately connected with it. The occasional praise they bestowed on the classical economists is by no means unimportant, but is actually supplementary evidence of their deviation from the dogmatic standpoint. Drucker relies solely on this evidence, while for Berki Marx's attitude towards his great bourgeois intellectual predecessors, especially Hegel and Ricardo, is more significant in this respect than other evidence. For instance, Drucker implies clearly that Marx used the *word* 'ideology' in different senses. I have found no textual evidence for this and Drucker offers none.[17] To argue, like Berki, that Marx thought

---

[15] Drucker, *The Political Uses of Ideology*, pp. 15, 24, 101.
[16] Drucker, p. 26.
[17] Drucker, pp. 30–1. Similarly Ollman, *Alienation*, p. 6, who says that

Hegel and Ricardo 'certainly not "ideological" in the sense of error, falsehood or illusion, otherwise Marx would not have spent so much time and energy in studying them',[18] is surely a *non sequitur*, apart from being wrong in substance. The passage from the postscript to the second edition of *Kapital* adduced by Berki to circumscribe Marx's aim to reveal 'the rational kernel within the mystical shell [of Hegel's philosophy]' attests no intention of rescuing that philsophy as it stands from the realm of ideology, but merely shows what Marx thought that philosophy ought to – or could – have been. Not only does Berki disregard the passage that begins with the words 'One must turn it [Hegel's philosophy] upside down', but also fails to take into account that in the same context Marx unmistakeably accused Hegel of having committed a fundamental error. It consisted in that

> for Hegel, the thought process, which he even transformed under the name idea into an independent subject, is the demiurge of reality, which represents only its external appearance. With me, by contrast, the ideational [*das Ideelle*] is nothing but the material [*das . . . Materielle*], transposed and translated in the head of man.[19]

' "ideology" . . . refers at times to all ideas', distinguishing furthermore two additional senses of 'ideology' which are actually variations of the same proposition. For textual evidence in the matter, he refers to G. Gurvitch, *Le concept des classes sociales de Marx à nos jours*, Centre de documentation universitaire (Paris, 1954), as having been 'able to provide supporting evidence' for 'thirteen meanings of "ideology" in Marx's writings'. In the first place, going by the edition just cited, Gurvitch only attributes the first eight meanings to Marx (pp. 29–30). Secondly, he supplies no detailed textual references to the Marxian texts he mentions in his inexact statements about these different uses, and he dispenses with references altogether in his summary presentation of the eight meanings. These are, moreover, far from overlapping only 'very partly' ('qui ne se recouvrent que très partiellement'). They are all reducible to the core propositions which in the following section of this Chapter will be shown to emerge from my textual analysis, which demonstrates that the term does not, for example, gradually assume a wider meaning (p. 28), nor does Marx apply it to his own communist doctrine or speak of 'l'idéologie prolétarienne', as would seem to follow from Gurvitch's use of the phrase (p. 30).

18 Berki, 'The Marxian Conception of Ideology', p. 98.
19 For further evidence for Marx's regarding Hegel as 'ideological', see, for instance, below, pp. 53–4. Here it bears repeating once again the core of Marx's own view of both his indebtedness and his opposition to Hegel: 'My dialectical method is in its foundation not only different from the Hegelian [method] but its direct opposite . . . I criticized the mystifying aspect of Hegel's dialectic almost thirty years ago, at a

Indeed the disregard of this clear-cut evidence is as strange as the fact that both Berki and Drucker, like others before them, should also neglect the crucial significance of the causal anchorage by Marx and Engels for the problem of ideology in the relationship between the spheres of the forces of production and of social relations.

The clarification of this key issue indeed will furnish the foundation for the accurate assessment of the facets of the original Marxist doctrine of ideology.

II. The original spectrum

In a famous statement, Engels used the phrase 'false consciousness' in order to define ideology in a generally applicable sense. He wrote:

> ideology is a process accomplished by the thinker consciously, indeed, but with a false consciousness. The real motives impelling him remain unknown to him, otherwise it would not be an ideological process at all.

As Engels explained, the delusion is helped by the fact that inasmuch as 'all action is produced through the *medium* of thought, it appears to him [the thinker] to be also ultimately based upon thought'.[20] It seems that Marx himself did not use the phrase 'false consciousness'. This makes no difference as far as his conception of ideological thought is concerned, since instead of

time when it was still the fashion of the day. But just when I worked out the first volume of *Kapital* it pleased the peevish, conceited and mediocre epigones ... to treat Hegel as ... "a dead dog". I declared myself therefore frankly as a disciple of this great thinker and even flirted here and there ... with the manner of expression peculiar to him. The mystification which the dialectic suffers from Hegel's hand in no way prevents his being the first to present comprehensively and consciously its general forms of movement. It stands with him on the head.' K. Marx, *Das Kapital, Kritik der politischen Ökonomie*, ed. F. Engels, Marx–Engels–Lenin Institut, Moscow, vol. I (Wien and Berlin, 1933), pp. 17–18. I have resorted to this edition in my library only when notes and references made from the edition cited in note 32 and available at the British Library required rechecking. It hardly needs to be added that Marx's words demonstrate the authenticity of Lukács's claim that his attitude towards Hegel is in Marx's spirit.

20 Engels in his letter to Mehring (14 July 1893), in K. Marx and F. Engels, *Selected Correspondence*, repr. (London, 1943), p. 511. Similarly, as early as his letters to Bloch (12 September 1890) and Heinz Starkenburg (25 January 1894), as well as in his Preface of 1895 to Marx's *Class Struggles in France*.

'false', Marx used 'incorrect', 'twisted', 'untrue' and 'abstract' besides nouns like 'illusion', 'block' (*Sparren*), *idée fixe*, etc.[21] We may thus take 'false consciousness' to denote Marx's view as well, the more so as Engels's definition of 1893 expressed the extreme to which both men went, separately and together, in their characterization of ideological thought. As we shall see, they also made statements from which it would appear that distortion is not a necessary corollary of the dependence of thought upon socio-economic conditions. However, they never ceased to reiterate the view that dependence issues in distortion. Rather than holding different views on the subject at different times, as is often asserted, they held the same variety of views at all times – and this indicates their failure to think the matter through systematically.

The unreconciled coexistence of the two views is already evident at the beginning of the co-authored *The German Ideology*. The fundamental postulate is that 'consciousness does not determine life, but life determines consciousness'. Men 'are the producers of their conceptions, ideas, etc.' in so far as these are determined by their social relations, which depend in their turn upon the development of the forces of production. While society, stratification and state are 'constantly reproduced out of the life process of the individuals', these are not the individuals 'as they *might* appear to themselves or to others', but as they really are, that is to say, 'how they produce in certain material conditions' which are independent of their will.[22]

Evidently, Marx and Engels do not here conclude that because men's ideas merely reflect socio-economic reality, without any free creation of it, their ideas must therefore be false. It is false to see oneself and others as creating social reality at will. Marx and Engels do not suggest here that men cannot help thinking that

---

21 K. Marx and F. Engels, *Historisch–kritische Gesamtausgabe* (Frankfurt, Moscow, Leningrad and Berlin, 1927–32), ed. D. Rjazanov and V. Adoratskij, v, 161, 271, 309, 334, 36, 217, 141 (hereafter cited as MEGA). In the *Economic and Philosophical Manuscripts*, Marx used Hegel's 'unhappy consciousness' to characterize Stoicism and scepticism (MEGA, III, 153). The late Professor Plamenatz, *Ideology*, p. 23, asserted, without a single reference to any Marxian text, that 'Marx often called ideology "false consciousness"'. He appeared to have been unaware that some scholars have maintained that Engels used 'false consciousness' only after Marx's death. Cp. E. Hölzle, *Idee und Ideologie, Eine Zeitkritik aus universalhistorischer Sicht* (Bern and München, 1969), p. 107.

22 MEGA, v, 16, 15; my italics.

way. They do assert, however, that such erroneous thought is itself causally related to men's material situation. The creation of ideas, conceptions and consciousness as such is immediately interwoven in the material activity and relationships of men: it is 'the direct emanation of their material postures'. Yet '*also* the fog-formations in the brain of men are necessary sublimations of their material, empirically ascertainable, life process and the material conditions tied to it'.[23]

Clearly, this is not to generalize and claim that men's consciousness is bound to produce unfaithful reflections of that from which it emanates. In the passages I have quoted so far, no more is said than that all thought is conditioned, including false thought. Marx clearly states the empirical ascertainability of the material conditions. It is out of 'the real life-process' that he intends 'to present' (or rather to explain) 'also the development of the ideological reflexes and echoes of this process'. To declare this to be the essence of Marx's conception of ideological thought would be in accordance with his plea, in the same context, for 'the real positive science' which 'begins where speculation ends, with real life', i.e. 'with the presentation of practical activity, the practical process of the development of men'.

However, this view, which is in accordance with the second thesis on Feuerbach, is not consistently maintained. In order to provide grounds for this interpretation, I had to pick quotations out of the same context that contains the formulation no less famous than the one Engels used half a century later in his letter to Mehring:

> If in the whole ideology [the entirety of ideas] men and
> their relations appear to be stood on their head as in a
> *camera obscura*, then this phenomenon derives to the same
> extent from their historical life-process as the reversal on
> the retina of objects [derives] from their immediate physical
> life-process. (MEGA, v, 15)

In the same context where illusory thought is said to be explicable by reference to empirically verifiable observation of real life, Marx announces as an unexceptional occurrence the inversion of cognition relating to the whole institutional and ideational superstructure.

Obviously the passage formed by the quotations adduced in this and the preceding paragraphs is not clear as a whole; it does

[23] MEGA, v, 15, 16; my italics.

not so much permit various interpretations[24] as impede the deduction from itself of a consistent standpoint. It does not, however, lend itself to the interpretation that 'ideology arises from the tendency to be taken in by phantoms' (*Nebelbildungen* being better translated literally by 'fog-formations'), for that, like such words as 'echoes' and the others already mentioned, quite simply denotes the same in Marx as 'ideology'. Likewise, 'ideological illusions', which is a pleonasm anyway, do not have their origin in 'the phenomenal form' of reality, if by that form one means how reality 'is presented [or rather misrepresented] to us',[25] since such 'phenomenal form' thus understood already *is* ideology. If, as Mepham argues, the profusion of metaphors indicates that Marx was not satisfied with any of them (though I side with those who think that the ones indicating removal from and distortion of reality all meant the same thing to him), then it is certainly highly precarious to draw distinctions between Marx's words and formulas not spelled out by him, and to construe on this basis differences between what Marx meant by ideology in the earlier writings and in *Kapital,* as distinct from developing certain and specifically interpreted Marxian premises into a theory of ideology more adequate than the Marxian. The evidence that seems relevant to me for appraising this last does not admit a distinction between the earlier and later conceptions. Mepham, too, eventually confesses that the metaphors associated with that of the *camera obscura,* which means the various ill-adjusted standpoints I have so far culled from *The German Ideology,* continue to occur throughout Marx's later works.[26]

To return to that aspect of the *camera obscura* passage according to which inverted (meaning distorted) cognition is universal, we find four pages later the foundation for holding Marx and Engels logically committed to the assumption that until the advent of communism the clash between consciousness and reality is unexceptional and inevitable.

After the stages of animal-like and tribal consciousness (*Hammel – oder Stammesbewusstsein*), and with the introduction of the division between mental and physical labour, 'the conscious [can] really imagine itself to be something else than the consciousness

24 J. Mepham, 'The Theory of Ideology in Capital', *Radical Philosophy,* II, 2 (1972), 13.

25 Mepham, p. 14, seems to be elaborating here on a distinction Acton imputes to Marx and Engels. See below, note 33.

26 Mepham, p. 18.

of existing practice'. It seems that the conscious is now assumed to indulge invariably in such imagery. For, bound up with the most elementary division of labour and its corollary, the apportioning of enjoyment and labour to different persons, is the contradiction, i.e. the lack of correspondence, between 'the existing social relations' and 'the existing force(s) of production'. Such a contradiction entails that philosophy, morals, metaphysics and all other 'ideological reflexes' are no longer in tune with reality (MEGA, v, 20). It could be argued that Marx wished to confine the clash between ideological reflexes and reality to the occasions when the character of social relations ceases to correspond to the nature of the forces of production. This is the qualification of the ubiquity of 'false consciousness', the qualification which, for all it is worth, Marx and Engels could be said to have adopted in principle. The worth of such an evolutionary conception would seem to be dubious, even if it did not qualify simply as an intermediary stage between degrees of 'false consciousness', but made part of the alternations of the two men between their affirmations of the merely possible and of the necessary falsity of conditioned thought. The latter view is expressed in the context from which I have just quoted.

It is now asserted without any qualification that

> whatever the conscious starts on its own [he uses the slang: *alleene*], we get only this one result out of the whole mess [*Dreck*]: that these three moments, the forces of production, the social situation and the conscious, *can and must* come into contradiction with each other,

the reason of the inevitability of the contradiction being the division into mental and physical labour.[27] Thus, what is expressed through the simile of the *camera obscura* assumes the significance of an inevitable occurrence in the life of society, for all the political struggles in the state are 'nothing but the illusory forms in which the real struggles between the various classes are conducted' (MEGA, v, 23). In the same work (*The German Ideology*), though in a different context, Marx and Engels again deviate from these unequivocal statements by saying that

> the more the normal form of relations [*Verkehrsform*] of society and therewith the conditions of the ruling class develop their contrast to the [more] advanced forces of production, the greater therefore the conflict becomes

27 MEGA, v, 20, the last italics are mine.

> within the ruling class itself and with the dominated class, the more untrue becomes naturally the consciousness *corresponding originally* to this form of relations, i.e. it ceases to be the consciousness that corresponds to the latter. (MEGA, v, 271)

It is assumed that the growing divergence between the forces of production and social relations causes a progression from correspondence of consciousness with social relations to discrepancy between them, or rather to an increase of that discrepancy. For original correspondence involves 'considering the real personal interests as general ones', which was appropriate to prevailing conditions, and constitutes 'adequate false consciousness', if I may use this self-contradictory phrase, which expresses, however, what is really meant here. This consciousness 'deteriorated into merely idealizing phrases, conscious illusion and deliberate hypocrisy'. In the same way utilitarian theory only slowly turned into 'a mere apologia for what exists' (p. 392). We are thus back at the evolutionary conception of 'false consciousness'.

This alternation of categorical assertions about the possible falseness and hence the possible correctness of thought, and its inevitable falseness, repeats itself in the various phases of Marx's writings. (It is only logical that the same should be true of vacillation between assigning a somehow creative function to consciousness and regarding it as irrelevant.) Already in *The Holy Family*, where Marx does not seem to have used the word 'ideology' and refers only to Napoleon's disdain of industrialists and ideologues, we find the qualified statement that 'the "idea" always made a fool of itself *in so far* as it was different from "interests"'.[28] Marx adds that it is easy to understand that each prevailing mass interest, when it first appears on the world stage, is expressed in a form exaggerated in ideas and conceptions. It goes so far beyond even its 'real barriers as to take itself for the human interest as such'. In accordance with the evolutionary conception, restricted falsification, because commensurate with what is accounted for by prevailing conditions, is placed here at the beginning of a process of deterioration which repeats itself in different phases of history.

In *Misère de la philosophie* (1847), Marx reiterated that 'the same men who establish social relations in conformity with their material production produce also the principles, ideas and categories *in conformity* with their social relations'.[29] The statement is

[28] MEGA, iii, 294, 253; my italics.   [29] MEGA, vi, 179–80; my italics.

typical in its ambiguity. Correct reflection of social relations instead of false reflection, but commensurate with social relations, could be meant here. Especially since the latter are said to conform with economic relations, Marx might therefore be supposed to have equated such threefold correspondence with correctness.

In the *Manifesto*, despite the noticeable influence of historism – bourgeois conceptions are not applicable to ancient and feudal property – the basic falseness of bourgeois consciousness is again clearly implied. The ideas and will of the bourgeoisie are rooted in their material conditions and not in eternal laws of nature and of reason (MEGA, vi, 541). As Marx specified elsewhere, he took exception to 'eternal laws of nature [conceived] independently of history'.[30] Indeed, for him, the core of bourgeois 'false consciousness' is the fixation on eternal laws sustaining the belief in the eternal domination of the bourgeoisie. Moreover, according to the *Manifesto*, diverse forms of class conflict and exploitation explain that 'social consciousness has assumed certain forms . . . which will dissolve only with the total disappearance of class conflicts'. Together with classes, all ideologies and ideological consciousness will disappear.[31] This can only mean that all hitherto known forms of consciousness have been 'false', that is, incongruent (although to varying degrees) with the objective conditions of production and yet conditioned by them. According to Marx and Engels it cannot be otherwise, since for them, false consciousness is a corollary of that most elementary division of labour, into mental and physical, which they declared to be at the root of all forms of class conflict and exploitation.

In *Kapital*, too, Marx retained the idea of the necessary distortion of thought. What appears to be

> the complete configuration of economic relations . . . in the conceptions in which the bearers and agents of these relations try to gain clarity about the latter is very different from, and [is] indeed wrong, [and] opposed to, their inner essential but veiled fundamental form [*Kerngestalt*] and its corresponding concept.[32]

---

30 *Zur Kritik der politischen Ökonomie*, ed. K. Kautsky, 7th edn (Stuttgart, 1907), pp. xviii, xxi.
31 MEGA, vi, 544, and i, i, 608.
32 K. Marx, *Das Kapital, Kritik der politischen Ökonomie*, ed. F. Engels, 4th edn, vol. i (Hamburg, 1890); 2nd edn, vol ii (1893); vol. iii (2 vols., 1894), i, 188.

As in the earlier works, a disparity is assumed between the conceptions of those involved in social action and the true nature of those actions. This includes the disparity between an inadequate and the adequate conception, the latter being available in Marx's 'real positive science'. He repeats this stance, together with the evolutionary conception, in the Introduction to the *Critique of Political Economy*. 'When the material forces of production' and 'the relations of production', meaning property relations and social relations in general, come into conflict, 'the entire immense superstructure' becomes involved in the convulsion. At the same time, he argues that the changes in the socio-economic base can be perceived 'truly in the manner of natural science', as distinct from 'the juridical, political, religious, artistic or philosophical, in short the ideological, forms in which men become conscious of this conflict and fight it out'.[33]

To conclude the examination of the evidence found in the pronouncedly theoretical or programmatical writings of Marx and Engels, I propose to turn briefly to the *Grundrisse*. According to David McLellan they present much more than a rough draft of *Kapital*. They are 'in a sense, the most fundamental of all Marx's writings' and apparently were unknown to Engels. If, however, the *Grundrisse* are indispensable in any discussion of the continuity of Marx's thought because they contain 'a synthesis of the various strands of Marx's thought',[34] the issue here treated must

[33] *Zur Kritik der politischen Ökonomie*, pp. iv–vi. This passage in particular, as well as some of those quoted before and in the following pages, obviously do not bear out the view of Acton, *The Illusion of the Epoch*, p. 173, that Marx and Engels set off as closer to social reality law and politics, and together with them legal and political ideologies, from art, religion and philosophy. Returning to the matter, Acton reiterates the same distinction as being one between the politico-legal superstructure and the ideological superstructure (p. 177), arguing that a distinction between the former and 'legal and political *ideologies*' ensues, as it were, from Marx's words: that is, Acton disregards the fact that for Marx both politico-legal institutions and theories are ideological. Indeed, when Acton comments that we can distinguish only between 'behaviour in which ideas and theories are neither explicit nor the prime object of attention, and explicit theorizing about such behaviour' (p. 178), he does not correct Marx and Engels on the basis of the passage he quotes (p. 161) from the Preface to the *Critique of Political Economy*, but gives an apt paraphrase of it. For in it Marx speaks of 'a juridicial and political superstructure ... to which definite forms of social consciousness correspond'.

[34] D. McLellan, *Marx's Grundrisse*, selections, trans. with Introduction (London, 1971), pp. 2–3, 14–15.

be an exception. As in the other works, no coordination of positions is discernible and, indeed, next to nothing is said directly on the relationship between conditioned and distorted thought.

In repeating his basic contention, Marx equates 'idea' with 'abstraction' – a word which he more often than not uses in a derogatory sense – and says that an idea is 'nothing but the theoretical expression of those material conditions which dominate it'.[35] That philosophers have assumed the contrary is characteristic of modern times because, as Marx puts it (very much like Engels in his letter to Mehring), conditions can be expressed only by ideas. It might seem that, just as in the metaphor of the *camera obscura*, the whole problem of distortion could be reduced to the reversal of the true causal concatenation of ideas and socio-economic conditions. However, neither in the *Grundrisse* nor anywhere else does Marx refrain from connecting this basic error with the falsity of specific conceptions and perceptions, and indeed with a whole world view. In continuation of his restatement of the fundamental causal misconception of bourgeois thought in particular, Marx remarked that 'this error was all the more easy to commit from the ideological standpoint . . . since this [causal] dominance of the [material] conditions appeared in the consciousness of the individuals themselves as the dominance of ideas'.

There can be no doubt that in Marx's view the basic error as much underlies as it conforms with other errors, and that all are likewise characteristic of 'the ideological standpoint'. Thus he uses the terminology of ideology *qua* illusory distortion or simply misconception, where he speaks of 'the pure semblance [*Schein*]' of 'the independence of money over and against circulation', when he discusses the errors of Bastiat and other economists, including those of Smith and Ricardo,[36] or when he exposes the misconception of the true nature of exchange value (*Grundrisse*, p. 80), and so on. In parallel with Marx's other writings, and especially with *Kapital*, we also find in the *Grundrisse* acknowledgment of the correspondence of consciousness to reality in so far as both are the inversion of what with respect to the given reality things can and

[35] K. Marx, *Grundrisse der Kritik der politischen Ökonomie*, Rohentwurf, 1857–8; Anhang, 1850–9 (Berlin, 1953), p. 81.
[36] *Grundrisse*, p. 942; cp. also pp. 435, 298, 335–9, 849–56 and 232–9, respectively.

ought to be. Regarding the process of appropriation of the labour of others, 'the process of alienation from the point of view of labour', distortion is 'a *real* one, not only *believed*, not only existing in the mental image of workers and capitalists' (*Grundrisse*, p. 716). The same measuring of mutually corresponding mental and actual distortions of social relations over and against what in their essence, or intrinsic nature, these relations are – i.e. over and against the form which is theirs ontologically and which they could have assumed were they not distorted by the nature of the capitalist system – this, and not the terminologically and substantively misleading distinction between 'real relations' and 'phenomenal form',[37] is involved also in Chapter 17 of Volume I of *Kapital* ('The Transformation of the Value of Labour Power into Wages').

Such a distinction could easily rest on a misreading of *Erscheinungsform* (better rendered by 'manifestation' than 'phenomenal form'), the form, that is, which something, like wage-labour relations, assumes in given circumstances, and not merely how something might appear to us. The first is in each case real and pertains to the domain of verifiable experience, whereas the second may be correct or not and pertains to cognition, a distinction Mepham is well aware of but does not apply in his distinction between 'real' and 'phenomenal' relations which he imputes to Marx, but then mitigates considerably, in his conclusion, though he avoids emphasis of the 'ought'-implication.

After all, the central problem for Marx here was that '*the form of wages extinguishes . . . every trace of the division of the labour day into necessary labour and surplus labour* [*Mehrarbeit*], *into paid and unpaid labour*'.[38] He stated in connection with 'the value of labour' that 'these imaginary expressions stem, however, from the relations of production themselves. They are categories for *manifestations* [*Erscheinungsformen*] of substantial relations', that is to say of both essential and real relations. 'That in their manifestations things often present themselves wrongly', i.e. not in conformity with their real nature (and here lies the science-coated ought-postulate, or, one may say, the notion of the true essence), 'is fairly well known in all sciences, except in political economy' (I, 562). What is hidden by phenomena, like the phenomena themselves, is real, but has to be recognized and consciously

---

[37] As Mepham, 'The Theory of Ideology in Capital', pp. 13–14, argues.
[38] *Kapital* (Moscow edn), I, 565.

apprehended. Thus, 'the relations of property hide the *working-for-himself of the slave*' and 'the relations of money *the working-for-nothing of the wage labourer*' (I, 565). The hidden obviously is as 'real' as the phenomenal. On these grounds we are asked to comprehend 'the decisive importance of the *transformation* of the value and price of labour power into the form of *wages* [*Arbeitslohn*] or into the value and price of labour itself'. If 'on this *manifestation* [*Erscheinungsform*], which makes the real relationship invisible and reveals just its opposite, rest ... all mystifications of the capitalist form of production' (I, 565–6), what becomes invisible is both the normatively and scientifically correct nature and actual essence of this relationship. What is manifest, phenomenally tangible but warping the essence, is not on this account less but rather more real than the relationship, both true and invisible. Indeed, in speaking of the task to discover through scientific endeavour 'the hidden background' of all 'manifestations' which 'reproduce themselves in immediate spontaneity as customary *forms of thought*' (I, 568), the discovery of 'the true nature of things' at once circumscribes explicitly the target of 'formulating it [that nature] consciously' and, by implication, the normative criterion, thus letting the Hegelian, if not Platonic, cat at least glimpse out of the materialistic bag.

The *Grundrisse* reflect, then, the various standpoints we have encountered so far in the works of both Marx and Engels, though in a less directly and clearly expressed form. This consonance seems to indicate quite clearly that the two men felt that basically they had settled the issue satisfactorily. The nature of Engels's later modifications only confirms this conclusion. So far Marx and Engels's express belief in the objectivity of their 'positive science' has almost alone provided secure ground for attributing to them the further view that men's perception of reality, which is conditioned by reality, can also conform with it. This view is also expressed unambiguously in other contexts and this fact (to be demonstrated presently) will buttress the assertion that they failed to reconcile this standpoint with their proposition that because thought is a mental reflex of material conditions, whatever its subject matter, and whether it contemplates action or guides it, thought is distorted. I shall henceforth refer to this derivation as Marx and Engels's programmatic or dogmatic conception of ideology because, as I have tried to show, they not only stand logically committed to it, but the statements made at all stages in the programmatical and theoretical contexts of their work point in that same direction.

Marx and Engels's use of concepts other than 'ideology' does not affect our conclusion. That they spoke sometimes, like Destutt de Tracy, of *Ideen* in a neutral sense[39] is only one example of the shifts of ground away from the dogmatic conception. This holds as central a place in Marx's work as those connotations of the various uses of the term 'class' that characterize his teachings as a whole. This is particularly true of the view that a class is a group which in virtue of its place in the process of production shares a common permanent interest and has an inexorably determined destiny; that it acts and believes (and here the dogmatic standpoints about class and ideology interlock) in conformity with objective necessity, whatever the degree of awareness displayed by individual members or even the entire class of its objective conditions and the transformations necessarily arising out of those conditions.

Since the absence of a systematic treatment of the issue of ideology did not prevent Marx from making the same kind of categorical statement throughout his career, it is unlikely that, had he attempted such a treatment, he would have modified the dogmatic theses in order to remove the quite considerable shifts in his exposition. True, in his drafts Marx often pointed out the need of further elaboration, but that need was always for further demonstration or fuller documentation of a thesis, not for tests of its validity. Yet even if he had unequivocally decided in favour of what I have termed 'the evolutionary proposition', and if, furthermore, we could say (which we really cannot) that his true intention was to say that correct (not less hypocritically nor less consciously idealizing) presentation of reality is possible as long as the forces of production are in harmony with social relations, not much would be changed. If only when the two collide does false consciousness arise, it would merely follow that permanently conditioned thought is not permanently distorted, but that it is totally distorted at the most critical junctures of development.

If it does not matter that at the cross-roads of development only entirely false thought is available, and since in the long run at least development proceeds rationally and irrespective of the will of men, it surely is of no great moment whether correct thought is

[39] Naess, *Democracy, Ideology and Objectivity*, p. 154.

unavailable only at the turning-points of known history or throughout its course. Even if the difference mattered and the evolutionary conception permitted us to identify cognition commensurate with prevailing conditions with correct cognition, the evolutionary proposition would still involve no more than the unreconciled existence in Marx's theory of two standpoints about the result of socio-economic conditioning. For Marx was not logically at liberty to postulate a frictionless relationship between the forces of production and social relations prior to the demise of the division of labour. The distortion of consciousness, we have been told, is a function of the division of labour, and the latter, we learn, will be obviated only when the proletariat abolishes itself together with private ownership and wage labour.[40] Logically, therefore, false consciousness must be the concomitant of all known history and at least of the more immediate post-capitalist future. The mere division between mental and physical labour which is held to induce illusions about reality can coexist with any form of production, as well as with any form of distribution and ownership, even with 'original' and post-capitalist communism, and in accordance with Marxian assumption at that.[41]

I doubt whether Engels was in a better position to extricate himself from these and other difficulties, although in the letter to Mehring, from which I have already quoted, he confessed that Marx and he had neglected 'the formal side' of the theory of ideology. He also admitted that one should not forget that to deny the ideological spheres an independent part in history is not to repudiate all influence of these spheres on even economic facts. Engels, however, leaves no doubt that his concession of some autonomy and adequacy to the ideological spheres leaves the causal preeminence of economics untouched.[42] In fact, his concessions can be derived from Marx's own deviations from the dogmatic position. In accordance with these, Marx, for instance, commented on the interaction between 'production, distribution

---

[40] MEGA, III, 206. Cp. *Die deutsche Ideologie*, MEGA, v, 64.

[41] See below, pp. 113–15, 119–21, 188.

[42] This is admitted by Z. A. Jordan, *The Evolution of Dialectical Materialism* (New York, 1967), p. 320, who attributes to Engels a qualified determinism on account of his utterances in later years (pp. 325ff); but in his *Philosophy and Ideology: The Development of Philosophy and Marxism–Leninism in Poland since the Second World War* (Dordtrecht, 1963), p. 477, Jordan somewhat plays down the adherence of Engels to the ultimate cause. For Engels's letter to Mehring, see above, note 20.

and the market' that such interaction 'is the case in each organic whole'.[43]

To attribute a greater significance to Engels's concessions than Engels did himself is legitimate in attempts to develop Marxism further and to mitigate among other things the deterministic stance in particular. For this purpose, philosophical revolutionists and some Marxiologists bent on presenting Marx's teachings in terms of a predominantly humanist philosophy quote mostly from the young Marx, while reformist social democrats and orthodox party philosophers rely on the old Engels,[44] just as 'humanist' and 'anti-humanist' explications of Marxism by communist philosophers in the West quite often do. That proposed qualifications of Marxist determinism need not obfuscate the mono-causal anchorage of Marx and Engels's conception is perhaps most readily evident in the attempts of Western Marxist Marxiologists to attribute to Marx and Engels an attenuated determinism, or those of Western communist philosophers like Goldmann and Althusser, who propose to go with Marx beyond Marx.[45]

In direct reference to 'the old Engels in 1890', Althusser speaks of 'the two ends of the chain' of determination which Marx has given us: determination 'in the last instance by the economic mode of production and relative autonomy of the superstructures and their specific effectivity'. Althusser also repeats Engels in saying that a theory of superstructures still awaits elaboration and points to Gramsci's sole effort so far.[46] Balibar enlarges on 'the matrix role' of the modes of production and concludes in essentially orthodox fashion that 'the economy is determinant in that it determines which of the instances of the social structure occupies the determinant place'.[47] Things tend to get out of hand when one wants to have it both the orthodox and the (unavowedly) reformist way. Mészáros agrees that human needs cannot be one-sidedly

[43] *Zur Kritik der politischen Ökonomie*, p. xxxiv.
[44] Labedz, *Revisionism*, p. 13 n.6. Ollman, *Alienation*, however, relies, regarding this point, on both the young Marx and the old Engels.
[45] For a 'humanist' interpretation to this effect see, e.g., L. Goldmann, *Recherches dialectiques*, 3rd edn (Paris, 1959), pp. 27f, 67. For a self-styled 'anti-humanist' reading, see L. Althusser, *For Marx*, trans. B. Brewster (London, 1969).
[46] Althusser, pp. 111, 140. For criticism of this view, see below, Chapter 6, ii, and in special reference to Gramsci, and Althusser himself, pp. 112–17.
[47] In L. Althusser and E. Balibar, *Reading Capital*, trans. B. Brewster (London, 1970), pp. 208, 224.

accounted for in terms of economic determination, and argues that by virtue of a 'dialectical methodology' the 'ultimate' economic *'determinants'* are at the same time 'determined determinants'.[48] In plain language this amounts to saying that a thing can be ultimate and at the same time not ultimate. Something like that ought to have followed from the particular variation of 'dialectical methodology' elaborated by Ollman. However, his notion of 'internal relations' reveals its interpretative indeterminateness in so far as the causal interdependence, if not interchangeability, of social factors, which this notion implies, is in fact not applied by Ollman when he deals with the 'long . . . debated' question of the compatibility of Marx's generalizing deterministic statements with his practical exceptions to them.[49]

Ollman admits that for Marx social conditions, in conformity with their relation to the mode of production, determine 'a psychological and ideological superstructure which is practically the same for all men caught up in a given set of material relations'.[50] As to the economic factor, Ollman asserts that in speaking of the economic aspect as 'the determining one', Marx wished 'to emphasize a particular link', or 'the influence most worth noting'.[51] Ollman offers here at best a modifying reading of 'numerous [?] statements by the elderly Engels on the role of non-economic factors', a reading which Ollman tries to read back into Marx, although not without a self-defeating qualification of Engels's retrospective emendation.[52] In sum, Ollman mutes somehow, and actually not more than Engels himself, the causal primacy of the economic factors, for he does not deny that this 'Relation' [*Verhältnis*] is for Marx 'most important'. Moreover, he concedes that Marx left room both for our uncertainty as to how much personal uniqueness the latter was prepared to concede, and for speculation about the explanation Marx would have given to

---

[48] Mészáros, 'Contingent and Necessary Class Consciousness', in Mészáros (ed.), *Aspects of History and Class Consciousness*, p. 86.
[49] See above, p. 4, note 5, and Ollman, *Alienation*, p. 125.
[50] Ollman, p. 121.
[51] Ollman, pp. 17–18. See also pp. 26, 30, 40–1.
[52] Ollman, p. 9 and note 17, pp. 256–7. Ollman admits that Engels made clearer what Marx and he did not mean than what they did mean. Ollman himself does not make it sufficiently clear that Engels did not waver in his adherence to the view that the economic cause remained ultimate, the independent variable, as we would say today. Ollman also fails to take into account that Engels's self-criticism bore on Marx and his neglect of 'the formal side', i.e. of their neglect of a systematic treatment, of the theory of ideology.

justify his admission of the fact that individuals escape socio-economic determination.[53] Ollman concludes rather misleadingly that 'exceptions are admitted . . . but Marx does not allow them to disturb his general rules'.[54] As we have seen, Marx simply made statements offending against his general rules without ever showing any awareness that he was doing so. In the same thematic context Ollman also jeopardizes his assertion that Marx's language requires non-ordinary language interpretation, a requirement taken to indicate that Marx's theorizing is 'relational'. Ollman claims that Marx's use of *bestimmen* as against *bedingen* is significant in that the second verb implies greater flexibility than the first. In fact the deterministic implication of either verb is the same, as is the case with their English translations: 'to determine' and 'to condition'.[55]

In any case, as far as Marx and Engels's conception of ideology is concerned, their deviations from the dogmatic definition are part and parcel of the shifts that arise from the basic ambiguity which I have tried to lay bare and which runs through all phases of their work. The shifts did not lead anywhere near to calling directly into question either the causal primacy of the economic base or the claims on this ground of both the necessary distortion of thought and the likewise ineluctable perception of the ultimate truth by putting oneself, like the founders of Marxist theory, and their (likewise bourgeois) successors, in the position of the proletariat. This is confirmed in Lukács's attempt to weave together the threads of Marx and Engels's argument, for he did so without infringing on its substance at a time when it was no longer a novelty even within the Marxist camp to recognize the need for modifications of some aspects of Marxist doctrine.

[53] Ollman, pp. 129, 124, 125.
[54] Ollman, pp. 126–7.
[55] Ollman, note 23, p. 259. In another instance Ollman tries to strengthen the case for his approach by rendering *anschauen* by 'being aware' (p. 84) instead of by 'looking at', and *Verhalten* by 'orientation' (p. 87) instead of by 'behaviour' or 'attitude'.

3

DISTORTED AND ADEQUATE THOUGHT

1. Ultimate understanding

Like Marx and Engels, Lukács made no attempt to square un-qualified acceptance of the notion of 'false consciousness' with admissions of the possible congruence of conceptions (especially theirs) with reality, or even of the impact of their conceptions on the course of events. Nor did Lukács's awareness of Marx's conceptual indeterminateness or of the absence in Marx's work of the systematic treatment of the class structure deflect him from drawing the conclusion that with Marx *the right method* of the understanding of society and history has been *at last* discovered'. Lukács conceded that the defence on these lines involves proceeding less by defining concepts than by revealing their methodological function.[1] Since the same concepts continued to be used, he argued, the changed meaning which they assumed in Marx's correction of Hegelian dialectics cannot be determined with terminological exactitude (they are not *terminologisch fixierbar*). Whatever the possibility of revealing the methodological function of concepts without defining them with precision, Lukács had no doubt about the inherited dogma that, once a social phenomenon is appraised by right dialectics (albeit in terminologically indeter-

---

[1] Lukács, *Geschichte und Klassenbewusstsein*, p. 17 n.1; pp. 7, 11. This is to rely on Engels's rebuttal of Marx's critics in the former's Preface to vol. III of *Kapital* (Moscow edn), p. 14. It is a mistake to assume 'that Marx wishes to define where he elaborates and that one can look at all in Marx for fixed and finished definitions, applicable once and for all. It is, indeed, self-evident that where things and their mutual relations are conceived not as fixed but changing, their thought images, the concepts, are likewise subject to change and transformation; that one does not encapsulate them in rigid definitions, but develop them in their historical or logical process of formation.' This noteworthy methodological qualification neither prevented Marx and Engels from reiterating, as I have shown in the previous Chapter, the same dogmatic conception of ideology (and from deviating from it), in all stages of their elaborations, nor did it hinder Lukács from attributing definite insights and conceptions to the founders.

minate concepts), the phenomenon is suspended forthwith,[2] i.e. the problem it poses is ready to be solved.

The admission of terminological indeterminateness is not only a sign of intellectual honesty; it is also useful. It preempts objections on the grounds of logical and conceptual consistency, though it does not prevent dogmatic pronouncements about reality – and extraordinary ones at that. Take the argument that once a problem is grasped in its dialectical significance it is 'suspended', because when an insoluble dialectical contradiction has reached its peak, it is condemned to self-dissolution. This derivation is based on a confusion of analytical cognition and prediction, and of both with actual occurrence; it is an empirically unverified, and indeed unverifiable, proposition. The emphasis of method over and against factual knowledge (*Sachkenntnis*) serves the obvious purpose of securing the method against objections on empirical grounds and thus buttresses the assumption of the unity of theory and practice. That unity is postulated in a circular argument: unity is the condition of the revolutionizing function of theory, and this function, on its part, is the condition for consciousness to 'possess' reality. It is quite simply assumed that what is deemed necessary is certain to occur when it is necessary. Marx had sanguinely decreed that 'mankind sets itself only such tasks which it can solve', and he supposed, therefore, that the task will surface 'only when the material conditions of its solution are already at hand, or at least in the process of taking shape'.[3] On this premise the disciple concluded that in a certain historical situation 'the correct appraisal of society becomes for a class the immediate condition of its self-maintenance in combat', and then its self-recognition is at the same time the correct perception of the whole society.[4]

A proper evaluation of reality by those immediately enmeshed in the social struggle is thus far from being dismissed; it is only postponed to a future stage in this struggle, and in any event seems to be the preserve of a specific class. From the empirically verifiable premise of the existence of the exploited proletariat (whose situation began ever so slightly to improve when Marx wrote that it was bound to deteriorate further),[5] the unverifiable

---

[2] Lukács, *Geschichte und Klassenbewusstsein*, p. 12.
[3] *Zur Kritik der politischen Ökonomie*, p. lv.
[4] Lukács, *Geschichte und Klassenbewusstsein*, pp. 13–14.
[5] Improvement cannot be questioned in cases where real wages rose

conclusion is drawn that this class is going to possess the fullest insight, one will and one objective. As Marx said, the proletariat is the 'dissolution of a society as a particular estate [*Stand*], and in announcing the *dissolution of the existing world order*, the proletariat thereby only reveals *the secret of its own existence*' and that of society as a whole. For 'in demanding *the negation of private property*, the proletariat merely posits as *the principle of society* that which society has made into *its* principle'.[6]

This is the highest stage of consciousness. Somewhat disappointingly it consists on the one hand in what hardly anybody could have failed to notice – the principle of private property as the mainstay of bourgeois society – and on the other in what nobody has ever proved to have been the demand of the majority of the proletariat – the negation of private property. Marx could have foreseen this attitude of the working classes perhaps less than the young Lukács.[7] In any case, Marx invested the proletariat with the unitary will to carry out in full consciousness of its 'mental and physical misery' the sentence which private property and wage labour had pronounced upon themselves.[8] Still, as Lukács points out reasonably, and in conformity with Marx's intention, this state of consciousness that encompasses in its understanding society as a whole is the consummation of a long process. It extends 'from the transcendent objectives of the first great thinkers of the workers' movement to the clarity [*sic!*] of the Commune of 1871'.[9] The clear implication is that until the proletariat reaches the highest stage of consciousness its knowledge is incomplete. This must mean that so far the proletariat's thinking too has been permeated with 'false consciousness'.

It therefore emerges by implication not only that bourgeois and proletarian perceptions of reality are comparable but that the difference presumed to exist between the two does not consist in that the proletarian perception is for the time being true only in part, whereas the bourgeois perception is completely false.

and working hours were shortened, even though the share of income to be spent on adequate housing was rising as well, as is argued by G. Best, *Mid-Victorian Britain, 1851–75* (London, 1971), p. 93.

[6] *Zur Kritik der Hegelschen Rechtsphilosophie*, MEGA, i, i, 619–20.
[7] Marx seems, however, to have taken this possibility into account, at any rate hypothetically. See below, pp. 72–3.
[8] *Die heilige Familie*, MEGA, iii, 206.
[9] Lukács, *Geschichte und Klassenbewusstsein*, p. 36.

II. The limitation of bourgeois understanding and the beneficiaries

'Ideology' appears to refer only to bourgeois thought because Marx and Engels developed the notion of the falsity of ideas in regard to the institutional and ideational characteristics of bourgeois society.[10] It is therefore important to recall that in Marx's view the bourgeoisie is not ignorant of the *factum brutum*. Its knowledge remains on the surface and partial[11] because it is the beneficiary of the prevailing socio-economic structure. Bourgeois 'coarseness and lack of conceptual grasp' (*Rohheit und Begriffslosigkeit*)[12] are, therefore, associated with the failure to apprehend the contextual significance of the facts actually perceived about capitalist society. In its turn, this limitation is the inevitable corollary of what delimits the objective situation of the bourgeoisie, the fact that 'the true barrier of capitalist production is capital itself'.[13] It follows, as Marx put it in 1859, that 'the bourgeois relations of production are the last antagonistic form of the societal process of production'. With 'this form of society [i.e. capitalist society] ends, therefore, the prehistory of human society'.[14]

From this contextual significance of bourgeois reality, that is, from what is actually a reality-transcending significance, the bourgeoisie averts its gaze resolutely but also inevitably. In each epoch the thinkers of the dominating class are 'the conceptualizing ideologues who make it their business to develop the illusions of that class about itself',[15] or rather about its fate. Bourgeois thinkers distinguish, for instance, between distribution subject to human decision and production following 'eternal laws' which are independent of men's will.[16] They foster thereby quite

---

[10] Cp. J. Y. Calvez, *La Pensée de Karl Marx* (Paris, 1956), p. 129.
[11] *Kapital*, I, 188, as quoted above, p. 36; and Lukács, *Geschichte und Klassenbewusstsein*, pp. 20, 75.
[12] Marx, *Zur Kritik der politischen Ökonomie*, p. xix. See also p. 11.
[13] *Kapital*, III, 1, 231. See also p. 242.
[14] *Zur Kritik der politischen Ökonomie*, p. lvi.
[15] *Die deutsche Ideologie*, MEGA, v, 36.
[16] *Zur Kritik der politischen Ökonomie*, p. xviii. See also p. xxi. Communist economies certainly do not disprove Mill's view that distribution depends upon the laws and customs of society, a view which Marx tried rather ineptly to confute. J. S. Mill, *Principles of Political Economy*, 7th edn (1871), re-issued with an Introduction by W. J. A. Ashley (London, 1909; repr. 1917), Book II, Chapter I, p. 200. See S. Feuer, 'Karl Marx and the Promethean Complex', *Encounter*,

naturally 'the illusion of the eternity and finality of capitalist production'.[17] Marx and Engels assumed, then, that in subjecting particular factual insights to its interests and, above all, to its efforts to perpetuate its moribund domination, the bourgeoisie becomes utterly incapable of understanding society, as a whole, and by the same token Marx and Engels's knowledge of the future millennium, or acceptance of communism, provides them with 'the relevant measure' for their analysis and condemnation of the capitalist order.[18] The Marxian argument is therefore that it is not any specific verifiable or falsifiable component which eludes the bourgeoisie but the context in which these components must be placed in order to make sense. The cause of this failure is the self-interest of the bourgeoisie which prevents it from including in its comprehension that which, according to Marx, must needs develop out of the existing order. The remarkable thing about this argument is that in the final analysis it makes understanding of the present dependent upon knowledge of the future.

We are faced with an epistemological somersault. We are asked to consider something which is not yet real as the condition of properly understanding the given reality. Hence the assertion that the rejection of the predicted future must engender, or flow from, an erroneous estimate of the given situation. The fallacy is obvious. Underlying it is Marx's false analogy between the anticipation of the end product of a planned process of labour, characteristic of that 'which distinguishes the first architect from the best of bees',[19] and the anticipation of the next stage of development of a complex socio-political system, a stage which in his

    XXXI (December 1968), 22, for a perhaps not sufficiently elaborate dismissal of Marx's attempt to derive distribution from production. For a long-overdue and highly perceptive comparative study to which I would take exception on some points, particularly to the somewhat excessive concern of the author with presenting his own view by way of updating problems, as distinct from his well-taken criticism (perhaps more severely applied to Mill than to Marx), see G. Duncan, *Marx and Mill* (Cambridge, 1973).

17 Engels to Mehring (14 July 1893), *Selected Correspondence*, p. 512.
18 Lukács, *Geschichte und Klassenbewusstsein*, pp. 85, 34, and Ollman, *Alienation*, p. 132, respectively. Throughout his book Ollman reveals no critique of this procedure. Only at the end does he admit the inadequacy of Marx's projections on the immediate future of capitalism (p. 232). He also points out there that one can neither agree nor disagree with what is non-existent, i.e. the communist conditions Marx foresaw.
19 *Kapital*, I, 178.

own view is not the product of overall planning. Now let us assume, nevertheless, that we accept as well founded a predicted solution of a problem besetting a complex organization, and act according to that prediction. These acts are likely to have side-effects that help to create a situation which in some respects we have not intended. Legislation to safeguard the freedom of association was not meant to make membership in unions almost inescapable or to lead to monopolies. Legislation to nationalize the means of production and distribution was not intended to lead to NEP and the growth of wage differentials.[20] Whether they are attendant upon following or not following a given prediction, such unforeseen and unwanted results of premeditated action do not necessarily attest a false estimate of past and present. The only thing they demonstrate is the failure to anticipate fully the effects of certain policy decisions. It should be remembered that the reversal, or merely the prospect of a reversal, of policies on the ground of the awareness of errors of anticipation is the essence of 'the rule of anticipated reactions'.[21] Errors of anticipation may be the result of assessing either correctly or incorrectly the situation in which the policy was adopted.

The Marxist explanation of the postulated necessity of bourgeois misapprehensions presupposes a conception of reality which defies both common sense and philosophical discrimination. It rests on the premise that one can reconstruct a comprehensive and exact causal nexus between the events of the past and the present; it is assumed to follow that such a nexus can, therefore, be established with the same degree of certainty between present and future events. Neither empirical social science nor historical science is in a position to confirm this highly presumptuous conclusion or its somewhat less presumptuous premise.[22] Both underlie the Marxist postulate of orientation towards 'concrete reality' and cannot hide its true meaning: orientation towards what is supposed to happen.

20 Those are instances that cause the bifurcation of ideologies and are reflected in it. The phenomenon has been explained briefly in the Introduction and is illustrated in Chapters 4–5 by the modifications Marx and Engels's immediate successors made in the founders' conception of ideology.
21 See C. J. Friedrich, *Constitutional Government and Politics* (New York and London, 1937), pp. 17–18, and *Man and His Government* (New York, San Francisco, Toronto and London, 1963), pp. 204ff.
22 Cp. K. Popper, *The Poverty of Historicism* (London, 1957), pp. 14 and 166, in special reference to Marx.

To be sure, a number of things can be derived as 'objective possibility' from 'objective reality', and orientation towards a desired possibility might deepen our understanding of a given reality. Yet in many situations more than one configuration of possible actions suggests itself. On this score alone it is unwarranted to defend the Marxian view that only those engaged in changing the world can see it correctly and that on this foundation Marx could affirm both historical relativism and claim exception from it for his views.[23]

Admittedly, what is true shows up in practice, but this is not necessarily what enables us to change the world. Lies do that as well, as thinkers like Plato, Montesquieu and Pareto assumed not unreasonably, and not only the none-too-remote past abounds with examples. If consciousness of the historical base means objective knowledge, it is unwarranted to suppose that such consciousness goes only with seeking to change the world, because those who do not seek this change need not for that reason be necessarily wrong about prevailing conditions. If they were, no political order could be preserved against structural change for any length of time. One needs also to consider that usually more than one project of change is peddled on the political market, each claiming the only fully true assessment of reality. It remains, therefore, an obfuscation of the notion of reality to stipulate that the condition of its correct perception is to know and opt for the 'objective possibility' of radical structural change. The notion of 'concrete reality' does not become more sensible if inferences about even just the basic outlines of such change are elevated to the rank of decisive criteria of correct perception. The obvious purpose of taking these liberties with the notion of reality is to rule out as unrealistic and unscientific any other prediction than the Marxist, and any evaluation of the present which is not based on that prediction.

Marx and Marxists do not demonstrate that bourgeois thought lacks concern with 'objective possibility', but only that they envisage this possibility differently. Moreover, while Marx regarded the difference in perspective as the reason for invalidating

---

[23] As A. MacIntyre, *Marxism* (London, 1953), pp. 60–2, argues on the basis of the argument I discuss in the following passages. For a similar re-elaboration, though on an official Marxist basis, of the fundamental Marxian vein, combined with some later Marxist and non-Marxist (Mannheim) standpoints, see J. J. Wiatr, 'Sociology–Marxism–Reality', *Social Research*, xxiv, 3 (1967), 416–34.

the bourgeois understanding of reality, he did not practise what he preached. He relied exclusively for his data on bourgeois literature, press and government publications, and accepted many of their evaluations. He was full of praise for the English commissions empowered by Government and Parliament 'to reveal the truth' and he expressed admiration for the 'knowledgeable, impartial and relentless men . . . like England's inspectors of factories . . . its medical reporters', etc. In this context, he again acknowledged generally the possibility of 'free scientific research' and defended it against its enemies.[24] He even admitted to having found support in the writings of classical economists for his view of the true nature and actual trend of economic and social development. He credited Ricardo with having been disturbed over the eventual outcome of the trends he discerned. Marx referred to him in connection with his own assertion that capital is the barrier of capitalism and admitted the existence 'within the boundaries of capitalist reasoning' of premonitions about the future of capitalism.[25]

He was, therefore, quite inconsistent when he intimated that only his way of analysing the economic forces reflected 'truly the manner of natural science' and when he classified Hegelianism and the whole German philosophy and historiography as false, lumping them finally together with all other non-Marxian products of the mind, from religion to classical economics and utopian socialism, under the name of 'ideology'.[26] Yet in order the better to depreciate German historiography and philosophy, he did not only comment on the ease with which the distortion of language could be redressed (MEGA, v, 424), the problem existing 'merely in philosophical consciousness for which it is impossible to gain clarity about its nature and the origin of its seeming separation from life' (p. 427). The possibility of another, correct, philosophical consciousness is assumed. In order to denigrate philosophy in its present state Marx contradicted again the core of his theory of ideology. For he said that the philosophers were unable to do

---

[24] *Kapital*, i, vii–viii. See also p. xii in the Preface to the second edition.
[25] *Kapital*, i, 231. See also *Zur Kritik der politischen Ökonomie*, p. 148.
[26] I have kept close here to the formulation used by R. C. Tucker, *Philosophy and Myth in Karl Marx* (Cambridge, 1961), p. 181. For the textual evidence, see *Einleitung zur Kritik der Hegelschen Rechtsphilosophie*, MEGA, i, i, 612; *Die deutsche Ideologie*, MEGA, v, 9ff, 15, 39, 97, 113, 154ff, 165–6; *Der Wahre Sozialismus*, MEGA, v, 435, 451, 499; *Zur Kritik der politischen Ökonomie*, p. lv. See also above, Chapter 2, note 19.

what any shopkeeper was capable of, namely 'to distinguish between what somebody pretends to be and what he really is'. If 'the ideologue reflects and the shopkeeper directs' (Der Ideologe denkt und der Krämer lenkt),[27] then by and large the bourgeoisie apparently know what they are doing.

The substance of Marx's contradictory assertions about bourgeois thought was that it was obsolete because it assumed capitalist society would continue to exist. In passing this judgment, he was undisturbed by the fact that bourgeois thinkers were well aware of the contradictions of that society and disagreed among themselves about whether its tensions would remain unsolved (Hegel and Spencer, for instance) or whether the tensions could be and would have to be alleviated (Mill, and later Green and Hobhouse, for instance). When it suited him, Marx also ignored how deeply indebted he was to 'Hegelian ideology' and Hegel's idealization of idealogy',[28] not least when it came to the analysis of 'bourgeois' or 'civic' society, for which he acknowledged his rather heavy reliance on the classical economists. Indeed, Marx had an explanation for making these admissions of the appositeness of bourgeois insights, admissions which ought to have prevented him from making his categorical statements about its incorrectness in the first place.

When a particular stage of development is on the wane, he explained, differences of opinion arise about the existing order and its future. Adapting again a Hegelian idea to his purposes, he asserted that in such a situation the consciousness of thinkers can advance beyond existing conditions with reference to issues which admit of being summed up. This is why one can rely on earlier theories.[29] Marx obviously meant theories about developments that had run their full course and had, so to speak, exhausted their potentialities. On the same grounds, he declared in the *Manifesto* that

> where the class struggle approaches the moment of decision, the process of dissolution . . . assumes such a violent and glaring character that a small section of the ruling class . . . joins the revolutionary class which holds the future in its hands. Just as, therefore, previously a part of the nobility

[27] MEGA, v, 39 and vii, 343 (on Ruge) respectively. Marx, of course, was adapting the German saying: *Der Mensch denkt und Gott lenkt* (Man proposes God disposes).
[28] MEGA, v, 166, 325. Cp. also iii, 303–4.
[29] MEGA, v, 62.

went over to the bourgeoisie, so now a part of the bourgeoisie goes over to the proletariat, and particularly a part of the bourgeois ideologists, who have raised themselves to the level of comprehending theoretically the historical movement as a whole.[30]

Thus, when the clash between 'existing social relations' and 'the existing forces of production', and consequently the disparity between ideology and reality, reaches its height, some bourgeois intellectuals can perceive what is going on. However reasonable the assumption (and only within its confines is it possible to say that, for Marx, ideas can prefigure the future without being its cause),[31] it is an exception that does not by a long shot come near to confirming the rule expressed in the dogmatic conception of ideology. Indeed, while Marx was hardly in a position to deny that socialist intellectuals of bourgeois provenance 'hold leading positions in the proletarian movement', the admission, which is perfectly in tune with his operative ideology, cannot be made to tally with his 'social epistemology'.[32]

---

[30] MEGA, vi, 535.

[31] Berki, 'The Marxian Conception of Bourgeois Ideology', p. 93, does not note the qualifications required for this rule.

[32] S. Avineri, 'Marx and the Intellectuals', *Journal of the History of Ideas*, xxviii, 2 (1967), 276, who makes the claim despite admitting Marx's 'radical ambivalence about the role of intellectuals' (p. 269), bases it on the interpretation of two Marxian *dicta*, without mentioning the fact that they are part of the context in which Marx made the relationship between being and consciousness dependent on the relationship between social being and the forces of production, and that it is on the relationship between the two that Marx grounded the distortion of human consciousness. The same disregard of these aspects underlies the assertion of the consistency in this respect of Marx's 'social epistemology' in Avineri's *The Social and Political Thought of Karl Marx* (Cambridge, 1968), pp. 75–7. Avineri thus apparently assumes that in this, of all instances, his admission that 'Marx's epistemology is sometimes divided against itself' (p. 69) does not apply.
Whilst I am commenting on colleagues, I might remark that another colleague, N. Rotenstreich, *Basic Problem of Marx's Philosophy* (Indianapolis, New York and Kansas City, 1965), pp. 50–1, 131ff, 158, does not exclude the problem of distortion from his treatment of the dependence in Marx of consciousness on existence. Maintaining that the problem of ideology arises when the determination of consciousness by existence is not acknowledged (pp. 50–1), he does not make it clear whether he thinks that Marx was inconsistently assuming that prior to the advent of 'the reign of freedom', that is prior to the cessation of dependence (p. 139), such acknowledgment is also possible. Still, the assumption of Marx's contradictoriness on the point easily follows from Rotenstreich's view that Marx did not

Following their teacher's lead, Marxists contradict the Marxian claim that, especially when social relations are out of tune with the relations of production, bourgeois thought cannot help being unaware of, or must needs conceal, the contradictions of bourgeois society. Thus Lukács, too, concedes to bourgeois thinkers insights reserved in principle for objective proletarian class consciousness. This does not apply only to those who, with commendable foresight, opt out of the doomed class. Repeating what Kautsky, Bernstein and Lenin had argued for more immediate practical purposes of party politics and doctrine,[33] and what was shrouded in ambiguity in Marx, Lukács laid the foundation for the vein later elaborated by Marcuse. He credited German classical philosophy with having risen to a level of philosophical consciousness that enabled it to face the problems of bourgeois society logically; as a result, the transition to another stage posed itself in philosophy as a methodological necessity.[34]

Since representative members of the bourgeoisie are held capable of more or less frequently evading false consciousness, the notion of bourgeois false consciousness could more easily pass muster if it were primarily a matter of deceiving others. However, as we have seen, the assertion of bourgeois misapprehension boils down to the failure – or unwillingness – of the bourgeoisie to fall in with the forecast of its doom. This remains the criterion of understanding. The refusal to accept the diagnosis is 'the highest degree of unconsciousness, the most blatant form of false consciousness' because it parades as 'the conscious domination of

even pose the question how consciousness can be both creative and derivative (p. 134).

   Ollman, *Alienation*, appears to be following Avineri. In conformity with the central theme, alienation, he refers repeatedly to Marx's view of the distortion under capitalism of both activity and thought and concludes that man's 'actions in religion, family affairs, politics and so on, are as distorted and brutalized as his productive activity' (p. 205). Yet although Ollman also comments on Marx's awareness of the limitation of our perception by the world as it appears to us (p. 90), as well as on his view of the transformation of consciousness through estrangement as a result of which 'species life becomes for him [man] a means' (p. 153), this is not seen by Ollman to have any bearing on Marx's belief in the trustworthiness of our sense perception (p. 41), or on our ability to be aware of what we are doing, 'to choose and to plan' (p. 153).

[33] See below, Chapter 5.
[34] Lukács, *Geschichte und Klassenbewusstsein*, p. 134. On Marcuse, see my 'Locke and Marcuse – Intermittent and Millennial Revolutionism', *Festschrift für Karl Loewenstein* (Tübingen, 1971), pp. 427–57.

economic phenomena', and this is 'the irremovable contrariety between ideology and economic base', a dynamic duality which presses towards 'the catastrophic rupture'.[35]

The ascription of distorted consciousness to the bourgeoisie is pinpointed on the central political and social issue between bourgeoisie and proletariat, the fate of the capitalist system. Indeed, only the emergence of the bourgeoisie and of capitalism gives rise to a pure class structure, and the clear-cut confrontation between the antagonists is the precondition for the proletariat to attain true consciousness.[36] The stand of the bourgeoisie in this confrontation is supposed to colour decisively its perception of the significance of facts, but not to render impossible the attainment on its part of factual knowledge. Misapprehensions about facts, however, intrude also into the consciousness of the proletariat.

Although the proletariat is the historic embodiment of the limitations of capitalistic society, and for this reason capable of the total understanding of society, such understanding is not 'immediately and naturally' given to it.[37] There is some lack of clarity about the time when fully-true consciousness will be attained. It is, however, clear that before this occurs the proletariat is involved in the class struggle. Mainly in order to bridge the gap between the proletariat's imperfect consciousness of its historic destiny (and hence of its unwillingness to achieve it) and the postulated inevitability of its victory, Lukács accounts for the false consciousness of the proletariat in terms of a distinction between actual and true class consciousness. The idea underlying the distinction is safely anchored in Marxian grounds and formed also a point of agreement between Kautsky, Bernstein and Lenin.

---

[35] Lukács, *Geschichte und Klassenbewusstsein*, pp. 76–7.
[36] Lukács, pp. 33–4.
[37] Lukács, p. 35. Cp. above, p. 48.

4

THE PRESSURE OF FACTS

1. Subjective and objective class consciousness

Treating false consciousness more and more as a universal phenomenon, Lukács distinguishes between the manifest thought and will of 'historical individuals', who may be persons, peoples or classes, and the laws that govern their actions. Their actually entertained consciousness does not – at least not invariably – reflect the true nature of the reality in which the individuals act and which they shape. The effectiveness which empirically observable consciousness displays is no proof against, but is even likely to attest, false consciousness. The really effective forces in history are ultimately independent of the psychological consciousness of men[1] and guarantee the rational course and outcome of historical development. At the same time, these effective forces also determine the degree of imprecise consciousness which classes entertain about their situation. Considered 'formally in an abstract manner', class consciousness, which is in conformity with the objective situation of a class, conditions the latter's unconsciousness of its situation,[2] that is, its 'false consciousness'. Put in the terms of the famous Marxian formula, Lukács is saying that, because being determines consciousness, actually entertained consciousness is false; whereas if objective consciousness were experienced, it would consist of the awareness of determination and of its outcome. So conceived and known to its self-appointed seers, objective class consciousness is attributable to a class without being entertained by it. It is, as Sombart had already explained, 'rationally imputed' consciousness, a notion which he irreverently, but to my mind appositely, appraised as 'a bluff'[3] – with a thoroughly anti-democratic intent at that.

[1] Lukács, *Geschichte und Klassenbewusstsein*, p. 61. Lukács relies here on Engels. See also pp. 58, 62.

[2] Lukács, p. 63.

[3] Sombart, *Der proletarische Sozialismus*, I, 373. For Lukács's explanation that the notion of 'imputed consciousness' was tantamount to Lenin's (undemocratic) view of the necessity of implanting proper

Men's actual consciousness is the agent of the unconscious not in terms of depth psychology but in the sense that its inevitable falseness is unconsciously determined by a consciousness outside the self: the objective class consciousness. It is thus 'objectively correct' that subjective consciousness consists of false ideas about

class consciousness 'from without', see below, p. 86. Ludz, 'Der Begriff der "demokratischen Diktatur" in der politischen Philosophie von Georg Lukács', offers a sympathetic account of Lukács's shifts between concessions to democratic practice and acceptance of the Leninist dictatorship. Whether or not one agrees with the attempt to relate dialectically democracy (hardly defined) to all-too-clearly-anti-democratic dictatorship, within a 'category of totality', one notes that Ludz cannot conclude that Lukács actually succeeded in overcoming 'Trotsky and Kautsky's overdrawn [*sic!*] question of democracy *or* dictatorship" ' (p. xvii). Eventually Ludz himself speaks of the 'contradictory unity' in which Lukács joined together philosophy of history and ethics in his early writings (p. xxxi). One wonders how a thoughtful commentator can still think that by the presumptuously naive and intrinsically illusory claim to 'total consciousness, the full knowledge of the situation' (p. xxiii), one can clarify anything philosophically and practically significant, or overcome by virtue of this notion of 'totality' existential and logical dichotomies, such as the chasm between those who claim to know all and those for whose benefit this claim is made. However, Ludz's account of the neo-Kantian attempts to overcome the dichotomy between 'is' and 'ought' (*Sein und Sollen*), issuing, for instance, in Georg Simmel's reaching out for 'a higher degree of reality in possibility' (p. xxiv), is a most instructive elaboration of Lukács's own retrospective account and helps us to understand this part of Lukács's immediate philosophical background, though it does not, in my view, make Lukács's, or Marx's, use of 'reality' or 'concreteness' – and for that matter of 'totality' – more sensible, or less overloaded.

The key to what seems to me wrong in this fundamental aspect is provided by Ludz's own pertinent observation that Lukács carried over from his aesthetics into his political philosophy the idea of 'classical harmony' (p. xxxiv; see also xlv–xlvii). This transfer is as illicit and dangerous as the unqualified transfer of the categories of coherence and derivation from epistemology into the determination of action-orientation. Ludz eventually also admits the susceptibility to 'arbitrary and uncritical interpretation' of the juxtaposition of 'the ideal-type conception of the communist party' (the embodiment of 'imputed consciousness') and actual party organization (pp. xlii–xliii).

Not entirely dissimilar, though on different levels, are the attempts of most contributors to Mészáros's collection to explain away the theoretical twists and their practical implications in Marx's and Lukács's conceptions of class consciousness. Notable exceptions are Bottomore, 'Class Structure and Class Consciousness', pp. 53–4 (but see note 35 below), and L. Goldmann, 'Reflections on History and Class Consciousness', pp. 71, 76, who at least admit the obvious anti-democratic implications of the distinction between the two kinds of class consciousness. Thus also Berki, 'Georg Lukács in Retrospect', p. 56.

itself, for men, classes and nations do not achieve the aims they set themselves but those only which are intrinsically rational and which men neither know nor will. The *contresens* of unconscious class consciousness could be regarded as a semantic oddity if a state of mind were meant in which people acted unconsciously in accordance with what a correct consciousness of their interests would require them to think and do. But according to the Marxist dogmatic position, nobody should in fact be capable of avoiding the adoption of false ideas about his interests. The rational laws of development impose upon men irrational deviations from them and irrational ideas about them. It could be argued that we could still get at the truth. Since we know that, because thought is related to social conditions, whatever we think and much of what we do about them is wrong, the implication would seem to be that the opposite must be right. To proceed in this way upon the assumption of 'the negation of negation' would be a weird but easy way to overcome false ideas. We need only accept that everything we believe and do according to these beliefs is wrong – and believe and do the opposite. But to say nothing of how we come to know the truth about the falsity of our ideas, to negate what is false, does not automatically provide us with the knowledge of what is correct. In social relations, unlike algebra, the negation of negation affords only the impetus to find a solution. The negation of a social evil does not normally carry with it one solution but – if any – a number of possible solutions.[4] The application of 'the negation of negation' is, moreover, precluded here, since *per definitionem*, our consciousness is and remains false so long as it is conditioned by economic factors.

A valid residue of the notion of unconscious class consciousness could also be extracted from Marxist theory in the following way. Judging by the conceptions upheld during the centuries, 'class systems have an enduring ideological superstructure independent of their particular social order'.[5] Put otherwise and amplified, principles of fundamental ideology persist, although in operative ideology, i.e. in actual policies, they are diluted, differently applied in various periods, and generally contradicted by important features of the class structure obtaining at any given time. To

---

[4] See my 'Herbert Marcuse's One-dimensionality – The Old Style of the New Left', in K. von Beyme (ed.), *Theory and Politics: Festschrift zum 70. Geburtstag für Carl Joachim Friedrich* (Haag, 1971), p. 213.
[5] Ossowski, *Class Structure in the Social Consciousness*, p. 180.

recognize these testable facts pertaining to the relationship between fundamental and operative ideology is a far cry from stipulating that, although class consciousness considered 'formally and in an abstract manner' reflects no psychological reality, its reality manifests itself in the ups and downs of the proletarian revolution (but not necessarily in the consciousness of all those involved in it). If this is why class conciousness so considered is no fiction,[6] then it is both an idealistic hypostatization (if not mystification) and a misnomer – and the latter fact alone precludes the comparability of 'imputed consciousness' with Weber's 'ideal type'. However, when the inclusion in our perception of that which has as yet not materialized is taken to be the criterion of the correct assessment of reality, and the illusory, not to say megalomaniac, presupposition is adopted of the perceptibility of socio-historical totality, of all that is actual and potential, it comes as no great surprise that adequate consciousness should exist beyond psychological consciousness.

The separation in the framework of this kind of dialectical relationship of subjectively conscious class consciousness from objective – but subjectively unconscious – class consciousness has obvious tactical advantages and must for the same purpose also be somewhat contradictorily qualified. The elevation of objective over subjective class consciousness is useful for explaining the unwillingness of the great majority of the working classes to behave according to the Marxist dispensation. On the other hand, to proclaim the irrelevance in the historical process of subjective consciousness and to put objective consciousness beyond the grasp of individuals, classes and nations,[7] is not, according to Lukács (and Marx), to deny their will any affluence whatsoever. They can slow down or hasten what is bound to happen anyway.

For the sake of allaying disappointment, as well as unperturbed compliance with delay in revolutionary progress, Marxists need a dam against what Lukács admitted to be 'the tempting influence ... on the thinking of the proletariat' of bourgeois concepts like 'ideas' (and their correlate, idealism);[8] it needs also reliance upon ideas and will which are at once conscious, subjective and correct. Marx certainly wished the dominated class to exercise their judgment when he said that they would attempt the impossible if they

[6] Lukács, *Geschichte und Klassenbewusstsein*, p. 88.
[7] Lukács, pp. 34, 61.
[8] Lukács, pp. 38 and 37 respectively.

had 'the will to abolish competition and with it state and society' before the forces of production were sufficiently developed.[9] If the master left this much to conscious perception and the discretion of will, Lukács was in no way at fault in insisting on the need to discern in the class struggle 'the direction-giving moment for action ... on the ground of the "natural" basis ... the bare, naked and raw experience (*Empirie*)'.[10] In principle, this 'moment' could be claimed to impose itself, so to speak, by its own weight, being the product of the determinant forces of the historical process. But imposing themselves within the Marxian framework are concessions over the possibility of consciously perceiving and pursuing objectively correct aims, which amounts to the concession that men's actually entertained consciousness, their ideology, can be correct. This is the inevitable result of overplaying the notion of 'false consciousness' and the determinist assumptions derived with it from the postulated dependence of consciousness on being. For on these grounds Marx and Marxists showed themselves unable either to interpret the world or to change it, as the famous eleventh thesis on Feuerbach specifically demanded of adequate philosophy.

II. Conditional concessions to conscious action

The dogma of the conditioned and therefore distorted character of beliefs invites contradiction and deviation in order to promote in the real world the belief that this dogma nourishes. Adherence to the dogma must be accompanied by, though not necessarily square with, a tolerable degree of consideration for how things do actually work out.

Marxism enters almost to the same degree into the realm of social philosophy and science as into ideology, and affords a telling example, in its original version no less than in its developments, of the interaction in social philosophies and party ideologies between values and facts, as well as between fundamental and operative principles. Facts, and among them those created in the attempt at implementing an ideology, often testify against the feasibility of fundamental principles or enhance their logical incompatibility.[11] Marxism also shows that the asymmetry in-

---

[9] *Die deutsche Ideologie*, MEGA, v, 308.
[10] Lukács, *Geschichte und Klassenbewusstsein*, p. 37.
[11] For a detailed schematization and general exemplification, see my *Ideology and Politics*, pp. 185–97.

herent in belief systems is enlarged by the influence on each other of the dimensions of fundamental and operative ideology. The shifts of argumentation we have analysed so far and the developments to which they gave rise are explicable both in terms of the tension between the factual and the normative components in the structure of a belief system, and in terms of the impact of operative on fundamental ideology. For operative ideology justifies what the holders of an ideology actually wish to be done and can do in view of the long-term and short-term exigencies that must be taken into account, however inconvenient they may be from the point of view of the fundamental principles, of the principles, that is, which bear on basic values and final goals and the general avenues of their realization.[12] In both the operative and the fundamental contexts, ideas are propounded which in the light of the facts they refer to, or help to create, cannot always be maintained or reconciled with one another without serious qualifications. These difficulties are sometimes simply ignored. More often than not they are glossed over or explained away so as not to impugn a fundamental principle. Such an evasion is also practised, wittingly or unwittingly, when changes of emphasis are implicit in certain lines of argument that run counter to the main contentions, as is the case in Marx and Engels's theory of ideology and Lukács's presentation of it, or when the connotations of a concept are changed without accounting for the change, as happened in Lenin's use of 'ideology'.

a. *The founders*

Once one ignores the nominal inflation involved in the notion 'totality' and the fact that to speak of class in terms of an action-unit is to reify a purely classificatory concept, it is perhaps not implausible to maintain at one and the same time that the will of a class to dominate distorts its perception of the totality of social relationships, and that this disability also condemns a class to subjection.[13] Only, one should be aware that in the first instance

---

[12] See above, pp. 4–6. As has been indicated there, the distinction between fundamental and operative ideology will particularly reveal its value in the present and the following chapters in the analysis of the nature and development of political and social theories. The reader will find another such exemplification – which in both instances has been incidental to the interpretation of the issue in hand – in the essay mentioned in Chapter 3 n.34.

[13] Lukács, *Geschichte und Klassenbewusstsein*, p. 64.

distortion is held to be attendant upon the will to maintain an advantageous class position, whereas in the second instance distortion perpetuates a class position enforced upon its members to their disadvantage. The relationship between socio-economic base and defective cognition is obviously not exactly the same in the two cases. In any event, it once more becomes apparent that false consciousness cannot be confined to the dominant class, and that the dominated class too is plagued by false consciousness. It would also seem to follow logically that only by relinquishing domination freely can a class overcome its cognitively defective way of seeing things.[14]

Indeed, as Marx argued, victory does not by itself make the proletariat 'the absolute aspect of society' (meaning presumably its embodiment). The proletariat will not gain even that victory, he continued not quite logically, unless it abolishes itself and its opposite.[15] Surely the proletariat cannot renounce the will to dominate and crush the opponent as long as the struggle lasts and its victory needs consolidation. How then can it achieve this victory or envisage its completeness if only the renunciation of domination clears the vision? Yet even if an anticipatory renunciation (to dominate in order to end domination) were feasible, and had any practical value, it would involve an act of will. Such a concession to the Platonic determinability of determination conflicts with what has been asserted all along, namely that free will is an illusion because what is willed that way suffers defeat from the laws of objective development, at least as long as classes have not disappeared. Yet the rigorously deterministic stance is quite clearly contradicted on the level of fundamentals themselves, as it must be in any belief system which calls for action, and revolutionary action at that. After all, what was the purpose of the *Manifesto* and of the founding of the International if not to enlighten the proletariat and prepare them to act upon correct insights? Even *Kapital* was intended to help in shortening and alleviating the birth pangs of the new order.[16] Thus, only the admission of operative deviations from fundamental tenets could be evaded, but not the deviations themselves.

Initially, Marx implied the informed exercise of will while engaging in the kind of abstract derivation which he criticized in Hegel. He postulated that the precondition of universal liberation

[14] Lukács, p. 65.
[15] *Die heilige Familie*, MEGA, iii, 206. [16] *Kapital*, i, viii.

is the existence of a class which symbolizes the sphere of universality 'through its universal suffering'.[17] There is no logical or
empirical reason why universal liberation should require the
existence of a class that symbolizes universality, nor is it self-
evident that the centrality of labour is unique to the proletariat
and that it therefore symbolizes universal suffering. It is not the
only 'working' class, although as a class of people it, or its majority, experienced for a long period the greatest amount of suffering.
But the proletariat did not experience all kinds of suffering, if it is
right to assume that no class position or any form of labour
guarantees immunity from suffering either in the physical or in
the mental sense. (After all, very few can make a living without
working and many would not stay with their work if they could
find or were suited to another way of earning a living.) Awareness
of suffering would seem to be sharpened precisely by its not being
universal, that is, by the contrast between those who suffer most
and those who suffer least. The sphere of universality can be
symbolized rather by what unites the members of different classes
of people.

The variegated frustration and manipulation suffered by almost
all classes, and the suffering of diverse minorities, may furnish the
basis of the quest for universal liberation, depending on what is
meant by that. To say the proletariat represents 'the complete loss
of man and can, therefore, regain itself only by a complete restitu-
tion of man' (MEGA, i, i, 619–20) is a morally defensible but
nevertheless metapoetical tautology. It needs to be shown how
beings who are completely dehumanized can regain their humanity. The proletariat may be 'the misery conscious of its spiritual
and physical misery'. But how can it be that 'the dehumanization
which is conscious of its dehumanization ... therefore, suspends
itself'? After all, 'the abstraction of all humanity, even of the
semblance of humanity in the fully developed proletariat is actually complete [*praktisch vollendet*]'. The young Marx's way out of
the difficulty was to ignore it.[18] Of particular importance here is,

---

[17] *Zur Kritik der Hegelschen Rechtsphilosophie*, MEGA, i, i, 619.
[18] *Die heilige Familie*, MEGA, iii, 206, 207. Ollman, *Alienation*, p. 239,
asserts that Marx never saw dehumanization 'in the workers as
complete but as almost complete'. Ollman disregards the passage
quoted in the text from MEGA, i, i, 619–20, and he relies on the
translation of '*praktisch vollendet*' by 'practically complete'. Yet the
connotations of the German *praktisch* do not include 'almost' as
'practically' does.

then, the conclusion that the proletariat 'can and must liberate itself' because it is forced into insurrection both by 'the theoretical consciousness of this loss' (of its humanity) and by the immediate experience of its irrefutable plight. Evidently, to hold the proletariat capable of being theoretically conscious of its situation is an implicit qualification of its dehumanization – and of dogmatic determinism. Complete dehumanization, like unreserved determinism and imputation of false consciousness, is revealed as an overstatement which remains uncorrected, though not uncontradicted.

Descending further from morally, though not logically, unimpeachable abstraction, Marx took it as self-evident 'that a great part of the English and French proletariat is already *conscious* of its historical task and is constantly engaged upon developing this consciousness to complete clarity'. Under the aspect of operative ideology which takes into account what Marx supposed to be the facts in England, the notion of 'false consciousness' might as well never have been conceived, or at least never have been taken as applicable to the proletariat in a class society, since 'complete clarity' is in such a society already within the reach of the proletariat. Harnessing each revolutionary happening to his cause, as he never ceased to do, Marx said in reference to the Silesian insurgents that they began with what came at the end of English and French insurrections: 'the consciousness of the nature of the proletariat'.[19] The flexibility in the thinking characteristic of the dimension of operative ideology is well illustrated by the fact that, fundamentals notwithstanding, a revolution is assumed to be either the cause or the result of the proletariat's self-consciousness about its situation.

The examples show that in the application of fundamentals to day-to-day politics, Marx was not impeded by concern with preserving their purity. When a practical posture was required, he viewed the differences in capitalist development of various countries exclusively under the aspect of the feasibility of having a revolution in whatever stage. The overriding consideration was to further the cause of a proletarian revolution indirectly or directly, whether or not this was in accordance with the mainstream of his theory of the development of the capitalist system towards its self-destruction. Preoccupation not with these fundamentals but with political orientation and indoctrination caused him to insist

[19] *Vorwärts* (10 August 1844), MEGA, III, 18.

that particular care be taken in Germany not to cloud 'the total contrast between communism and the existing order' because in that country 'philosophical phrases had for centuries acquired a certain power' and class conflicts were as yet not incisive enough.[20] He was well aware of the advantages accruing to the bourgeoisie from the spread of such 'false' ideas, and hence of the importance that the proletariat entertain correct class consciousness. We thus find in the *Manifesto* that one of the tasks of communists is 'the moulding of the proletariat into a class' (MEGA, vi, 538), although he and Engels had spoken before and were to continue to speak of the proletariat as a class already in existence. Their fundamentals required them to do so, just as operative ideology demanded of them to deviate from or even contradict themselves on the point.

b. *The faithful disciple*

Lukács followed Marx and Engels in these turns of their argument. Like them, he assumed that free will and consciously pursued aims do not invariably attest false consciousness, but may also conform with the rational course and factual base of historical development. Like the masters, he could not avert his gaze from what was in practice conducive to furthering the class struggle of the proletariat. He did not tilt the scales in favour of conscious action as far as Bernstein and Lenin did, although he followed them in going terminologically against Marx and Engels.

Conceiving the struggle about 'the concealment and the revelation of the class character of society' in terms of an ideological confrontation, he said that it required 'the ideological maturity' of the proletariat.[21] Thus proletarian as well as bourgeois ideology, and ideology as such, can be correct, as proletarian ideology is for the most part supposed to be. Having used 'ideology' most of the time in the pejorative sense established by the founders, Lukács was inconsistent in taking it occasionally in a positive sense, as Bernstein and particularly Lenin had been doing. But what he meant was in line not so much with the cautious reshuffle of emphases we shall witness in Kautsky's approach as with Marx

---

[20] *Rheinische Jahrbücher oder der wahre Sozialismus*, MEGA, v, 443.
[21] Lukács, *Geschichte und Klassenbewusstsein*, pp. 71 and 81 respectively. See also p. 89, for another use of 'ideological maturity' with respect to the proletariat. Plamenatz, *Ideology*, p. 27, was unaware of these passages, as well as of the others I shall refer to, for he said that Lukács did not use the term 'proletarian ideology'.

and Engels's own concessions, already mentioned, to the conscious element. From them Lukács could also draw the conclusion that it is not only the ideology of those who want to overthrow bourgeois domination that gains strength from an adequate appraisal of the situation.

This admission is again shrouded in the ambivalence and contradictoriness which distinguish the Marxist attitude towards facts. On one side it extols by way of its self-glorification as 'real positive science' its empirically and methodologically unfounded claim of the disclosure of the ultimate material *qua* real determining forces of history. On the other, an orthodox Marxist, like Lukács, speaks derogatorily of 'the so-called facts which are the object of idolatry in the whole revisionist literature'.[22] This derogation seems to stem not solely from impatience with the revisionist and bourgeois invocation of facts against Marxist evaluations and predictions, but also from the awareness that the opponents of the proletariat know how to seize upon facts. How else can one explain Lukács's warning against the attempts to press down the class consciousness of the proletariat to 'the level of its [actual] psychological condition'?[23] This real condition must evidently somehow be correctly appraised by whoever wishes to perpetuate it.

To say by way of supplementing, if not contradicting, the deterministic stance, that correct insight is a power factor 'of the *first order*' for the proletariat[24] is to leave room for admitting that for the bourgeoisie, too, correct insight is not irrelevant. Such an admission is certainly not ruled out by Marx's scornful utterance to the effect that the individual bourgeois is always ready to sacrifice the overall interest of his class to this or that private matter, and that at each moment the bourgeoisie is prepared to sacrifice its general interest to the most narrow-minded and squalid of interests.[25] Marx gave rein here to his penchant for strong language and hasty generalizations, but although these were part of the attempt to validate the unexceptional applicability of his theory, in this particular instance its terms clashed with those employed to characterize the regime of Louis Bonaparte. It clearly follows from Marx's overall comment that the regime of Napoleon III was an exception to the rule according to which the

[22] Lukács, *Geschichte und Klassenbewusstsein*, p. 17.
[23] Lukács, p. 88.
[24] Lukács, p. 80; my italics.
[25] K. Marx, *Der 18. Brumaire des Louis Bonaparte*, in K. Marx and F. Engels, *Werke*, viii (Berlin, 1960), 172, 185.

government is 'the executive committee' of the bourgeoisie. In the normal situation the subjective beliefs of the bourgeois ruling class are supposed to strengthen its fighting power. They assuage its conscience and deceive the oppressed at the same time.[26] Since Marx meant 'false' beliefs, one is entitled to wonder how long one can effectively deceive others by deceiving oneself in the first place, let alone maintain domination for any length of time in unawareness of the real nature of prevailing conditions. But as we have seen, not only Royal Commissions, government inspectors and even some bourgeois scholars, but shopkeepers as well, know what is what.

In fact, the bourgeois who offends as a matter of course against property and family knows that he must insist on the sanctity of these institutions because they are the foundation of the dominance of the bourgeoisie (MEGA, v, 162). The admission that the bourgeois ruling class practises its deceptions not only unconsciously but also more or less consciously is, therefore, only the opening for a flagrant contradiction of the assertion that the will to perpetuate domination conceals the perception of reality. As has been noted earlier, the rule that the servitude of a class is proportionate to its inability to apprehend reality comprehensively, calls into question the normally assumed causal relationship between social base and false consciousness. In accordance with the rule which diverges from the norm, Lukács arrives at the conclusion that the capability of a class to maintain itself in power increases or decreases to the extent that the class acts consciously or unconsciously.[27] This now means quite simply to act either in awareness or in unawareness of the real nature of the situation. (It will be recalled that according to the distinction in principle between subjective and objective class consciousness, to act consciously is to act in conformity with subjectively correct but objectively false consciousness of reality, whereas actions in conformity with reality and objective class consciousness are performed unconsciously.)

To envisage a typology of class consciousness on the supposition that it is 'clear' that there are effective structural and qualitative gradations of falsity is a commendable, though by and large contradictory, modification of the basic assertion that bourgeois ideology exhibits 'the sterility of an ideology cut off from life',[28]

26 Lukács, *Geschichte und Klassenbewusstsein*, p. 78.
27 Lukács, p. 65.
28 Lukács, p. 79.

and is engaged in 'a desperate struggle against the insight into the true nature of society it has created against the real consciousness of its class situation'. Recourse to overstatements concerning false consciousness is needed here in order to link dialectically the growing estrangement of bourgeois ideology from reality to its growing perception by the proletariat, so that it acquires 'ideologically . . . the same increasing insight into the nature of society in which the slow death-struggle of the bourgeoisie reflects itself'. Practically this entails 'an increase of power', since 'for the proletariat the truth is the weapon which brings victory'.[29]

The gradation of ideological falseness is retained inasmuch as it is the logical corollary of the gradation of ideological correctness whose increase is claimed for proletarian ideology. This is in substance, though not terminologically, in conformity with Marx's view of the progress of English and French workers towards gaining 'complete clarity' about their task. Hence, apart from using in this context the term 'ideological', Lukács does not say something different from Marx in speaking of 'the ideological overcoming of capitalism in the proletariat'. In the terminology he had introduced and which he normally used, he meant the proletariat's overcoming of subjective *qua* ideological class consciousness by objective class consciousness, which at an earlier stage of historical development was the preserve 'only . . . of extraordinary individuals'.[30]

Ideology, which is by definition false consciousness, is thus redeemable from it. The truth, which in principle resides outside psychological *qua* ideological consciousness and is unattainable by the bourgeoisie, is at least occasionally grasped by its members, and indeed must form part of the psychological *qua* ideological consciousness of the proletariat if the latter is to win its preordained victory. The distinction on principle and the subsequent confusion between the conscious or unconscious attainment of truth or the conscious and unconscious adoption of falsehoods help to ensure that whatever the observable facts, and however the workers relate to the truth, the truth itself remains wedded to proletarian ideology. In the ideological battle with its enemy, the proletariat can decisively rely on conscious action in so far as truth is objectively on its side. Yet since truth is in any case on the side of the proletariat, errors in matter of fact are of no great consequence; indeed they contain 'an intention directed towards what is correct'. This intention, again, is due to the growth of instinctive awareness of what causes the bourgeoisie to shy away from 'the real consciousness of its class situation'.[31] However, the faith in neither the instinctive nor the conscious proletarian awareness of the truth is, or can be, unreserved.

Belief in the possible adequacy of the subjective class consciousness of the workers must be confessed even at the price of bringing to the fore the asymmetry of the belief system. Otherwise appeals for organization for the sake of political education and action would be self-defeating. Why should workers join hands if their beliefs are condemned to be false and their total liberation will occur anyway? Yet is was precisely the nature of the actually prevailing, that is, largely false, working-class consciousness that forbade going as far as Bernstein in reducing the decisiveness, and particularly the unequivocalness, of impersonal determinants for the advent of socialism, unless one were prepared to exchange belief in revolutionary transformation for revisionism. In this point, as in other points (and other ideologies), the requirements of operative and fundamental ideology coincide. For the practical purposes of ideological debate and mass mobilization in support of the orthodox Marxist camp, Lukács, like Marx, occasionally had to relegate determinism into the wings while being able to summon it back at a moment's notice.

Lukács was not saying anything new or remarkable when he said that to view its position according to bourgeois ideology would be more fatal for the proletariat than for the bourgeoisie.[32] This is not merely stating the obvious in a way which does not tally well with the notion of the preordained doom of the bourgeoisie and victory of the proletariat. That the proletariat is held capable of adopting bourgeois ideology is a *reductio ad absurdum* of the determinist foundation of false consciousness. Although the fear of such a blunder on the part of the proletariat explains the need for keeping the concessions to voluntarism well under the umbrella of determinism, the inescapable implication is that the objectively determined false consciousness of the proletariat

---

[31] Lukács, pp. 60 and 85, relied here on the Preface of Engels's *Das Elend der Philosophie*, where Engels said: 'What can, however, economically-formally be false may for this reason nevertheless be correct from the point of view of world history.'
[32] Lukács, p. 81.

can lead it to adopt the likewise objectively determined false consciousness of its opponent in the class structure and class war. Hence, if Lukács did not want to change one of the most basic propositions of Marxism and admit that in principle different class positions can give rise to identical consciousness, he was forced to admit by implication that such consciousness can and must be also a matter of persuasion.

Indeed, if the bourgeoisie practises deception not only upon itself, the proletariat must be deceivable. This is then probably what Lukács meant here, the more so since to warn against a fatal mistake would be pointless, if one thinks it cannot be averted. If the proletariat is held capable of shedding the false 'subjective' consciousness which its class position normally forces it to entertain, only to adopt the false consciousness conditioned by the class position of its opponents, it can equally be assumed capable of exchanging in decisive moments of the class struggle its false for its correct class consciousness. Since the implication of free choice, the choice of either false or correct consciousness, cuts both ways, to be on the safe side it is necessary to postulate that just as the pursuit of its class interests leads the bourgeoisie ultimately to its downfall, so any misunderstanding by the proletariat of its interests is no decisive obstacle to its victory. For even if the proletariat were to commit the fatal mistake of adopting the ideological outlook of the bourgeoisie, this would no more than militate somewhat against the necessities of action, 'towards which the economic situation drives the proletariat – no matter what it might think about it'.[33]

In sum, nothing more than this attitude towards the thinking of the proletariat is involved in Lukács's distinction between subjective and objective class consciousness. And this distinction is therefore fully compatible with Marx's views. In the context where Marx identified the proletariat as the consciousness of its misery and dehumanization, and derived from that consciousness the proletariat's 'world historic role', he made it clear that this role does not mislead socialists

> to regard the proletarians as gods . . . The question is not what this or that proletarian or even the whole proletariat for the time being *considers* as its aim. The question is *what it* [the proletariat] *is* and what in accordance with that *being* it will be historically compelled to do. Its aim and its

[33] Lukács, p. 82.

historical action is palpably and irrevocably prescribed in its own life situation as in the whole organization of bourgeois society today.[34]

This is immediately followed by the remark that 'it needs no elaboration here' of the fact that the English and French proletariat is for the most part already '*conscious* of its historical task'. In the same spirit Lukács supplemented his 'no matter what it [the proletariat] might think' with the view that the nearer the predetermined goal, the more important become the conscious over and against the blind forces and, therefore, 'the ideological maturity of the proletariat'.[35] On the whole, Lukács's presentation thus reflects Marx's alternation between the possibility and even necessity of consciously rational action, and a determinism which, while it precludes such action and accounts for men's necessarily false consciousness, simultaneously guarantees the ineffectiveness of false consciousness in the long run, and in this way ensures the rational outcome of irrational action-orientation.

For long Marxists have accused those who point out any contradictory alternation in Marxist theory of disregarding, as Lucien Goldmann has again put it, 'the dialectical nature of human reality',[36] and, accordingly, of Marxist theory. It therefore needs stressing (again) that such an argument confuses the issues. It behoves a thinker to reveal both the contradictions in the human condition and the dialectics of these contradictions, which may also be said to characterize the relationship between judgments of fact and value judgments. One can also elucidate, as Goldmann perceptively does, how thinkers arrive at embracing 'the tragic

[34] *Die heilige Familie*, MEGA, III, 207. See also *Die deutsche Ideologie*, MEGA, v, 15, 25–6, 62, 66–8, 226, 307–8, 357–9; the Prefaces to the first and second edition of vol. I of *Kapital*, vol. III, I, 242, 426 and vol. III, II, 309.

[35] Lukács, *Geschichte und Klassenbewusstsein*, p. 82. Bottomore misses the evidence from Marx just quoted (text to my note 32) and that contained in the references of my preceding note 34, when he asserted in 'Class Structure and Class Consciousness', p. 53, that Lukács diverges here widely from Marx. Mészáros, 'Contingent and Necessary Class Consciousness', pp. 94, 99, 101, sees the connection and defends the notion of two kinds of class consciousness on the assumption that for Marx, the proletariat was a class '*against* capital but not yet for itself'. One wonders whether this elaboration on Marx's distinction between a class 'by itself' and 'for itself' issues in, or brings to the fore, the proximity of the notion of two kinds of consciousness to the clinical concept of split consciousness.

[36] L. Goldmann, *The Hidden God*, trans. P. Thody (London, 1964), p. 303.

vision' and thereby become involved in contradictions. Thus, Pascal's act of faith and its independence of any theoretical consideration illustrate the problem which in Goldmann's view is equally characteristic of 'all forms of tragic and dialectical thought (Kant, Hegel, Marx, Lukács, etc.)'. Yet no amount of dialectics can justify the suspension of critical judgment when a thinker is found to make contradictory statements about reality. One can, after all, state the contradictoriness of the nature of various phenomena, and of the relationships between them, without making contradictory statements about their contradictoriness. In point of fact, one is led to wonder how Goldmann can criticize the criticism of contradictoriness in the first place, if it is also in the nature of 'the tragic mind' to become aware of its own paradoxical character.[37] Why then do Marxists not admit their master's paradoxicality, but censure others for revealing and criticizing it?

The Marxian and Marxist alternation between the insistence on historical inevitability and the plea for purposive action is due, I suggest, to the interference with fundamental principles of the more or less realistic assessment of requirements normally met in terms of operative ideology. The asymmetric profile of an ideology, or of a belief system which combines, like Marxism, philosophy, social science and ideology, is likewise explained by the advantages which the asymmetry between the fundamentals themselves affords for the propagation and preservation of the ideology in question. In the recruitment and guidance of followers the orthodox Marxist can, in reliance on Marx, appeal to men's free and rational will, to the extent of inducing them to perceive properly the destiny of their class or espouse the cause of the class with which the future lies. Alternatively, refuge can be taken in the haven of historical inevitability when, as more than once happened to Marx, history disowns one's prediction – or when communist politics profane the humanitarian ideals attributed to communism. However, what is most important in our discussion is that the alternating retreat from and resort to socio-economic determination, as well as the highly variegated results ascribed to it, illustrate the impossibility of upholding the identification of ideology with false consciousness.

This failing, which epitomizes the explanatory shortcomings of orthodox Marxist theory, is an asset in so far as it becomes manifest that the application and propagation of its fundamental

[37] Goldmann, p. 58.

principles, that is, its very functioning as an ideology, require infringements of the dogmatic position. Moreover, various degrees of consideration for logic and empirical evidence impose themselves at the outset, since otherwise no tolerable degree of credibility could be claimed for fundamental principles and aims in the first place. Since, for reasons like these, dogmatic standpoints are impaired in the orthodox Marxist theory of ideology, it is more than an exercise in partisan scholastics, more that is, than 'mere ideology' in the terms of its own extreme definition of the concept. This will become evident as we now summarize the main steps of the argument which has led us from the general philosophical premise to the proclaimed extreme of the negative conception of ideology on the one hand and to the evident implication of the opposite on the other.

III. The tenable substratum

The fundamental postulate is that consciousness derives from social being. How men are engaged in production according to prevailing material conditions constitutes the forces of production, and these determine how men mould their social relationships. The existential base formed by the interaction of these two factors gives rise to the ideational and political superstructure. On these grounds, all ideas are therefore conditioned. To the extent that men's ideas are correct, this does not mean that in the same degree as the socio-economic reality confirms ideas, it has been created according to preconceived ideas; cognitive adequacy signifies merely that men's ideas mirror this reality without refraction. Whether or not they are correct, ideas are conditioned reflexes and men could not have created reality otherwise than it has emerged.

It does not follow directly from these propositions that men's ideas about the world they live in must be false, though they have been used for this conclusion. It might appear that false perceptions and illusory opinions are a function of a certain stage of transformation in which the network of social relationships falls behind the development of the forces of production. The question of adequate criteria for establishing when we are faced with such a lag becomes immaterial, for a lag merely aggravates false consciousness, which is regarded as the corollary of the most elementary form of the division of labour. Being coeval with all known forms of production, the division between mental and physical labour, and with it false consciousness, cannot therefore be dependent upon any changes in the conditions of production.

In this way the argument proceeds from the basic propositions to the negative pole by identifying the bourgeois belief systems, specifically, with ideology, and ideology as such with socially determined and therefore false consciousness. It then becomes necessary to admit that bourgeois ideology is not bare of factual insights or even entirely wrong about causal relationships and predictive evaluations. It is also conceded that the proletarian belief system is coloured by false consciousness. Consequently, the argument reaches the point where the original absolute juxtaposition of objective or total perception of reality and ideology, of objective and subjective class consciousness, breaks down.

In a few instances, but only in reference to the proletariat, 'ideology' and 'ideological' are used by Lukács in a non-pejorative sense. This break with Marx and Engels's exclusively pejorative, truth-excluding use of 'ideology' is inadvertent, for Lukács uses the term most of the time in their sense. But even in his terminological deviation he means what they meant. Notwithstanding their declaration on principle that the course of development does not depend upon it, they also envisaged the eventual achievement by English and French workers of full consciousness of their situation, without relating that achievement to the demise of capitalism. Lukács preserved the tendency of the founders to stamp as essentially false the bourgeois and as essentially correct the proletarian belief system when he considered bourgeois ideology above all as false, and properly proletarian ideology as coming nearest the truth, if not on occasion at least, and certainly in the end, identical with it. For the proletariat, Lukács states, 'its "ideology" is no flag ... no cover ... but the positing of the aim and its weapon itself'; only unprincipled tactics degrade historical materialism to 'mere "ideology"'.[38]

Rather than being used in two clearly differentiated, if not supplementary, senses,[39] the meaning of 'ideology' is stretched over a continuum which ranges from the negative pole – 'mere ideology' as unconsciously false consciousness and the unprin-

---

[38] Lukács, *Geschichte und Klassenbewusstsein*, pp. 82–3.
[39] Jordan, *Philosophy and Ideology*, pp. 495, 523 n.146, reports that the Polish Marxist philosopher Schaff and the political scientist Wiatr attribute such a differentiation to Marx.

cipled manipulation of ideas – to the positive pole – 'ideology' as consciously correct consciousness. 'Ideology' in the second sense stands in absolute contradiction to 'ideology' in the first and explicitly stipulated sense. 'Ideology' in either of the two extreme senses is empirically a non-datum. There never has been and there is not as yet an ideology which contains only verified and verifiable statements – and then it would not be an ideology; or one containing only unverified and unverifiable statements – and then it might be an ideology but a totally ineffective one. Shorn, therefore, of its two extreme poles, or considering them as ideal-types, i.e. as the two diametrically opposed theoretical points of reference, the continuum which I have extracted from the vacillations of the Marxist theory of ideology encompasses that which finds its place in the definition which I have offered at the outset and defended, as well as expanded in *Ideology and Politics*.

According to this curtailed span of the Marxist continuum, it could be said that ideology characterizes the aims posited and pursued more or less consciously by the bourgeoisie and the proletariat. Ideology can therefore be oriented towards more or less radical change, or oppose any change. The assumption that the extent to which ideology contains correct insight depends upon the extent to which it envisages total structural change, belongs to the unverifiable elements of ideology itself. If adopted by a political movement, the assumption might have the effect of a self-fulfilling or self-denying prophecy. The assumption is the object of an analytical theory about ideologies and not a conclusion proved by any such theory, Marxian or otherwise.

In Marxist country, this is not yet journey's end. The perceptible growth in the socialist camp after Marx's death of the explicit emphasis on conscious action was accompanied by the adoption of a usage of 'ideology' which avoided particularly the prominence of the extreme negative pole of orthodox theory, if that pole was not dispensed with altogether. These developments in fact issued in the dismissal of both extreme poles of the continuum I have outlined. At the same time, those admissions in the original theory were more or less discreetly enlarged upon which contravened its dogmatic claim that ideology is determined by class.

PART TWO

THE REDEMPTION OF IDEOLOGY

5

UNACKNOWLEDGED AND ACKNOWLEDGED MODIFICATION

1. Lenin's *de facto* breakaway

a. *The setting*

Whether or not a movement seeks total structural change, once it enters the political arena and prospects for mass support its leaders will not handicap themselves by raising doubts about the adequacy of conscious will and action. Quite early, therefore, the original pejorative connotation of 'ideology' had to be relegated into the background, or dropped altogether, by the leaders of Marxist social-democratic parties. If, like Lassalle, Kautsky, Bernstein and Lenin, one stressed the importance of politics, one had to restore the importance of 'the conscious element', since it would have been self-defeating to go on insisting that as a matter of principle all consciousness is false consciousness, as Marx and Engels's dogmatic conception of ideology required. Indeed, in the course of pressing for centrally organized and professionally guided revolutionary action, Lenin in *What Is to Be Done?* made a clean sweep of the restrictive use of 'ideology' and its unexceptional derogatory meaning.

The change in the Marxist attitude towards the role of consciousness has been widely noticed. The same cannot be said of the corollary of that change, the departure from Marx and Engels's use of 'ideology'. None too often mentioned, its significance has never been explored.[1] Thus, for example, Delany in his debate

---

[1] As Hölzle, *Idee und Ideologie*, p. 112, points out. His comment, however, is too brief to fill the *lacuna* and is contained in that of Acton, *The Illusion of the Epoch*, p. 132, for whom the acknowledgment of the partisanship and class character of Marxism–Leninism affords the natural explanation for calling it an ideology and yet continue regarding it as 'scientific'. Acton overlooks the fact that Lenin had already used 'ideology' in this sense, although Acton quotes from *What Is to Be Done?* a famous passage which is almost immediately followed by passages in which the new use of 'ideology' occurs. The change seems to have escaped Mepham, 'The Theory of Ideology in Capital', pp. 12, 16, who proceeds as if Lenin used 'ideology' as Marx did.

with Bell[2] praised Lenin for having improved the Marxian conception of ideology and for having acknowledged that Marxism was an ideology. Although Lenin did only the latter, this was enough to upset the original Marxist theory of ideology. Delany does not even hint at the nature of the break and the difficulties it created for Lenin's claim to defend Marxism against revisionism. Similarly, in a recent review in *The Times Literary Supplement*[3] of the translation into English of Lukács's *History and Class Consciousness*, Lenin's innovation is noted and commented upon to the effect that it 'might have been significant'. The significance is not clearly indicated, for it cannot be meant to consist in the possibility of the party's imposing through 'a regime of "reified" laws and institutions . . . a false consciousness or ideology'. Such a view is as little attributable to Lukács as to Lenin.

Bell, who appositely reintroduces Kautsky into the picture and raises the question of the reconcilability of both Kautsky's and Lenin's views of conscious action with 'the entire theory of Marxist materialism', leaves things at that.[4] On a later occasion, he again raised the question of reconcilability, this time in regard to Lenin's considering Marxism as an ideology on the one hand and Marx's views on the other.[5] For Bell, the significance of Lenin's non-Marxian use of 'ideology' consists almost exclusively in Lenin's adoption of the language of conflicting belief systems in the temper of the wars of religion and hence in 'casting ideology in these "either-or terms"', as if this had not been the significance of Marx's restrictive usage in the first place. Moreover, Bell evidently follows here Loewenstein's identification of the 'either-or terms' with totalitarianism.[6] He says that owing to conceiving ideology in these terms, 'Lenin more than any other thinker or leader gave politics its totalist framework and made ideology synonymous with total belief.'[7] Yet Bell ignores the

[2] W. Delany, 'Ideology – A Debate', in C. I. Waxman (ed.), *The End of Ideology Debate* (New York, 1968), p. 273.

[3] *Times Literary Supplement*, 2 June 1971, in reference to Livingstone's translation.

[4] D. Bell, *The End of Ideology – On the Exhaustion of Political Ideas in the Fifties* (New York, 1960), rev. edn, Colliers (New York, 1961), p. 377.

[5] D. Bell, 'Ideology and Soviet Politics', *Slavic Review*, xxiv, 4 (1965), 593.

[6] K. Loewenstein, 'Political Systems, Ideologies and Institutions: The Problem of their Circulation', *Western Political Quarterly*, vi, 4 (1953), 705.

[7] Bell, 'Ideology and Soviet Politics', p. 594.

significance of the fact that in the passages he quotes from Lenin, Lenin used 'ideology' for both the bourgeois and the proletarian belief systems. On this count, Lenin cannot be said to have regarded only that kind of doctrine as ideology which is synonymous with 'total belief', and this restrictive meaning of ideology is what the author of *The End of Ideology* most probably still had in mind here, although he had meanwhile modified, but not entirely abandoned, such a conception of ideology.[8]

In his comment on Bell's article, Lichtheim strictured Lenin's 'misuse of a terminology which a Marxist might have been expected to treat more carefully'.[9] Lichtheim chose to ignore the full correspondence with Lenin's revolutionary voluntarism of the latter's break with Marx and Engels's use of the term, a voluntarism which implied the unacknowledged but none the less palpable contradiction of orthodox presuppositions. It was thus as ill-founded to put Lenin on the carpet for his 'carelessness', as it was to declare as 'slightly overdrawn' Carr's quite precisely drawn judgment that 'in Marx "ideology" is a negative term', whereas in 'Lenin, "ideology" becomes neutral or positive'.[10] Indeed, in speaking of socialist ideology and bourgeois ideology, Lenin retained the idea that the latter, but not ideology as such, was false. He thus laid the foundation for what has become known as the Marxist–Leninist 'dual' theory of ideology.

It is not surprising that Lenin offered no explanation for his drastic change of the use of the term, since he did not, to my knowledge, confess to this change in the first place. (And the same seems to apply to Lukács.) Although generally Marxism was for him 'not a dogma but a guide to action', he did not admit the need for any change of principles but merely for shifts of emphases. With the change of the aims and direction of immediate action, in such 'a living doctrine *various* sides *were bound* to come to the fore'.[11] The explanation of quite an incisive change in the original doctrine would have been necessary if Lenin had made the attempt to account for his accommodating within its bounds his political voluntarism, which indubitably was at the root of his inclusive and in this respect neutral, use of 'ideology'. Those of Marx's pronouncements according to which the consciousness

[8] See my *Ideology and Politics*, pp. 65–7.
[9] G. Lichtheim, 'Comments', *Slavic Review*, xxiv, 4 (1965), 606.
[10] E. H. Carr, *What Is History?* (London, 1962), pp. 132–3.
[11] Lenin, SW, i, 481.

actually informing the attitude of some (and in principle even all) proletarians might be false[12] could have served Lenin as the point of orthodox anchorage for his elitist voluntarism. However, avant-gardism means conquering and leading the masses. Lenin there-fore denied the irrelevance in the short and long run of inadequate consciousness on the part of the masses. In his unequivocal em-phasis on the decisiveness of correct conscious action he thus went far beyond the orthodox position. This transgression is clearly reflected in his inclusive use of 'ideology', and any admission, let alone explanation, of this semantic change would of itself have involved Lenin in a confrontation with the masters, and one well beyond the semantic level at that.

Any explanation and demarcation of what amounted to a rup-ture with orthodox doctrine would have called also for spelling out the difference between Lenin's conception of ideology and that of Kautsky, whose authority he invoked in *What Is to Be Done?*, in his fight against those who preached exclusive reliance on econo-mic development. Worse, intellectual honesty would have de-manded that, in the context of stigmatizing his opponents as 'Bernsteinist revisionists', Lenin acknowledge fundamental affi-nities between his and Bernstein's conception of ideology. In view of his struggle against the Russian 'Bernsteinists' and the break be-tween Lenin and Kautsky in later years over the attitude towards the First World War and, after the Bolshevik Revolution, over 'the dictatorship of the proletariat', one might be inclined to see the seeds of this break as already embedded in Lenin's not quite faithful reliance on Kautsky, and in his unawareness, pretended or genuine, of his much greater closeness to Bernstein with respect to the unorthodox emphasis on conscious will and action. How-ever, there exists no stringent correlation between different politi-cal attitudes and the degree to which the elements of conscious-ness and will are accorded an influence of their own.

Kautsky condemned the Bolshevik dictatorship as a deviation from Marxian principles. He linked the proletarian revolution with the maturity of the proletariat, in elaborating, like Lukács after him, on the basically Marxian tautology that the nearer the victory the more urgent does it become to accelerate 'the develop-ment to a higher stage of the proletariat'. Unlike Lukács, Kautsky did not speak of the proletariat's *ideological* maturity, although he meant the same thing, since the maturity he had in mind consisted

[12] See above, pp. 72–3.

in the proletariat's enlightenment and knowledge, which it was supposed to acquire in the class struggle and which it needed 'to make itself master of . . . [political] power, and to use it' in order 'to transfer democracy from politics to economics'.[13] In principle, Kautsky thus gave no cause to Lenin for controversy over the importance of politics. Their serious differences of opinion about the political regime which should (and could) ensure the realization of socialism therefore had nothing to do with the somewhat different ways in which they related economic determination and conscious political action to each other.

In defending conscious action, as on other issues, Kautsky kept closest to the orthodox position, in contrast to Bernstein, for instance, who straightforwardly rejected the centrality which Marx accorded to economic causation. In substance, Lenin, whom Stalin followed in this respect, evaluated economic causation much as Bernstein did, but pretended to remain within the confines of orthodoxy. Although in this doctrinal issue Lenin had actually more in common with Bernstein than with Kautsky, Bernstein and Lenin were not less at loggerheads about 'the dictatorship of the proletariat' than were Kautsky and Lenin. The lack of correlation between the attenuation of economic determination in order to enable insistence on the need for consciously directed political action on the one hand, and the choice of the form and institutional framework of such action on the other hand, is strikingly revealed in the irony of fate that in Poland, for instance, Stalin's voluntarist modifications of orthodox theory helped eventually to free 'the intellectual scene . . . from the mental strait jacket' of Stalinism.[14] The same reversal of the relationship between base and superstructure, effected originally by Lenin, contrary to Plekhanov's defence of the orthodox position, had served Lenin to buttress authoritarian centralism of the party, and even within it, and afterwards Stalin to perfect it.[15]

[13] Kautsky, *Die proletarische Revolution und ihr Programm*, p. viii, and *The Dictatorship of the Proletariat*, trans. of *Die Diktatur des Proletariats* (Wien, 1918) by H. J. Stenning with an Introduction by J. H. Kautsky (Ann Arbor, 1964), pp. 15, 19, 21, 23–4, 96 respectively.
[14] Jordan, *Philosophy and Ideology*, p. 479.
[15] On Lenin's share in the creation of a 'bureaucratic monster' and the 'zigzags' of his misinterpretation of Marx's misinterpretations of the 'commune state', see, for instance, G. Ionescu, 'Lenin, the Commune and the State – Thoughts for a Centenary', *Government and Opposition*, v, 2 (1970), 131–65. On the famous zigzag patterns of Leninist policy and their explanation in reference to changing

It is permissible to doubt whether even at the early stage of his career as a writer, and certainly not in *History and Class Consciousness*, where he largely reproduced the orthodox doctrine with its unsolved tensions, Lukács did, like Kautsky, identify the maturity of the proletariat with its maturity for democratic government. In fact in his retrospective recantations, Lukács quite rightly explained that by his 'subjectively' derived notion of 'imputed' class consciousness he meant the same as Lenin in *What Is to Be Done?* with respect to implanting in the workers the proper class consciousness 'from without', and there is indeed no doubt whatsoever that on the score of divorcing proletarian maturity from the maturity for democracy it was not Kautsky but Lenin who followed the lead of Marx and Engels. To the extent that some transient concessions to reformism can be attributed to them, no commitment to political democracy need be in any way involved.[16] Thus, leaving his philosophical endeavours apart, in his political writings Lenin can be seen to gainsay unavowedly, but none the less clearly, that which in the founders' conception of economic determination foreclosed the preeminence of political education and action. At the same time, however, he provided the frank and consistent transformation into the form appropriate for political action of Marx and Engels's determinism (in the spirit of their action-oriented deviations from it). What is historically determined, or expedient, is understood by a minority and must be communicated to the majority so as to mobilize them as far as

situations, see A. G. Meyer, *Leninism*, 6th impr. (Cambridge, Mass., 1971), pp. 89, 103.

16 For Lukács, see his Preface (1967), pp. xxviii–xxix. Even Avineri, *The Social and Political Thought of Karl Marx*, p. 218, who stresses the reformist aspects of Marx's theory, does not present him as committed to democratic values. On Marx's scorn for general suffrage, see below, p. 125. Since they did not cut themselves off from Marxism, Bernstein and other democratic socialists of course invoked Marx's authority whenever this suited their revisionism. That this was not unfounded, although a case of eclecticism, was clear not only to Sombart. Thus, G. Schmoller's views, held since the 1870s, are reflected in his posthumously published *Die soziale Frage: Klassenbildung, Arbeiterfrage, Klassenkampf* (München and Leipzig, 1918), p. 613, where he said that 'initially Marx himself was a frenzied revolutionary in a bloody sense, in the sense of [aiming at] a coercive dictatorship of a Robespierre; later he became a more quiet and scholarly evolutionist'. Sombart, *Der proletarische Sozialismus*, I, 388, found that 'there is a Marx, there is, above all, an Engels whom one must by all means and exclusively consider as opportunist [revisionist] socialists'.

possible for a goal they would not embrace of their own accord. This is why the leaders must 'ascertain the *actual* state of class consciousness [in Lukács's terminology, 'subjective class consciousness'] and preparedness of the whole class', not in order to abide by its will but in order to fan and direct it.[17]

What political form one associates with the insistence on the importance of consciously directed political action, then, shows itself not to be in principle a function of the degree of this insistence. Rather, a logical connection exists between the amount of influence accorded to conscious decisions and free will, and therewith to politics, on the one hand, and the acceptance or rejection of a purely pejorative and restrictive conception of ideology, on the other. In other words, the less influence one attributes to 'the conscious element' as compared with the supra-individual determination of the rational course and outcome of history, the easier and, indeed, the more imperative it is, to identify ideology, i.e. action-oriented thought, with false consciousness and to ascribe it to specific belief systems, particularly to those one condemns, and not to one's own. Conversely, and by the same token, the greater the influence which is ascribed to conscious decisions, the less sense it makes to retain the indiscriminately pejorative connotation of ideology and its restrictive conception, i.e. the less sense it makes to refrain from applying the term in a neutral meaning to all political belief systems.

b. *The rupture*

In the debate about what both sides called 'the ideological development of socialism', Lenin took up the charge levelled by the Economists against those for whom, as Lenin put it, 'the economic base of the movement is eclipsed by the effort never to forget the political ideal'.[18] Defending the overriding importance of the political pursuit of the ideal, Lenin rejected in the name of

---

[17] Lenin, *Left-wing Communism, An Infantile Disorder* (1920), SW, II, 600. As Meyer, *Leninism*, pp. 295, 29, points out, the English translation is faulty in general. The translators ignored the fact that Lenin 'consistently and inevitably used the word "consciousness" without any modifier'. I have, however, retained 'class consciousness' where the consciousness of either the bourgeoisie or the proletariat as a whole is meant. Lenin's consistent rejection of political democracy before and after the Bolshevik Revolution hardly needs documentation. For samples of this attitude throughout his political career, see SW, I, 167, 177, 224ff, 245, II, 565, 585ff, 603, 620.

[18] SW, I, 162, 174.

orthodox Marxism the belief that the proper consciousness of the workers would spontaneously emerge in their economic struggle with the capitalists. Evidently, the view Lenin rejected could lay at least as much claim to being Marxist as his emphasis on the paramount importance of 'all-sided political agitation' and of action against '*all cases* of tyranny', whatever class it affected.[19] In point of fact, Lenin's attack on the Economists' 'retreat to the purely trade-union struggle' led him rather far afield, and not just terminologically. His emphasis on 'the importance of ideology', reflecting the stress he laid on 'the role of the conscious element' over and against revisionist 'spontaneity', is in the spirit of orthodoxy in so far as he underscored on these grounds 'the role of the Party of Social-Democracy' in leading the way, with no nonsense about hoping that everything will turn out right if one only lets the workers take their fate into their own hands (SW, i, 174). However, his persistent use of 'ideology' in the inclusive sense, never adopted by Marx or Engels, or their major Russian interpreter, Plekhanov, is a clear indication of the extent of Lenin's deviation from orthodoxy.[20] Indeed, although Plekhanov also

---

[19] SW, i, 202, 196. Cp. 186ff.

[20] The statement on Lenin's persistent use of 'ideology' for either bourgeois or proletarian belief systems relies on the evidence of the *Selected Works*. Cp. SW, i, 293 (1904), 344, 647 (1917): ii, 41 (1917), 273 (1918), 472 (1919), 505, 576 (1920), 600 (here he juxtaposes 'political–ideological attitude' and 'actual fact'), 603, 629. Lenin also used 'ideology' and 'ideological' synonymously with 'theory', e.g. 'Marxist theory' (i, 291), or 'Marxism, the only correct revolutionary theory' (ii, 575), and 'scientific modern socialism' (ii, 510). He further used 'doctrine' (i, 481, ii, 143), and spoke of 'political work' when he meant ideological indoctrination (ii, 512). In *State and Revolution*, which is most pronouncedly concerned with the exegesis of Marxian tenets, 'socialist ideology' is not used. Lenin employed 'ideology' there in connection with the bourgeoisie (ii, 144, 192, 205), but he also spoke of Kautsky's failure as 'the ideological leader of the Party' (ii, 193), so that there is really no break in his usage of the term. Deviations in the *Collected Works* would merely testify to inconsistency, but they would not alter the fact that throughout the years Lenin used 'ideology' in what I call the inclusive sense. This did not preclude, of course, his using it also, with respect to the ideology of opponents, as pejorative and opposed to facts. Having used the English translation, and knowing about its inexactness (see note 17), I have found it necessary to check with *Sochineniya* (4th edn), for which I am indebted to my colleague Dr A. Unger. Discrepancies have appeared in so far as in the original the Russian equivalent of 'ideas' is sometimes used where the translators use 'ideology'. It thus emerges that like Marx, Lenin used 'ideas' and 'ideology' synonymously. The Russian original also confirms that

modified the dogmatic conception of ideology and allowed for intermediate stages between the economic base, social relations and the superstructure, his reinterpretation retained enough of the original doctrine to serve as a source of criticism of Lenin for turning that doctrine into mere rules of action, thus eroding Marx's determinism.[21]

Lenin did not just warn that the Economists' 'crude vulgarization of "economic materialism"' would benefit only the ideology of the opponents and strengthen their influence upon the workers. He did not only point out that 'the only choice is: either the bourgeois or the Socialist ideology ... Hence to belittle Socialist ideology in any way, *to turn away from it in the slightest degree,* means to strengthen bourgeois ideology' (SW, I, 177). In making it clear what it means to turn away from socialist ideology, he turned squarely against the substance of the orthodox Marxist theory of causality. Pronouncements about 'the efforts of the most inspired ideologist [as] not being able to divert the labour movement from the path that is determined by the interaction of the material elements and the material environment, are *tantamount to the abandonment of Socialism'.*[22] This is no casual remark. Rather it reflects how far Lenin strayed away even from Engels's mitigation of one of the most basic Marxist fundamentals, the view that the factors emanating from the economic base may react back upon it, and yet remain ultimately determined by it.[23] Lenin did not merely stretch Engels's concessions a little further. Having offered official obeisance to the fundamental principle that economic factors have decisive influence, he added the proviso that ' "decisive" interests of classes can be satisfied *only* by radical political change in general'.[24] The satisfaction of class interests requires political radicalism, because to rely on 'the spontaneous development of the labour movement' leads only to 'pure and simple trade unionism ... *Nur Gewerkschaftlerei,* and ... the enslavement of the workers to the bourgeoisie' (SW, I, 177–8). Rejecting

    Lenin used 'ideology' over the years as Marx and Engels never did, i.e. for both bourgeois and proletarian beliefs.

[21] G. V. Plekhanov, *In Defence of Materialism: The Development of the Monist View of History* (1895), trans. A. Rothstein (London, 1947), pp. 189–202; and Jordan, *The Evolution of Dialectical Materialism,* pp. 341 *passim,* 285, and Chapter 12 respectively.

[22] SW, I, 177–8. Lenin referred here to Lassalle as a shining example of steering the labour movement away from trade unionism.

[23] See above, p. 42.

[24] SW, I, 182n.

trade unionism as the adequate manifestation of socialist consciousness and the trustworthy vehicle towards socialism, he remorselessly pressed the point that the economic base cannot by its own momentum induce socialist consciousness in the workers. Lenin did not thus put 'political' beside 'economic' materialism as Weber did,[25] but actually accorded greater importance to political and educational than to economic influence or practice, as we might say with the Marxian *Praxis* in mind.

Lenin invoked history to confirm that by their own efforts the masses of workers were able to produce not 'an independent ideology', but only 'trade-union consciousness'. 'Social-democratic consciousness could only be brought to them from without' (SW, I, 176–8). Lenin always returned to this standpoint and applied it also to proletarian state construction. Sixteen years after *What Is to Be Done?* he condemned the ignorant and self-conceited belief that the working people were capable of overcoming capitalism and the bourgeois order without learning from bourgeois experts.[26] Socialism, Lenin maintained in reliance on Kautsky, grew out of the 'philosophical, historical and economic theories' which were conceived not by members of the proletariat but by bourgeois intellectuals. To them belonged Marx and Engels as well as the Russian revolutionary intelligentsia. Proudhon and Weitling, who came from the working class, were notable exceptions.[27] The theories of the bourgeois intellectuals, Lenin

[25] For Weber's view and terms, see below, pp. 110–11.
[26] *Izvestia* (9 July 1919), SW, II, 512. Here, then, we have an indication that the stance in *What Is to Be Done?* fits the last Jacobin phase of Lenin very well. Dispute among Lenin scholars pertains to the question whether or not the unorthodox strain is counterbalanced by the one which puts the economic struggle more in the forefront. The impression one gains from attempts to show this is, however, that Lenin elaborated theoretical arguments only to provide orthodox-looking cover for whatever seemed to him conducive to his revolutionary drive and political tactics. The importance of tactical polemical purposes is attenuated by Meyer, *Leninism*, p. 48, inasmuch as he attributes to Lenin self-deception and ambivalence. Concerning Lenin's attitude towards democracy, for instance, on the basis of the evidence referred to in note 17, I find it difficult to accept Meyer's view that Lenin was unaware of self-contradiction (p. 66), since he had no reason to be aware of any self-contradiction in the first place.
[27] SW, I, 176. These are the two names mentioned by E. Bernstein, 'Das realistische und das ideologische Moment im Sozialismus' (The Realistic and the Ideological Element in Socialism), *Die Neue Zeit* (1897–8), repr. in *Zur Geschichte und Theorie des Sozialismus*, 2nd edn (Berlin and Bern, 1901), p. 270.

continued, caught on because they coincided with the spontaneous awakening of the masses. Thus he did not rule out spontaneous development due to the determining power of economic conditions, but conceded no more to them than the fostering of the potential of the masses to imbibe socialist class consciousness.

From the point of view of Marxist principles, the implicit paradox is that socialist consciousness had to be created for the working class by members of the bourgeois intelligentsia, in disregard both of the consciousness which their own class position ought to have induced in them and of the consciousness which the class position of the workers had actually produced in the workers. Proper, not to say pure, 'class political consciousness' is clearly assumed to exist 'only outside of the economic struggle, outside of the sphere of relations between workers and employers'. It can be gained only from 'the sphere of relationships between *all* the various classes and strata and the state and the government' (SW, I, 203–4). It was only logical and consistent in its unorthodoxy that Lenin should have held the ideologist capable of diverting the labour movement from the course determined by economic factors. This conclusion is borne out even by the words which reflect his tribute to orthodox theory. In accordance with it, he asserted that even the cleverest members of the bourgeoisie have become muddled and 'cannot help committing irreparable stupidities' which will cause their downfall, while 'our people may commit stupidities . . . and yet in the long run come out the victors'. Yet Lenin interspersed the rider 'provided, of course, that they ['our stupidities'] are not too serious and are rectified in time'.[28]

Lenin's shift of weight from economic determinism to political voluntarism is a classical example of ideological change which is so incisive that the ideologue feels that he cannot acknowledge it. Indeed, the shift goes beyond Kautsky's reinterpretation of Marxist theory, to which Lenin referred in order to establish the appearances of orthodox appositeness for his intrinsically unorthodox

---

[28] *Left-wing Communism*, SW, II, 619. Lukács, Preface (1967), p. xviii, quoted the passage referring to the existence of class consciousness 'outside the economic struggle' and said that this made plain what he had meant by 'imputed consciousness'. He not only refrained from admitting that Lenin's argument departed from Marxist orthodoxy but stressed that, as distinct from his own 'subjectivism', Lenin's argument was 'the result of an authentic Marxist analysis' (p. xix).

attack on the 'Bernsteinist' Economists.[29] In support of his un-
ambiguous preference of political action to the purely economic
class struggle, Lenin quoted from 'the profoundly true and important utterances by Karl Kautsky'. In the lengthy quotation
bearing on the contention central to Lenin's voluntarist argument
we also find the phrase which he took over almost literally:
'Socialist consciousness is something introduced into the proletarian class struggle from without (*etwas von Aussen Hineinge-
tragenes*), and not something that arose within it spontaneously
(*urwüchsig*)'.[30] As the rest of the quotation shows, one of the
reasons for this declaration was the widespread impact of the
revisionist argument according to which orthodox Marxism was
disproved by the lack of socialist consciousness of the workers of
England, the most advanced capitalist country. Kautsky retorted
without adducing any evidence that, according to Marx, economic
development and the class struggle create the conditions for
socialist production, but do not create simultaneously and directly
the conditions for 'the perception of its necessity'.[31] Hence the

29 SW, I, 176. See below, pp. 106–7, for the demagogic use of
'Bernsteinists'.
30 The quotation is from Kautsky, 'Die Revision des Programmes der
Sozialdemokratischen Partei in Österreich', pp. 79–80. I am indebted
to Professor Leonard Schapiro for having drawn my attention to this
point. His remarks on Kautsky in a lecture delivered at the Hebrew
University have induced me to follow the matter up. The evidence I
discuss in this and the following section confirms Professor Schapiro's
views, as expressed in his letter to me of 22 July 1969, from which I
quote with his permission the following passage: 'The phrase "Nur
Gewerkschaftlerei" comes from a commentary on the Erfurt
Programme which he [Kautsky] published in 1892 and which was
translated into Russian in 1893. Similar views are to be discovered in
many of his articles in vol. XVII for 1899 [*Die Neue Zeit*] and in his
Bernstein und das Sozialdemokratische Programm. Eine Antikritik
(Stuttgart, 1899). It seems to me quite obvious that these views of
Kautsky are not accidental but in fact formed a part of his general
thinking, and that Lenin had been reading them for years. We know
for certain that *Die Neue Zeit* was part of Lenin's regular reading.
Actually the views which we associate with *What Is to Be Done?*
first appeared in an article by Lenin published in 1899 called 'Our
Immediate Task', where he in fact quotes a phrase from Kautsky
about the union of socialism with the worker's movement. This article
already contains practically the whole essence of *What Is to Be Done?*.
I stress these facts because I have had the objection raised when I
have discussed these matters at seminars that the Kautsky phrases
were accidental. I think they were nothing of the kind and I think
that Lenin in fact was imbibing these views over a period of years.'
31 For Kautsky's assertion that this was Marx's view, the passage quoted
above, pp. 72–3, could have served as evidence, were it not for the

indispensable role of bourgeois intellectuals in the creation of socialist theory. Not only did Bernstein and Lenin repeat the view, but Weber extended it to charismatic leaders – the Hebrew prophets, the leaders of the Reformation, etc. – in so far as he pointed to the frequent lack of class identity between such leaders and the followers who eventually embrace some of the new ideas.

As a whole the argument Kautsky elaborated in his article is not faithfully reflected in the passage quoted by Lenin. In the first place, Kautsky said that socialism and the class struggle 'arise side by side'. Therefore he connected the role of the Social-Democratic Party 'to organize the proletariat politically and fill it with the consciousness of its situation and task' much more evenly with the economic struggle than Lenin did.[32] Only if, like Lenin, one disregards these views and the mediating tendency they reflect and, in addition, quotes Kautsky's words out of their context, does the conclusion of his article read like a retreat from what in Lenin's quotation seems to be the centrepiece of Kautsky's argument. The new programme of the Austrian party, Kautsky concluded his article, contained, besides the new, the old version also of the party's doctrine, for it declared that the consciousness of the historical task of the proletariat arises from the class war and is carried into the proletariat by the Social-Democratic Party.[33] Lenin's conclusion was very different. He said that 'there has never been too much of . . . pushing from the outside. We professional revolutionaries', he promised, 'will make it our business to

deterministic conclusion Marx allied with it. The quotation of Kautsky's words by Lenin furnishes a characteristic example of the apparently deliberate inexactness of the translators. They use 'consciousness' where the German original says *Erkenntnis*. Hence I have used 'perception'. The translation also adds emphasis by rendering 'das ist aber falsch' (but this is false) with 'but this is absolutely untrue'.

[32] *Die Neue Zeit*, p. 72. Since this was Kautsky's considered opinion, it is characteristic of Lenin's continuous subjection of theoretical argument to polemical tactics that he should have accused Kautsky, especially after the break with him, of detaching politics from its economic base, and that he gave this as the reason, for instance, for branding Kautsky's interpretation of imperialism as 'un-Marxian'. See *Imperialism: The Highest Stage of Capitalism* (August 1917), SW, I, 711–12. Lenin himself, however, felt free to go on maintaining in the same context his rejection of the inevitable coincidence of ideology and the socio-economic base, as when he concluded from the fact that Hobson spoke of 'Fabian imperialism' that the ideology of imperialism had also penetrated into the working class (p. 725).

[33] *Die Neue Zeit*, p. 80.

continue *this kind of pushing* [as exerted by students on workers] a hundred times more forcibly than we have done hitherto' (SW, I, 232–3). Characteristically, Lenin disclaimed the phrase '*pushing from the outside*' only in so far as it was likely to arouse distrust against all 'who bring them [the workers] political knowledge and revolutionary experience from the outside'. He did not disown his rejection of amateur leaders in favour of 'a circle of heroes ... capable of performing political tasks', or his assignment of a subsidiary role to the economic class war.[34] On his part, Kautsky did not rescind in his later writings the compromise he had put forward in the conclusion of his comment on the new programme of the Austrian Social-Democratic Party. He continued his attempts to account for the necessary modifications of orthodox theory in the terms of that theory. Much less than Lenin, therefore, did he dissociate the concessions he made to 'the conscious element' from the economic base. For the same reason Kautsky also does not seem to have used 'ideology' in the same way as Lenin did.[35]

II. Reverential revisionism: Kautsky

Whether they appear in a more practical or more theoretical context, Kautsky's concessions to the ideological spheres did not go considerably beyond what Engels had in his later days agreed to. Writing after the Bolshevik and German revolutions, Kautsky still thought that the English, and by this time also the German, proletarian mass parties were on the verge of the democratic conquest of power which he assumed, like Lenin, in unorthodox fashion and with respect to the use of state power as such, would enable these parties to direct economic development towards socialism. Yet in conformity with orthodox theory, Kautsky warned Marxists not to forget that during this process all political ideas and institutions remain conditioned by the economic and social substructures and that therefore 'socialism is impossible in

[34] SW, I, 222. Given that Lenin's adoption of centrally directed and eventually dictatorial action was based on the deepest respect for organization as both the guarantor of strength and the embodiment of rationality (Meyer, *Leninism*, p. 97), he thus again implied salient aspects of Weberian theory, the more so as organization naturally meant for him bureaucratic organization.

[35] I refrain from using more determinate language, since thorough study of all Kautsky's works has not been my object here. From the key works I have checked, I feel fairly certain that my inference is correct.

an early stage of development', just as the advent of socialism is guaranteed by the nature of capitalism and its corollary, the class struggle.[36] Objective conditions remain decisive, even though their comprehension and informed attempts to steer development can by no means be dispensed with. The materialist conception of history is 'a proletarian philosophy' in so far as it is accessible only from the standpoint of the proletariat, which members of the bourgeoisie, like Marx and Engels, could adopt. Indeed, such crossing from one camp into the other is essential, since the proletarian revolution cannot be successful without organizations of long standing, well-considered programmes and experienced leaders, just as technological development and adjustment are inconceivable without conscious direction.[37]

Kautsky's conception of the interaction [*Wechselwirkung*] between the constituent factors of historical development is circumscribed by these examples. Within these confines he was ready to acknowledge that some of Marx's views stand in need of correction. For as he acutely observed, Marx was apt to be carried away by his 'revolutionary temper' and often saw 'the future which he clearly envisaged nearer than it was'.[38] This, it would seem, is not to visit the sins of Lenin on Marx, but it does provide the basis for assessing both men correctly. Generally and in principle, Kautsky held that, because a conditioning effect is exercised by a variety of external material factors, among which the technological is most important, the conscious element can play a relatively independent role. For Kautsky this role might have been somewhat greater than for Engels. Apart from suggesting that morals and other ideological factors influence social and economic developments, he also admitted that moral norms can outlast technological change for a considerable time. 'The whole ideological superstructure' can actually separate from the base 'and lead for a while an independent existence'.[39]

Moreover, and most importantly, Kautsky did not conclude that in leading such an existence ethical conceptions need immediately become false, that is, turn into ideology in the Marxian sense. While he likewise did not believe that in order to be adequate ethical conceptions need only respond to specific material condi-

---

[36] Kautsky, *Die proletarische Revolution und ihr Programm*, pp. vii, 89.
[37] K. Kautsky, *Ethik und materialistische Geschichtsauffassung* (Stuttgart, 1906; repr. Berlin and Stuttgart, 1922), pp. 76, 82; *Die proletarische Revolution*, p. 77.
[38] *Die proletarische Revolution*, pp. 2, 68.
[39] *Ethik*, pp. 113, 128, 129.

tions, he argued that independence from material factors rendered ethical conceptions unfit to contribute to new developments. Precisely because they retain a power to resolve contradictions within prevailing conceptions, independent ethical norms 'merely fortify the ideological superstructure' and 'do not raise it above itself'. This they can only do if they are related to the contradictions and problems arising under the influence of external conditions on the human spirit. In Kautsky's terms, this influence can be evaded temporarily and in the long run only at the price of obstructing progress and eventually causing immorality and self-contradiction in the dominating class (after it has had the power, for a while, to resolve such contradictions).

Still, what is implicit in Kautsky's argument concerning the importance of 'the conscious element' is that informed effort and will are needed to prevent the superstructure from becoming dysfunctional and 'raise it above itself', i.e. to a new and more adequate level. In the ascending class, the same contradictions which the ruling class evades in the end only at its peril, engender enthusiasm for a new 'moral ideal'.[40] Its success, too, depends upon its correspondence with material conditions, the milieu, the stage of technology, historical development and the immediate neighbours of the country.[41] Yet even such ramified correspondence does not ensure that 'ethical idealism' provides the adequate answers to the problems which cause its emergence. The reason is that it does not 'originate from an in any sense deep perception of the social organism', but from 'a deep social want, and ardent longing' for something different from what exists, and indeed opposed to it. In this negating function the moral ideal is a motivating force of the class struggle, but it 'has no place in scientific socialism, the scientific research into the laws of the development and movement of the social organism for the sake of perceiving the necessary tendencies and aims of the proletarian class struggle'.[42]

In Kautsky's conception, the discrepancy between ideology and

---

[40] *Ethik*, pp. 129, 132–3.
[41] *Ethik*, pp. 136, 138. Marx, *Kritik der politischen Ökonomie*, p. xlvii, had already included external relations among the conditioning factors. Neither he nor Kautsky gave the matter fuller consideration. As evinced in R. N. Berki's thoughtful 'On Marxian Thought and the Problem of International Relations', *World Politics*, xxiv, 1 (1971), 80–105, commentators overlook the attribution by Marx of a codeferminant, besides a derivative, status to foreign relations. Berki also does not note another Marxian deviation discussed below, pp. 123–4.
[42] *Ethik*, p. 141.

reality is thus quite clearly neither absolute nor permanent. The residue of what was 'false consciousness' in the orthodox theory is reflected in the view that the ethical conceptions of the dominant class become eventually dysfunctional. It is likewise assumed that although the critical and forward-looking ideals of the ascending class reflect existential contradictions and the conditions generating them, so that in this sense the ideals of the ascending class have a higher truth-value, they nevertheless fall short of scientific truth. Kautsky distinguishes, therefore, not simply between ideology and science. He sets off from one another dysfunctional norms (ideology), the socialist ideal which is by and large in accordance with the entirety of prevailing conditions (and this ideal he does not call 'ideology'), and science in the form of 'scientific socialism' which alone can vouchsafe the realizability of the socialist ideal. Kautsky explicitly wished to make it plainer than Marx that a line ought to be drawn between the two. 'Science', he declared, 'stands above ethics; its results are as little ethical or unethical as necessity is ethical or unethical.'[43] This statement is in no way at variance with Marx's views, nor is the fact that Kautsky does not speak of 'socialist ideology'. Yet his use of 'socialist ideal' and its juxtaposition to scientific socialism contravene Marx's semantics and intention.

The commendable distinction between a scientific theory of socialism and the critical and forward-looking, yet nevertheless moral, ideal of socialism is immediately impugned by harnessing the Weberian notion of *wertfreie Wissenschaft* (anchored in Marx's ideal of the 'real positive science') to the socio-ethical 'ism'. To warn, as Kautsky did, that the acquisition of political power still leaves the questions open how to adapt to prevailing economic and social conditions the realization of socialism, and whether or not conditions are ripe for it, is to provide an opening for scientific inquiry. It is stretching scientific predictability too far if it is presumed to encompass the scale of social change which 'scientific socialism' claims to reveal as a necessity. Kautsky also widened the unavoidable gap in social science between prediction and verification to an extent that blurred the already precarious demarcation between prediction and belief, because to all intents and purposes he aligned, if he did not, like the founders, confuse, the claim of scientific prediction with the belief in historical inevitability. In other words, Kautsky clearly failed to establish a

[43] *Ethik*, pp. 141–2.

strict separation between 'scientific socialism' and the ethical ideal, precisely because he attempted to relate to the orthodox framework his concessions to the relative independence of political consciousness from economic causation.

The political experience of the socialist parties had made these concessions mandatory and Kautsky could not overlook the fact that it was – and had to be – the same people who wished to serve both scientific truth and the ideal of the ascending class. The combination, Kautsky explains, is feasible so long as the wish to serve the two objectives manifests itself only in negation,[44] that is, in the exposure of what is morally opposed and from which development leads away in any event. Despite the *caveat*, scientific socialism and socialism as an ethical ideal overlap to a much greater extent in Kautsky's own conception. He himself admitted that ethics did play a part in the dissemination, and even the attainment, of scientific knowledge. He also spoke of 'the wonderful perspectives of the ethical ideal gathered from sober economic analysis'. He thus did not succeed in making plainer than Marx the distinction between scientific socialism and the ethical ideal of socialism. However, in submitting both bourgeois and proletarian beliefs under the same category of 'ethical ideals' and in relating Marxian scientific socialism and the ethical ideal of socialism to each other, Kautsky went against Marx and Engels's theoretical claims in general and their conception of ideology in particular. Characteristically, neither Kautsky nor Lenin did so explicitly. Yet in substance, and above all also in terminology, Kautsky kept closer to Marx and Engels than did Lenin.

Kautsky used the term 'moral ideal' for the norms and beliefs of the two contending classes, but like the founders he did not apply 'ideology' and 'ideological' (terms he used rarely) to socialism. He employed 'teachings' and especially 'theory', as was most fitting for a proponent of 'scientific socialism', He spoke of the 'ideological superstructure', particularly when he related to it an ideal which leads 'for a while an independent life' and collides with social development only in the longer run. This assumption can be regarded to follow from, and to be open to the same ob-

---

[44] *Ethik*, pp. 142, 144. Lukács's distinction between political and spiritual elites (Ludz, 'Der Begriff der "demokratischen Diktatur" in der politischen Philosophie von Georg Lukács', p. xlv) is thus implied in Kautsky's conception, without being part of an undemocratic elitism.

jection as, Marx and Engels's evolutionary thesis, according to which the superstructure is entirely out of tune with reality whenever the state of social relations falls behind the development of the forces of production.[45] Kautsky also retained the notion of the irreducible disparity between ideals and reality and remained close to the founders in maintaining that, unlike proletarian ideals, bourgeois ideals were bound to become an impediment to development. He did not take over the formulas which indicated that the dependence of consciousness on being invariably entailed false consciousness as long as classes and the division of labour continued to exist. Rather he fastened, above all, on the most sensible implication of the idea that consciousness depends on being. He stipulated that the degree to which consciousness corresponded to the actual stage of socio-economic development was the criterion of 'scientific socialism', i.e. the criterion of the adequacy and effectiveness of the ways and means to advance the socialist ideal. On these grounds it was possible to adhere to what is a modified residue of the idea of 'false consciousness': the varying disparity between ideals and prevailing conditions. On the same grounds it was also possible to maintain that socialist consciousness grows in conjunction with the class struggle and that this spontaneous growth can be supplemented by direct efforts to raise the consciousness of the workers to the level of their actual position in the class war.

III. Intrepid inferences: Bernstein

In placing class consciousness 'outside the economic struggle', Lenin therefore went beyond Kautsky's attempt to reconcile conscious action and economic causation. On this account, as in his use of 'ideology', Lenin was nearer to Bernstein than to Kautsky.

Bernstein's conception of ideology may represent a return to Lassalle.[46] He quite obviously drew the logical conclusion from

[45] See above, pp. 34 and 41–2, for the impossibility of reducing their theory of ideology to this position.

[46] P. Gay, *The Dilemma of Democratic Socialism: Eduard Bernstein's Challenge to Marx* (New York, 1952), p. 139. The author deals only with Bernstein's attempt to undermine Marx's determinism and not with the evaluation of Bernstein's deviations from Marx and Engels's use of ideology. Similarly, P. Angel, *Eduard Bernstein et l'évolution du socialisme allemand* (Paris, 1961), pp. 188ff, asserts in addition that economic and ideological factors were adjusted to each other in Marx, and on these grounds maintains that Bernstein was not in some points

Kautsky's identification of socialist as well as of bourgeois norms with 'moral ideals' when he called 'ideological' the reliance on, or influence of, ideals. Socialism was originally 'pure ideology' or idealism, because whatever the motivation of theorists and the masses for aspiring to a socialist society, the argument always took its cue from an 'idea' like Christianity, justice, equality and so forth.[47] Unburdened by the self-imposed commitments of Kautsky and Lenin to minimize or not admit any break with orthodox Marxism, Bernstein called in question the claim of historical materialism to have purged socialism from ideology. The attempt to assign to ideal factors a derivative status was unsuccessful, because the supposition of motivation by interests includes and presupposes motivation by 'ideal forces'.

Although historical materialism derived motivation by interest from material factors, group interests, argued Bernstein perceptively, could not emerge without the intervention of social and ethical orientation. To be shared, interests must be perceived as ideas, and participation in their pursuit requires at least partial renunciation of purely self-oriented perspectives, if not the temporary sacrifice of personal advantages. Concerning the other ideal force, the insights and perceptions themselves which make up the 'proletarian ideas' about state, society, history and so on, Bernstein repeated, like Lenin, Kautsky's view that these ideas were not produced by the proletariat but by bourgeois intellectuals.[48] But only Bernstein recalled the fact in order to expose the weakness of historical materialism. Similarly, regarding the most moot point, that is the original claim that moral considerations have nothing to do with the nature of socialism,[49] it was again not the affirmation of moral influence which separated Bernstein from Kautsky and Lenin but the explicit insistence on the failure of Marxist theory to uphold in its elaborations the claim it made in principle. Bernstein had no qualms about arguing that the Marxian negation of the role of moral convictions in the conception of socialism was strikingly confuted by the moral judgments implicit in concepts like 'relations of exploitation [*Ausbeutungs-*

altogether fair to Marx and Engels. Angel does not offer any documentation of the premise, which on my reading of Marx (see above, Chapter 2.ıı) is false.

[47] 'Das realistische und das ideologische Moment im Sozialismus', pp. 267, 279.
[48] Bernstein, pp. 270–1.
[49] Bernstein, p. 276.

verhältnis]', and the evaluation of 'surplus value' in terms of 'cheat, theft or robbery'.[50]

Bernstein's use of 'ideology' for all ideals and theories about them enabled him to some extent to treat the lack of correspondence between ideal and reality even more in accordance with orthodox theory than did Kautsky, and at the same time to make such use of the dogmatic conception of ideology as to turn what he retained of it against the notion of 'scientific socialism'. Bernstein again dealt with the discrepancy between ideal and reality as inherent in the nature of 'ideology' and consequently as characteristic of all belief systems.[51] In saying that to attribute the creation of 'the proletarian ideas' to the proletariat is to perpetrate 'an ideological inversion of the real occurrence',[52] he employed the terminology of the dogmatic conception. He did not interpret the occurrence of such falsification as a necessity predetermined economically, socially or otherwise. On the contrary, the inversion is an obfuscation, particularly unpardonable on the part of the spokesmen of scientific socialism, who ought to take seriously Marx's words in the Introduction to the *Critique of Political Economy* about the unprejudiced recourse to facts.[53] Bernstein thus agreed with Kautsky on the separation of the ideal from science. He did so in accordance with Antonio Labriola's and Benedetto Croce's opposition to the alignment of socialism and science. Bernstein reported that, 'in order to stop this nonsense', Labriola suggested the use of 'critical communism' instead of 'scientific socialism'.[54]

It follows that in Bernstein's view ideological falsification can be exposed like falsehoods in science. Marx thought the same but confused the issue hopelessly by his dogmatic conception of ideology. But we also must challenge Bernstein and ask: can we avoid falsities if, as Bernstein argues, the results of scientific

---

[50] Bernstein, p. 278. It perhaps deserves recalling, as Schmoller, *Die soziale Frage*, p. 281, had done, that Charles Hall had already pointed out in 1805 that the poor work only one hour out of eight for themselves and that Owen's friend William Thomson used 'surplus value' for workers' labour unjustly appropriated by the owners of land and capital. As Schmoller concluded, these were 'the thoughts and words which afterwards served Rodbertus, Marx and his disciples'.

[51] In his political writings, Lenin touched on the problem only in passing (Cp. SW, ii, 600, 603, 629), as one would do in comparing thought and approach on the one hand and actual fact on the other.

[52] Bernstein, 'Das realistische und das ideologische Moment', p. 270.

[53] Bernstein, p. 271.

[54] Bernstein, p. 280n.

verification themselves can never be final or escape the influence of its presuppositions? To go by Bernstein's elaborations, designed to expose the ideological character of Marxism, it does not follow that it is in the nature of an ideological argument to impose upon reality ideas which can never stand up to facts. Rather, Bernstein seems to have assumed that varied degrees of verification and verifiability are attendant upon the interaction in ideology of ideas and the reality they are intended to shape. 'Proletarian ideas', for example, are ideological because, as Bernstein cogently remarks, they are 'turned towards' [*zugewandt*], i.e. facing material factors and thought reflexes in the sense of 'conclusions built on the summing up in thought of established facts'. These conclusions are 'necessarily coloured by ideology' since no future-oriented theory can avoid such colouring.[55] Although Bernstein retained the idea that 'ideological' signifies the inversion of reality, he moved far away from the Marxian notion of necessarily distorting thought reflexes triggered off more or less automatically by economic and social conditions.

First he assumed that, once economic factors have in modern society given rise to other factors, these can henceforth operate independently.[56] Moreover, economic factors in the first place concur generally with a plethora of other factors – social, political, historical, religious, geographical and other natural ones, including the nature of men and their mental capabilities. They all have a bearing on the thought and actions of men.[57] Second, although Bernstein did not make the point with sufficient clarity and explicitness, he unmistakeably assumed that thought which emerges from the interaction of a multiplicity of existential factors is not fully identical with ideological thought. Rather, the latter emerges from thought coming to grips with both existential factors and the thought and action they give rise to. The conceptual presuppositions of the thought process which go into the 'summing up' of facts, the reflection in that process of intellectual trends and of moral motivations, are taken to assume a weight of their own and to colour as the ideological factor *per se* any theory which pertains to future developments, no matter whether the theory is materialistic or does not relate to tangible economic

---

[55] Bernstein, pp. 272, 275.
[56] E. Bernstein, *Die Voraussetzungen des Sozialismus und die Aufgaben der Sozialdemokratie* (Stuttgart, 1899), p. 9.
[57] Bernstein, pp. 7–8.

phenomena at all.[58] This is clearly reflected in Bernstein's discussion of the conditions in England which in his view confuted, more than did anything else, the core of Marxist theory.

On the assumption that the attitudes of people are formed also in spheres of life other than the working place, Bernstein held that the confrontation between classes and parties in England had been assuaged by the shortening of the working day, the habit of living in cottages (an antidote to collectivist orientation), and the democratization of sport and of other spheres of common interest, not to mention the history of England's political parties and religious communities.[59] He foresaw the faster growth of the numbers of white- than of blue-collar workers in the course of the expansion of industry and commerce. The alleviation of class and party antagonism in such circumstances is, in Bernstein's view, in conformity with historical materialism in so far as social conditions account for the political outlook. Yet he brought upon himself the wrath of orthodox Marxists by asserting at the same time that Marxist theory is refuted by the developments in England, since these show the impact of factors which 'tone down or, if you wish, "falsify"' the influence of the relations of production on the thought and action of the workers.[60]

Bernstein tried to beat Marx at his own game. He is saying that the consciousness rooted in the complex life situation of workers 'falsifies', that is, is different from, the consciousness which according to Marxist theory corresponds to the class position of the workers, if that position is defined exclusively in terms of economic relations. In other words, Bernstein regarded Marxist theory as disproved by what Marx had assumed to be irrelevant in the final analysis and what – apart from Bernstein – Kautsky and Lenin, too, estimated as a fact to be reckoned with, namely that the class consciousness which the proletariat ought to exhibit according to Marxist theory is not entertained by most proletarians.

[58] 'Das realistische und das ideologische Moment', p. 285. In saying that political ideas and institutions exercise a mediating and integrative function in relation to the social structure and that, while they originate in the latter, they can outlast it, L. Dion, 'An Hypothesis Concerning Structure and Function of Ideology', in R. H. Cox (ed.), *Ideology, Politics and Political Theory* (Belmont, Cal., 1969), pp. 317, 331, 326, actually follows Bernstein's advance beyond Kautsky's admission of the temporary independence of the superstructure (see above, pp. 95–6).

[59] Bernstein, 'Das realistische und das ideologische Moment', p. 274.

[60] Bernstein, p. 275.

In Bernstein's opinion it could not be otherwise. The empirically observable consciousness of the majority of the working class is no mirror of the relations of production because it is wrong to assume in the first place that economic position alone determines consciousness. Moreover, as Bernstein perspicaciously observed, the ideas about state, society, history etc. which Marxist theory attributes to the proletariat are not derived from the specific life situation of the workers but from the common traits of the different life situations of the workers in advanced societies. No wonder that such derivations (i.e. second-order generalizations about facts) are misleading and that 'what we call "proletarian conceptions" are for the proletarian himself – for the time being – ideology'.[61] For Bernstein, historical materialism thus stands contradicted, in part by facts that conform with its own terms and in part by facts which invalidate those terms. Bernstein's pertinent polemics, which are designed to uncover the ideological character of Marxism, add up to the conclusion that socialist ideology – and hence all ideology – clashes in varying degrees with reality, with the actual consciousness people entertain about that reality as well as with the scientific appraisal of that reality.

Kautsky, Bernstein and Lenin were thus at one in asserting that socialist consciousness did not come naturally to the workers. The three socialist ideologists were not of one mind over the explication and the implications. However, their explicit disagreements and even their explicit agreements often obscure that which really unites and divides their views (and this is true of most ideological controversies). In consideration both of their relation to the original doctrine and of their future importance, it is worth while to sort out and clarify the actual agreements and disagreements in the case in hand.

[61] Bernstein, p. 275.

6

AN INTERIM BALANCE

/

1. Affinities and differences

Marx himself was aware of the discrepancy – resulting, in his view, from the division of labour, and bound to last until 'the reign of reason' – between the historically adequate and effective consciousness that fitted the class position and historical mission of the proletariat and its actual inadequate and, in the long run, ineffective consciousness. He was contradictory on the importance of the point, since apparently it also seemed to him important to demonstrate the attainability of adequate class consciousness; hence his singling out as exemplary the stage of consciousness already reached, as it were, by the English and French workers. He was justified in attaching no decisive importance to such progress in so far as he believed that ultimately consciousness must follow economic and social developments.

Lukács kept closer to that position than Kautsky, with whom Bernstein and Lenin agreed about the importance of the issue and the necessity of laying greater stress on the conscious element. The young Lukács abided much more than his elders by the masters' conception and kept his concessions to the conscious element within the limits of merely repeating Marx and Engels's deviations (without in any way intimating that they were deviations) from the primacy of economic determination and their constant return to it.[1] Kautsky squarely faced the problem of the lack of correspondence between adequate, though for the time being insufficiently effective, class consciousness and inadequate, but for the time being most effective, class consciousness. He asserted that to recognize the discrepancy and to act in order to impart the right consciousness to the workers was in accord with Marx's teachings. This is probably one reason why Lenin sought support in Kautsky for the far more pronounced importance he

---

[1] Lukács's attempt in the Preface of 1967 at retroactive adjustment of his views to those of *What Is to Be Done?* (see above, Chapter 5, note 28) patches over the deeper-lying original incompatability.

attached to political over and against economic activity, although his views in this respect were much better accounted for by Bernstein's arguments.

According to Kautsky, the more the political ideal is in harmony with the predominantly economic conditioning factors, the more effective it is. Bernstein reversed this conclusion and held that the influence of the relations of production on the workers' consciousness is toned down, if not actually offset, by the influence of the other existential factors. Such a drastic reduction of the significance of the economic factor was the logical precondition of Lenin's demand to divert the workers from their spontaneous penchant for trade unionism and bring them the socialist consciousness 'from without . . . the economic struggle'. The explanation Bernstein offered for the lack of conformity of the class consciousness of the English workers with that which, according to orthodox theory, they were presumed to display, could have served Lenin as a striking example of why workers match the development of capitalism with that of trade unionism and largely fall in with bourgeois ideology, and why, therefore, socialist ideology and the way of thinking of the workers do not necessarily coincide. Acknowledged or not, Lenin's insistence on the power of ideology and politics to overcome economic determination reflects Bernstein's explicit exceptions to Marxist theory.

Thus it was a double sleight of hand on Lenin's part to dub his Russian adversaries 'Bernsteinists'[2] and argue against them that it need not be deduced from the decisiveness of economic factors that trade unionism embodies the struggle of the proletariat for socialism. In the first place, Bernstein did not derive trade-union consciousness from the premise of the decisiveness of the economic factor, but from the premise that it was 'toned down' by other factors. He had not only, much like Lenin, practically qualified away his acceptance of the primary impact of economic factors, but had done so in open defiance of Marxism, although he credited it with having disproved the notion that socialism had been arbitrarily derived from ideas,[3] and even agreed that economic conditions were conducive to evoking socialist convictions in the workers. But Bernstein insisted that, contrary to Marxist theory, those who acted on these convictions were the workers not in the most advanced but in the retarded and ancillary indus-

[2] E.g. SW, I, 153, 185, 197.
[3] Bernstein, 'Das realistische und das ideologische Moment', p. 285.

tries in England and Germany.[4] There is a clear affinity between this and Lenin's views on village capitalism and class war[5] and the justification of the occurrence of the Bolshevik Revolution in economically and socially backward Russia. Even if Lenin had been aware of the extent to which he adapted Bernstein's views to his purposes, to admit this was tactically irreconcilable with his political controversy with revisionism. After all, his business was not scholarly accuracy but ideological controversy. Even if overdrawn, there is something to be said in favour of Sombart's judgment that the Marxist doctrinairism displayed by Lenin was largely a means to his political power struggle.[6]

Lenin was miles apart from Bernstein not merely in separating 'trade-union consciousness' from 'social democratic consciousness'. While Bernstein, too, had put a premium on political action, it was an altogether different kind of action each man had in mind. Since on vital issues Lenin fought the Russian Economists *qua* Bernsteinists, and saw fit to do so under the banner of orthodox Marxism, he could not admit that Bernstein in point of fact explained what was implicit in Lenin's own inclusive and non-pejorative use of 'ideology', i.e. that socialism cannot claim to be something else, and that the term 'scientific socialism' is therefore out of place. This unacknowledged affinity with Bernstein is all the less spurious, since Bernstein as little as Lenin maintained that socialism had no social roots, but that, like any ideology, it collided in important respects with reality and the thought reflecting it faithfully. The affinity is certainly not logically disturbed by Bernstein's explanation that 'proletarian ideas' are above reality because they are second-order generalizations about it designed to lead beyond it. Lenin could also have had no objection to Bernstein's observation that socialism cannot claim to be free of ideology because 'no future-oriented theory can be'.[7]

[4] Bernstein, p. 273.
[5] See *The Agrarian Programme of Russian Social Democracy* (1902). Bernstein's idea is also confirmed if extended to generally backward regions, by, for instance, the analysis of the communist vote in Finland. See E. Allardt, 'Patterns of Class Conflict and Class Consciousness in Finnish Politics', in E. Allardt and Y. Littunen (eds.), *Cleavages, Ideologies and Party Systems* (Helsinki, 1964), pp. 104ff, 112ff. Allardt adds the very important distinction between the different social roots of traditional and emerging communism or radicalism (pp. 125ff).
[6] Sombart, *Der proletarische Sozialismus*, II, 504.
[7] Bernstein, 'Das realistische und das ideologische Moment', p. 285.

However, it is one thing to argue along these lines. It is something else – and this made the admission of the affinity impossible for Lenin – to admit, let alone stress, that Marxist socialism is contradicted in its essential fundamentals by facts and considerations that weighed equally with the two men. Among these, particular importance attaches to Bernstein's exceptions to the negative role which historical materialism assigns to ideology. They represent the core of the arguments required for Lenin's consistent use of 'ideology' in an inclusive sense never intended by Marx and Engels. For the same reason, Bernstein's views circumscribe a tenable and coherent conception of ideology which can be related to, by being sifted from, the original Marxist theory of ideology.

Forming a far from well-knit and self-consistent whole, that theory has been shown to move between (and hence to diminish the admissibility of) two extreme poles: the postulate of unexceptionally false bourgeois consciousness, and the implicit, but none the less obvious, postulate of inherently correct proletarian consciousness. A conception of ideology free of these overstatements can be related to the original Marxist theory, partly because it has been shown to alternate between an uncompromising determinism and concessions to the necessity, and possible appositeness, of purposive action. On both counts the original Marxist theory provided an opening for the successors to modify in varying degrees the unilateral dependence of both correct and distorted consciousness on class and socio-economic conditions. It should, therefore, perhaps not come as a surprise that Lukács made the attempt to justify on orthodox lines a disjunction of ideology from economic conditions, which matches to some extent Bernstein's idea of the general progress towards 'free ideology'. Given the at first sight strange affinities between the anti-revisionist and Bernsteinian attitudes so far considered, it seems appropriate, before dealing with the specific issue of the dissociation in different ways and contexts of ideology and cognition from economic conditions, to outline first the case for the attempt to retrieve Kautsky and Bernstein's theoretical achievements from what might be called 'ideological repression'.

In continuation of the preceding discussion, and within its thematic confines, I propose therefore in the remainder of the present chapter to indicate briefly some reverberations of the views of Kautsky and Bernstein in latter-day revaluations of Marxian theory. This will round off our interim balance of the degree to which, and the ways in which, the bond was loosened between ideology on the one hand and impotence and falsity on the other.

ii. Unrequited debts

It is certainly strange, though characteristic of New Leftism, that people should assert that reinstating 'the subjective element' in its proper place in the Marxist conception of ideology occurred as late as the 1920s in opposition to the 'official' orthodox and revisionist Marx interpretation of a Kautsky and Bernstein.[8] The truth of the matter is, as I have amply documented, that Kautsky and Bernstein in their varying responses to the situation which their party had to face, and *in their wake* Lenin, did the decisive spade-work in explicit and implicit extension of Engels's misgivings about the one-sidedness of the theory of history and ideology as Marx and he had left it.[9] The contributions of a Bloch, Korsch, Lukács, Marcuse and others, hailed by the contemporary New Left, actually did no more in the twenties or early thirties than elaborate on the ideas Kautsky, Bernstein and Lenin had advanced in their different ways some decades earlier. And so, by the way, did Stalin, who in his *Marxism and Problems of Linguistics* revised the theoretical framework of historical materialism. Contemporary Polish Marxist scholars, like Adam Schaff, could without pangs of conscience acclaim the revision as 'a further step in the long development initiated by Lenin in *What Is to Be Done?*'.[10] Party logic flawed the historical record only slightly in so far as it apparently forbade the invocation of Kautsky as the

---

[8] Thus Lenk, *Ideologie*, pp. 38–9. See also N. Harris, *Beliefs in Society: The Problem of Ideology* (London, 1968), pp. 84, 162, for the misjudgment of Kautsky's conception of 'the role of human activity and consciousness' and the contention that Kautsky expanded the deterministic vein beyond Marx to a 'crude materialism' (pp. 147, 161). No shred of evidence is produced to support these allegations.

[9] See above, p. 42.

[10] Jordan, *Philosophy and Ideology*, pp. 480ff. As Jordan explains, Stalin made a sharp distinction between social consciousness and the superstructure. He accorded to the former a wider scope so as to make room in it for elements, like language, which were not to be regarded as superstructural and hence not as class-bound. Moreover, in its new and narrower confines the superstructure is invested with the power to advance or retard the growth of the base (pp. 478–9). Like the revolutionary revisionists themselves, Jordan ignores that in these matters their views are in the spirit of Bernstein's revisionism.

patron saint of the 'development', as Lenin did. It is only fair to add that, while Lenin to all intents and purposes actually accepted Bernstein's denial of the primary importance of the socio-economic class struggle as the instrument of change, Bernstein on his part followed in this respect the lead provided by Sidney Webb.[11]

It is furthermore worth recalling that in both their critique and their appreciation of Marx and Engels, the older and younger generations of Marxists who immediately succeeded the founders posed a challenge to bourgeois scholars who, like Gustav Schmoller, Werner Sombart and Max Weber, took issue with Marxism. These scholars too adapted and enlarged upon the reinterpretations of Kautsky and Bernstein, though they did not necessarily refer to them. Yet there is a tangible connection between the rehabilitation of political and ideal factors by Kautsky and Bernstein, and particularly Bernstein's explicit rejection of Marx's notion of economic mono-causality, and the critique of that notion by Weber in conjunction with his delineation of what 'economically determined' can sensibly be taken to mean. In obvious refinement of Bernstein's criticism, Weber argued that institutions, groupings and even 'the finest hues of aesthetic and religious feelings' are indirectly influenced by social relations in which reverberates the pressure of material interests. In other words, the superstructure is 'co-influenced' by social relations reflecting also material interests, 'just as the sum total of the phenomena and conditions of life act upon the form of material wants, the manner of their satisfaction ... the formation of material interest groups ... and their instruments of power and therewith upon the direction which economic development takes ... The economic is a specific element of cultural phenomena', and to trace it alone furnishes only a partial picture.[12] Just as Kautsky, Bernstein and Lenin recognized the elaboration of socialism by (bourgeois) intellectuals and the cleft to be bridged between prevailing attitudes and those believed to be adequate, Weber stressed the personal (and charismatic) origin of socially effective ideas to-

[11] G. D. H. Cole, *A History of Socialist Thought* (4 vols., London and New York, 1959–60), III, I, 278.
[12] M. Weber, 'Die "Objektivität" sozialwissenschaftlicher und sozialpolitischer Erkenntnis', in *Gesammelte Aufsätze zur Wissenschaftslehre* (Tübingen, 1922), pp. 163–4. It is worth mentioning, especially in view of Marx's rather thoughtless acceptance of racialist premises (see Chapter 7, note 15), that in his rejection of *Kausalmonismus*, Weber put historical materialism on a par with racial theories (p. 170).

gether with their initial clash with prevailing economic and other orientations.[13]

In the same line lies Weber's supplementation of Marx's economic by a political and even military 'materialism'. In quite close affinity to Bernstein, he distinguished between the influence of 'material and ideal interests' and that of ideas, assuming that 'world images' created by ideas acted like 'switchmen' (Trotsky's simile) who determine 'the tracks along which action has been pushed by the dynamic interests'.[14]

Given the original predominance in the socialist camp of the German SPD, and the fact that the struggle between Bernstein and his opponents over the adaptation of official party theory to the principles actually underlying its political course was conducted in the limelight of history, one is justified in speaking of the unacknowledged debt owed to Kautsky and, above all, to Bernstein by critics of Marxism, as well as by those who pose as opponents of revisionism but cannot (and sometimes even do not) for this reason claim to be faithful to the letter of Marx and Engels's teachings. To the ungrateful debtors belong also the proponents of the revisionism that emerged into the open with 'the thaw' and of the revisionism inherent in the 'humanist' and anti-humanist reinterpretations of Marx in the West.

The neglect of Bernstein's anticipation of later trends is not without exceptions. Labedz has noted that 'most of the ideas pronounced by modern revisionists [a designation more often than not shunned by the 'humanist' interpreters and the other sympathizers or adherents of the New Left] were already pretty clearly stated by their predecessors'.[15] The point is made with special reference to Bernstein by a number of contributors to

---

[13] M. Weber, *Wirtschaft und Gesellschaft*, 2nd enlarged edn (half-vols. I, II, Tübingen, 1925), pp. 760, 763–4.

[14] *Gesammelte Aufsätze zur Religionssoziologie* (Tübingen, 1922–3), I, 252, as quoted in H. H. Gerth and C. W. Mills, *From Max Weber: Essays in Sociology*, repr. (New York, 1969), p. 63. Generally, Weber seems to have juxtaposed 'ideal and material consideration' or 'interests' to the exclusive preponderance of the cash-nexus. See R. Bendix, *Max Weber: An Intellectual Portrait* (New York, 1960), p. 260. The connections indicated here between Marx's successors and Weber are not considered in Roth's brief 'Critique and Adaptation' in R. Bendix and G. Roth, *Scholarship and Partisanship, Essays on Max Weber* (Berkeley, Los Angeles and London, 1971), pp. 227–52, the intent of which is to show that Marx's influence on Weber has been overestimated.

[15] Labedz, *Revisionism*, p. 26.

Labedz's collection. However, even the more specific acknowledgments, as in Kolakowski's adoption of Bernstein's insistence
on the ethical foundation of socialism, or the explicit reliance on
his general demand, shared with Kautsky, for the subordination
of the socialist programme to the democratic process,[16] are essentially summary and fragmentary. They only bring home the need
(which I trust is underscored by what has been revealed in the
present thematic confines) for a study in depth of Bernstein's
ideas, which have been proved vital and for the most part assimilated tacitly into various contexts – very much in Lenin's way,
that is, under the cover of calumny or disdain.[17]

The ideological foundation of the neglect becomes all the more
evident in view of the fact that it has become fashionable among
scholars with more or less radical leftist leanings to lavish praise
on Gramsci, in particular, for, among other things, developing the
Marxist theory of ideology. For the most part this is done by
selective quotation. It must be said, however, that Gramsci's
efforts in this connection, as in that of other subjects treated or
rather adumbrated by him, are more elaborate but no less fragmentary in substance than the writings available in English
translation generally are. He conceived a broadly indicated
framework for a philosophical and historical comparative theory
of development, of which Marxism formed the basis and at the
same time the object of its own further development. Whether or
not his failure to relate his contribution to the theory of ideology
to the contribution made by Kautsky and Bernstein, or even in
any detail to Lenin's views, is due like other shortcomings to the
cruel hardships of his imprisonment, it emerges clearly that
Gramsci actually made explicit the idealist assumptions underlying Lenin's voluntarism and avant-gardism. Gramsci hailed the
blending of idealist tendencies with Marxism as most significant
for making the latter a potent force, as well as for bringing to the
fore the philosophical potential of Marxism,[18] over and against the
preoccupation in original Marxism with economics, and, as a

---

[16] K. Reyman and H. Singer, 'The Origin and Significance of East
European Revisionism', in Labedz, pp. 216–17.

[17] Even Jordan in his richly documented *Philosophy and Ideology* does
not identify the reverberations in communist thought in Poland of
Kautsky and Bernstein's ideas.

[18] A. Gramsci, *The Modern Prince and Other Writings*, ed. with an
Introduction by L. Marks, 4th impr. (New York, 1970), pp. 82,
84.

result, with 'fatalistic' economic determinism, 'fatalistic finalism', in short, 'mechanicalism'.[19]

For didactic reasons, Gramsci argued, original Marxism was only slightly above the very low average of popular culture and only implied a philosophy.[20] Since Marxism 'true and proper' consisted, however, of its philosophical parts, the time has come for 'the fatalist interpretation' to receive its 'funeral eulogy' and submit to 'the necessity of burying it with all honours'.[21] True, 'mechanical determinism' was 'a formidable power of moral resistance ... and ... perseverance'; it was 'a form of religion and of stimulation' in adversity and desperation, but it became a danger after the situation of the subordinate groups changed. The belief 'in favourable conditions ... predestined to come into existence' caused 'the loss of all voluntary initiative aiming to predispose this situation according to plan'.[22] While Gramsci pointed out, just as Bernstein had, the fundamental limitation of the founders' theory, he, like Kautsky, admitted of no break with it. Apart from explaining 'the historical role' of the pronounced determinism of the 'primitive' phase as having been once adequate and necessary, he also held in Kautsky's vein that industrial techniques '(in a certain sense)' are independent of systems of appropriation (or rather allocation) of products.[23] He eventually gave a pragmatic answer to the question of whether or not cultural (ideological) reform could precede economic reform: since the relationship between 'economism' and 'ideologism' is difficult to determine, the useful application of free will is like seizing upon an opportunity in foreign relations.[24]

[19] Gramsci, pp. 84–5, 93 and 67, 69, 160, respectively.
[20] Gramsci, pp. 83, 95.
[21] Gramsci, pp. 96, 75.
[22] Gramsci, pp. 69, 160. Thus Gramsci also said that 'mechanical causation' is 'a mere myth which was *perhaps* [my italics] useful in the past' (p. 101). He also strictured the scientific and political wrongness of assuming 'a statistical law' (p. 95), and postulated that there existed an interaction between education and environment (p. 100).
[23] Gramsci, p. 25. For Kautsky, see below, p. 177.
[24] Gramsci, pp. 140, 173. It needs to be pointed out that Gramsci's conception of economism was wider than that of Lenin inasmuch as he grounded it in liberalism and found it to express itself in syndicalism, as well as in other political postures (pp. 153–7). One should also note that he criticized the 'historical economism', purportedly produced by liberalism, for confusing permanent and complex class interests with self-interest 'in a direct and "dirty" Jewish sense' (p. 156). The view is not precisely that of the master; the language certainly is.

Thus in his explicit concessions to idealism and voluntarism Gramsci went as far as Bernstein did. This indirectly confirms that, as I have argued, Lenin's evaluation of ideology and politics can best be explained in the terms of Bernstein's overt criticism of Marxism. In fact Gramsci abided by Lenin's intention in following Kautsky more than Bernstein, in so far as he not only attenuated his critique of original Marxism but also tried time and time again to convey the impression that he relied on the essence of the founders' teachings. In the last resort, however, he justified his often drastic emendations of these teachings by reference to the most often used, most flexible and hence least convincing piece of already post-orthodox evidence: the late Engels's self-criticism which, taken strictly (as it never was), did not affect the causal decisiveness 'in the last instance' of the economic structure.[25] On these grounds, or rather as part of them, Gramsci outlined his theory of the role of 'traditional' and 'organic' intellectuals who serve the cultural and political concerns of ruling and subordinate groups respectively.[26]

Although Gramsci's numerous statements on the subject are neither wholly reconcilable with one another nor uncontroversial, they are always worthy of attention. They amount to an elaboration of Marx's own statement about the defection of middle-class intellectuals into the proletarian camp and proceed along the lines according to which first Kautsky and Bernstein and then Lenin actually opposed the founders to the point not only of unambiguously admitting the creation of socialism by middle-class intellectuals but also of connecting their leading role with the rehabilitation of the conscious element over and against the immediate and decisive influence of the economic factor. These views clearly reverberate in all that Gramsci says on the relationship between the leaders and the led, for his 'organic' intellectual is not only the creator of a new culture but is also, for instance, the entrepreneur, the intellectual technician and the political economist in emerging capitalism; all represent 'the new social type'[27] and fulfil a political integrating function. So do the 'traditional' intellectuals who mediate between the rulers and bearers

25 Gramsci, p. 160.
26 Henceforth I shall refer only to *The Modern Prince and Other Writings*. However, see also Q. Hoare and G. N. Smith (eds.), *Selections from Prison Notebooks of Antonio Gramsci* (London, 1971), pp. 5–23.
27 Gramsci, pp. 43, 118.

of 'the higher' culture or philosophy on the one hand and the masses on the other in order to secure their compliance with the established institutional and belief system.[28] Prior to the conquest of state power, the proletariat is unable to produce its intellectuals from its midst, and even afterwards does so only 'very slowly and laboriously'.[29] An essentially political function is played also by the intellectuals who are capable of defecting to the proletariat. They render the proletariat and the new ideology predicated on the situation of the proletariat coherent, homogeneous and, above all, disciplined. As little as his predecessor does this new type remain a specialist. He becomes a leader, a 'specialist plus politician' – a builder, an organizer, 'permanently persuasive'.[30]

In accordance with the explicit redemption of the superstructure and its officiants by the two most prominent reformist successors of Marx and Engels, and in the spirit of the outstanding architect of the first communist revolution, Gramsci said: 'There is no organization without intellectuals, that is, without organizers and leaders.'[31] For, like Lenin, Gramsci did not accept the two reformists' demand that the relationship between leaders and led rest on the commitment to formal and parliamentary democracy.[32]

28 Gramsci, pp. 62, 65–6, 90–2.
29 Gramsci, p. 50. Cp. also p. 89. Here, as in other instances, Gramsci was not quite consistent. Much of what he said about the subject rests on the assumption that the middle-class defectors are joined by intellectuals emerging from the subordinate groups. Indeed we are told that the more simultaneous the process, the more rapidly the concerns of the rising groups will be espoused by traditional intellectuals (p. 122).
30 Gramsci, p. 122.
31 Gramsci, p. 67.
32 One should not be misled by his stress on the participation of even the most primitive industrial worker in social change (p. 128), the necessity of the simultaneous thrust forward by intellectuals and the masses in 'an intellectual-mass dialectic' (in which contact might be lost) (p. 68), the suggestion of minimizing and eventually disposing of the leader–led relationship (p. 143), by his opposing, like Trotsky, 'democratic centralism' to 'bureaucratic centralism' (p. 153). The prime consideration is that, for the time being, the question is how to prepare leaders and gain obedience (p. 144). Gramsci provided no clue as to how to reconcile factory self-government (p. 23) and democratic self-government. He rejected 'the canons of formal democracy' on the basis of denying the appropriateness of identifying representative with parliamentary democracy (pp. 183–6). Nothing he said in *The Modern Prince* on the formation of 'the collective will' attenuated his view of the preponderance of 'the solid frame of the apparatus of rule' (p. 178) in the adjustment of the thrust from below to the command from above. Thus, as to the conditions which ensure the existence of a

The more recent and orthodox, that is to say both 'anti-humanist' and officially communist, reinterpretations of Marxism also show traces of early revisionism. Thus Althusser, for instance, without acknowledging it elaborates on Kautsky's distinction between socialism as a new moral ideal and scientific socialism.[33] For, according to Althusser, 'egalitarian communism is still an ideological conception of the aim of the workers' movement', i.e. it is not yet (as Kautsky said of socialism) 'scientific communism'. Althusser's statements that Marx the philosopher strayed into the very ideology he fought against[34] also recall Kautsky's criticism of Marx. In view of this attitude towards Kautsky, it is not surprising that the more or less official French party philosopher who displays nevertheless an astonishing measure of intellectual independence (at least at the time of writing), should not only use 'ideology' as Lenin did in his political writings[35] but should also fail to note any consonance with Bernstein in this respect. The omission of any reference to Kautsky, however, weighs more heavily, since Althusser follows Kautsky more closely than did Lenin, who merely invoked his authority. Although used in a positive sense and hence applicable to communism and Marxist philosophy, 'ideology' is distinguished by Althusser (*vide* Kautsky) from science and from Marxist theory as well. 'In the strict Marxist sense of the term', says Althusser, 'Marxism itself is not an ideology.'[36] Thus we find Marxist 'philosophical ideology' set apart from 'the theory of Marxist philosophy'.[37] While Althusser presents us with a highly sophisticated and confessedly further development of Marxism, he fails to admit that Kautsky's views furnish at least the grounds for his recasting of the distinction between Marxism *qua* philosophy and ideology on one side, and Marxist science and theory on the other; between Marx's new science of social formations and that of which it is the basis, 'a new theoretically and

party, the principal element 'endowed with a highly cohesive, centralizing and disciplinary power' is 'the generals', as it were, and while 'this element alone would not form a party, . . . it would do so more than the first element', i.e. 'the widespread element of common average men' (p. 150). If generals disappear the army is destroyed, but if they exist they are able 'to form an army even where none exists'.

[33] See above, pp. 96–7.
[34] Althusser and Balibar, *Reading Capital*, pp. 58, 90.
[35] Althusser and Balibar, p. 15 and *passim*.
[36] Althusser, *For Marx*, p. 69. See also Althusser and Balibar, *Reading Capital*, pp. 17, 30, 39ff, 53ff, 60, 69.
[37] *Reading Capital*, p. 31.

practically revolutionary philosophy', which, however, still lags in its elaboration behind its breeding-ground, the Marxist science of history.[38]

The logical corollary of the redemption in the Marxist camp of ideology from its exclusive association, in principle at any rate, with falsity and of the application of the term to Marxism itself, was, of course, the relaxation of the ties between ideology and the economic base. Some evidence to this effect has already been adduced in the preceding discussions, and it now needs to be augmented in order to show how far the successors went in this direction and how much ground was provided by the founders themselves for these developments which therefore attest the extent to which the seeds of the refutation of Marxism are embedded in Marxist theory itself.

[38] Althusser, *For Marx*, p. 14.

7

IDEOLOGY BEYOND ECONOMIC CAUSATION

1. The version of the successors

Like Marx, Bernstein also viewed the relationship between ideological thought and economic conditions in historical perspective. It was a very different perspective, though. Bernstein believed that in earlier epochs ideology served the purpose of concealing the economic motive through political arrangements of domination. Formerly, peasants and workers were kept, like primitive peoples, under the spell of ideologies which put men at the mercy of nature. Modern economic and technological development leaves a greater latitude to ethical and other ideological factors and determines social institutions in ever-diminishing degrees. Modern society has become 'richer in ideology which is not determined by economics and nature as it manifests itself in economic power'. Such 'free ideology' has for the first time become relevant for the most numerous class in modern society.[1] We witness here another un-Marxian application of Marxian principles and a very cogent one at that: the freedom to choose between ideologies is derived from economic developments within the capitalist structure. Evidently, only on the strength of such an assumption of the freedom of choice between ideologies could Lenin argue that 'all belittling' of the socialist ideology 'means ... strengthening the influence of the bourgeois ideology among the workers' (SW, i, 175–6).

Lukács, too, postulated a liberation of ideology from economic conditions. He predicated it, like Bernstein, on modern society, but he meant the post-capitalist society established as a result of the Bolshevik Revolution. Lukács, too, tried to explain the liberation in terms of orthodox theory, and in the attempt he also brought it, however inadvertently, a little more into the orbit of an empirically tenable theory of ideology.

It will be remembered that Lukács is at one with Marx in holding that, in the course of the clear-cut confrontation possible only in bourgeois society between the two classes, the bourgeoisie

---

[1] Bernstein, *Die Voraussetzungen des Sozialismus*, pp. 10–11.

and the proletariat, the oppressed class will become fully conscious of reality. This will coincide with the announcement by the proletariat of the dissolution of the existing order. As I have shown, there is a lack of clarity as to the precise juncture at which the proletariat will attain true consciousness. It is not even clear whether this is really necessary in order to achieve victory in the class struggle.[2] It does not seem wrong to assume that, while Lukács was not prepared to underwrite the voluntarism of *What Is to Be Done?*, he tried to provide orthodox cover for the palpable deviations of the Bolshevik Revolution from the Marxist blueprint (as recapitulated shortly before the event in Lenin's *State and Revolution*). This is evidently the reason for Lukács's assertion that the victory of the proletariat provides only the condition of the eventual attainment of fully objective knowledge and that gradations of distance between objective and subjective class consciousness continue to obtain. This is to say that although the victory of the proletariat has abolished classes, it has not entailed the disappearance of ideology. Yet by the same token, the discrepancy between ideology and correct insight is no longer due, according to Lukács, to economic causes, but to stratification in the proletariat. Thus, although 'the political-economic overcoming' by the workers' Soviets 'of capitalist reification [*Verdinglichung*]', that is of alienation in its social and political aspects, has severed the link between socio-economic conditions and ideological thought,[3] stratification and with it ideology survives.

In *What Is to Be Done?* Lenin also had not excluded the survival of ideology in a classless society. 'In a society torn by class antagonism', he said, 'there can never be a non-class or above-class ideology.'[4] It follows that in a society without class antagonism there can be a non-class ideology. It is the disappearance of class ideologies that is logically implied in Lenin's words, not of ideology as such. (There is nothing strange about this implication, once we cease to conceive the term 'ideological' as being necessarily bound to polarized divisiveness.) For Lenin, the decisive achievement of the Bolshevik Revolution was the abolition of property by the proletariat and, forthwith, the establishment of its own supremacy. Indeed, in that abolition 'lies its domination as a class'.[5] Obviously, Lenin could not connect the

---

[2] See above, pp. 57, 48, 58, 72–3, respectively.
[3] Lukács, *Geschichte und Klassenbewusstsein*, pp. 92–3.
[4] SW, i, 177.   [5] SW, ii, 564.

domination of the proletarian class with the disappearance of classes. He acknowledged without beating about the bush the continuation of class antagonism and of 'the revolutionary class struggle'.[6] In the same year (1921), he also presented 'the concessions policy' as 'a form . . . of the class struggle'. Earlier he saw the small commodity proprietor 'encircle' the proletariat with 'a petty bourgeois atmosphere', and he spoke of 'the bourgeois revolutionary peasantry', the millions of private producers and the bourgeois experts, as well as of capitalism in conjunction with NEP, and so affirmed the coexistence of 'particles' of both capitalism and socialism.[7] The class domination of the proletariat was thus one over class opponents, active and alive.

Lukács apparently felt that on grounds of doctrinal purity one could not admit a plurality of classes in the post-revolutionary society, although like anybody else, he knew that the early endeavours to ensure equality of incomes or even to do without money altogether were short-lived.[7a] He therefore decreed away classes and their corollary, the impact of economic conditions, and made stratification within the proletariat deputize for socioeconomic class division as the causal agent of the remnants of false consciousness, that is, of the undeniable continuance of ideological diversity, as well as of the availability through the Party of the indubitably correct ideology.

Only on these apologetical grounds could Lukács, who knew his Weber, ignore the fact that stratification by status is not entirely, or even decisively, detachable from economic class, although the former is not stringently related to the latter. As Weber said, 'with some oversimplification one might say that classes are stratified according to their relations to production and the acquisition of goods, and status groups [*Stände*] according to the principles of their *consumption* of goods, as evinced in specific forms of "ways of life".' Assuming as obvious the interdependence of economically determined class situation and prestige-oriented status position, Weber also considered the rebound of status stratification on the market.[8] Just as production and distribution

---

[6] *The Fourth Anniversary of the October Revolution* (1921), SW, II, 749.
[7] SW, II, 715, 589, 713, 506, 565, 712 respectively.
[7a] On the developments and the present state of the disparities of income, see now K. von Beyme's comprehensive and richly documented *Ökonomie und Politik im Sozialismus: Ein Vergleich der Entwicklung in den sozialistischen Ländern* (München and Zürich, 1975).
[8] Weber, *Wirtschaft und Gesellschaft*, pp. 639, 638, and generally 631–40; see also on the different status attitudes in various Western

are not subject to the same degree to laws bearing 'the character of physical laws', as Mill argued and Marx contested,[9] and distribution is not entirely independent of the conditions of production, so too status stratification is not wholly unrelated to stratification according to economic class. For instance, in terms of status, lower income groups might rate higher than higher income groups. In both capitalist and communist societies such asymmetry occurs for the most part within the range of higher and lower income groups respectively. In other words, despite disparity of status and income in the two groups, the highest and lowest status groups still belong to the highest and lowest income groups. If in the lower income groups a lower-rated group gets better pay than a group enjoying a higher status, the status of this latter group will normally be lower than that of the lowest income group that belongs to the highest status groups. One can imagine the grounds of status stratification to vary – or not – according to different forms of economic and social organization, but not in the main without any relation to them at all. Moreover, the communist surely is as much of an economic order as is the capitalist order; it does not even lose its conditioning effect in Marxist futurology. A particular form of economic organization, the socialization of the means of production and distribution, figures as the *conditio sine qua non* of the classless society. Thus Lukács misused for polemical purposes the Weberian distinction between various forms of stratification by his substitution of largely unspecified 'stratification' for socio-economic differentiation in Soviet Russia, in order to justify the continuation there of phenomena which, according to Marxist theory, were typical of capitalist society. His inane and self-contradictory manoeuvre should not, however, obscure the importance of the stratagem.

It is important to note, in the first place, that the manoeuvre was carried out because, among other things, it had to be admitted that proletarian ideology continued to be afflicted by false consciousness even after having been instrumental, in accord with 'objective class consciousness', in triggering off the most decisive

(the American and German) and other cultures. For an elaboration of Weber's view and convincing arguments for abiding by his terminology, see W. G. Runciman, *Social Science and Political Theory* (Cambridge, 1963), Chapter 7. On the political significance of the fact that class and status do not always coincide, see below, pp. 203–4.

9 Mill, *Principles of Political Economy*, p. 200, and see above, Chapter 3, note 16.

step, supposed to make possible all others, towards total structural change. The admission further confirms my dismissal as untenable of the extreme positive pole of the continuum which I have culled from the original Marxist theory of ideology: the complete congruence of proletarian ideology with truth.

Secondly, to postulate, even at the cost of a sleight of hand, the continuation of ideology in independence of socio-economic organization and men's position in it, is to admit in principle the detachment of ideology from the economic base. In his desperate attempt at rescuing a central principle of the original Marxist doctrine from being refuted by the attempt to realize it, Lukács unrealistically restricted to the post-capitalist stage the detachment of ideology from economic determination and, therefore, dealt with the phenomenon in a less sensible manner than either Bernstein, in his remarks on 'free ideology', or Lenin, in connection with showing the necessity of imbuing the proletariat with socialist consciousness 'from without'.

Thirdly, Lukács's adaptation by way of semantic subterfuge of inconvenient facts to orthodox theory nevertheless gains in stature if compared either with Lenin's dissimulation of the very existence of a problem of adaptation or with the disregard of both facts and consistency displayed in wily speculations such as those proffered, for instance, by Goldmann a generation later. Goldmann explained on orthodox lines that for dialectical materialism, false consciousness always implied action which, though necessary, did not put an end to exploitation and alienation. Dialectical materialism itself represents a practical attitude which Goldmann styles in unorthodox fashion, though partly in the language of Marx's eleventh thesis on Feuerbach, 'the ideology of a class wanting to transform the world'. Leaving it unclear whether false consciousness is separate from, or both separable from and identifiable with, ideology, Goldmann spells out the implication of Bernstein and Lenin's use of 'ideology' and says that it can be not only conservative and progressive, but also revolutionary. Yet he concluded again in orthodox fashion – and without reference to the more than a generation-old Bolshevik experiment – that there can be no 'proletarian' ideology, because in a classless society there remains no reason for dissimulating anything, nobody being left who might want more radical change than that already achieved.[10]

[10] Goldmann, *Recherches dialectiques*, pp. 17, 18, 22. Goldmann's use of 'proletarian' here is careless. For it follows that 'dialectical

What unites Lukács with the more immediate successors of Marx and Engels is the fact that their far from identical assumptions about the separability of ideology from economic conditioning accord with the substance of the findings of modern historical and behavioural research about the relatively high degree of disharmony between class membership and ideological motivation in the political process of capitalist society. Original Marxist theory itself is by no means consistent in confining the detachment of ideology from the conditioning economic class base to the aftermath of the proletarian victory. It is certainly not less true in this respect than in others that the differences between Marx and Engels's successors are manifestations of the difficulties and contradictions inherent in the founders' own thoughts.[11] One might, therefore, regard these differences and the systems of thought in which they manifest themselves as attempts at the necessary correction of the original doctrine.

II. Point of departure

Marx's internationalism did not prevent him from viewing the stages of socio-economic development, and hence of the superstructure, primarily in the context of existing state-societies. Yet he was not oblivious to the traffic of ideas between states in unequal stages of socio-economic development. To square the fact with his theory of the causal primacy of economic conditions, Marx argued that the relationship of dependence and contradiction between consciousness and reality could also take effect by way of consciousness in one society relating to the reality of another society.[12] In other words, although normally the contents of consciousness emerge in immediate relation to the specific conditions in which men produce, some people are able to take their cue from what has emerged in relation to a different socio-economic base in another society. Thus in a given country, beliefs can be entertained which are more advanced than its material

---

materialism' cannot be called 'proletarian' because it is an ideology, nor can the working class qualify as proletarian if the term can only be used in equivalence with classlessness. Goldmann is perspicacious enough to put his amalgamate of not easily reconcilable views on the matter 'beyond any reference to this or that quotation from Marx and Engels' (p. 11), to whom he could have added some other names.

[11] Calvez, *La Pensée de Karl Marx*, pp. 15–16.
[12] *Die heilige Familie*, MEGA, III, 261.

development, because an extraneous form of being can serve by proxy, as it were, as the frame of reference and account for the adoption of beliefs for which indigenous class foundations are not yet ripe. In this way ideology is on Marx's own terms detachable from its immediate socio-economic base. Marx can be said to have made a further dent in the dogmatic position in the course of yet another attempt to reconcile a generally accepted fact to his theory. True, he argued in connection with the same phenomenon that Kant's adoption of the principles of French liberalism meant turning what was rooted in socio-economic class interests into a pure self-determination of 'free will', i.e. into 'pure ideological conceptualization and moral principles'.[13] The point here is not the implicit criticism, but the admission of the possibility of such materially rootless ideology.

The bond between ideology and class-base is also loosened, as we have already noted, when Marx held ordinary single bourgeois and proletarians, even a class as a whole, capable of adopting standpoints which are not only in advance of, but immediately opposed to, their socially and economically determined class interests.[14] It is particularly instructive that Marx even went so far as to interpret the situation obtaining under the rule of Louis Bonaparte in terms of the detachment of the entire political superstructure from the dominant socio-economic class-base. With the connivance of the dominant class, i.e. the bourgeoisie, the state is said to have 'reverted to its oldest form, to the brazenly simple rule of sword and cowl'. It has achieved complete independence of and mastery over bourgeois society by relying upon the most numerous class, the small farmers (not to forget the *Lumpenproletariat*), whose interests, like those of all other classes, were

---

[13] *Die deutsche Ideologie*, MEGA, v, 177.

[14] See e.g. above, pp. 53–5, 68, 72–3. In an aside in *Neue Rheinische Zeitung* (12 December 1848), Marx spoke of the different conscience (*Gewissen*) of a royalist, republican, proprietor and a propertyless person as well as of the conscience of those who think and those who do not (MEGA, vii, 501). Only two of the categories on which conscience is predicated are socio-economic. Indeed, Marx believed also in the determining of power of racial predispositions. Cp. *Die deutsche Ideologie*, MEGA, v, 62, 435, on 'cross-breeding' (*Rassenkreuzung*); *Zur Kritik der politischen Ökonomie*, pp. xvii, xlvii. He never faced the problem of adjusting the race perspective to the class perspective. This has to be considered if one argues, as does Ollman, *Alienation*, p. 126, that the hereditary transmission of racial qualities is one of the answers Marx would have given to meet the objection to the exceptions he made to socio-economic determination.

basically opposed to those of the bourgeoisie.[15] Marx concluded with a broad sweep that 'the collective will of the nation whenever it speaks in general suffrage seeks its adequate representation in the inveterate enemies of mass interests'.[16]

The bond between socio-economic base and ideological superstructure thus becomes tangled in the original Marxist conception. This is the result mainly of ascribing contradictory effects to the same causal forces and of likewise ill-adjusted conclusions about the perceptibility of the nature and directions of these forces and the impact of that perceptibility, or of its falsification, upon the course of events. Thus a good deal of rein is given to the liberation of ideology on more than one occasion not just from its putatively unexceptional falsehood, but likewise from its dependence upon socio-economic conditioning. The unmodified Marxist theory of ideology is thus highly inconsistent, though not on that account less susceptible to relevant insights.

Take the last-mentioned generalization about the ill-advised exercise by the masses of general suffrage. It comes at the end of one of the quite frequent deviations from the assumption of uniformly and inescapably operating causation, and the concluding generalization itself is not easily reconcilable with other dogmatic derivations related more or less tightly to the assumption of economic and social conditioning. If in virtue of their position in the economic process, proletariat and bourgeoisie are necessarily locked in a life-and-death struggle, how is it that the masses confirm their 'inveterate enemies' in power? Indeed, this assertion, like those I have mentioned before and others, only shows that Marx himself detracted in his interpretation of specific events and phenomena from the explanatory value of his deterministic theory of causation. It is, however, not less significant that the assertion in question should point in the direction of the findings

---

15 Marx, *Der 18. Brumaire*, pp. 118, 140, 178, 182f, 196, 198–200. According to Ollman, *Alienation*, p. 9, Engels's advice to look in *Der 18. Brumaire* for how Marx's materialist conception of history was applied by him has not been followed often enough. I think the opposite is true and that what Ollman actually is complaining about is the fact, strongly indicated by the evidence adduced here and also above, pp. 68–9, namely that such recourse is more often than not (justly) used to reveal the extent to which Engels and Marx contradicted fundamental principles in their explanation of specific events. Engels's advice attests that he shared Marx's unawareness of such contradictoriness, except, of course, if one accepts Ollman's interpretative postulate that such contradictions *must be* reconcilable.

16 Marx, *Der 18. Brumaire*, p. 136.

of modern empirical research. Based upon elaborate techniques of data collection, this has confirmed asymmetry between class membership and voting behaviour. It has thereby deflated, as Marx certainly wished to do, cherished assumptions about the conclusiveness of the electoral test as an expression of the informed will of the electorate, to say nothing of the direct bearing of that will upon policy decisions.

In any event we have arrived at the final turn taken by the original argument concerning the nature of ideology. One could even say that we have arrived at the point where the Marxian argument finally turns against itself. It moves, as I have noted before,[17] from the identification of ideology with bourgeois false consciousness *via* qualifications of that falseness (implied in the interpretation of specific phenomena and events but not acknowledged as qualifications) to the extension of false consciousness to actually entertained proletarian beliefs. The argument arrives at the identification of mature proletarian consciousness with correct consciousness. At the same time the argument moves from the postulate of the stringent dependence of ideology upon economic and social conditions (and the relationship between them) to ideology's dissociation from their impact. It emerges thus from the turns and twists which characterize the original Marxist theory, and its faithful elaboration by Lukács, that this theory can maintain the identification neither of ideology with false consciousness nor of proletarian ideology with correct consciousness. Nor can it deny in its extension by Lukács to post-capitalist society, that so long as there is politics, ideology, that hybrid between real and putative knowledge, will be with us, no matter whose politics it is.

Deviations from axiomatic propositions or their implicit qualification reveal the merits and demerits of the Marxian and Marxist conception. They do not, however, reveal that Marx and Engels distinguished between two conceptions of ideology,[18] but that they were unable to uphold one conception consistently. Yet, though we cannot give them credit for having established an adequate theory of ideology, their alternating positions contain the foundation of such a theory. Awareness of the inadequacy of the original programmatic (and dogmatic) conception is implicit in Lenin's radical, though unadmitted, departure from the

[17] See above, pp. 75–6.
[18] See above, pp. 76–7.

Marxian use of 'ideology', a departure which is less covered by Kautsky's cautious reinterpretation of the role of 'the conscious element' than by Bernstein's straightforward critique of Marxist theory. Apart from his sudden use of 'ideology' and 'ideological' in a positive sense, Lukács's presentation conveys little of these developments. It reflects, but it does not critically expose, the fact that Marx and Engels made diverse statements of principle in different contexts and that they left the statements unadjusted to one another. Lukács made scarcely any attempt to tackle clashes between generalizations or between them and sensible concessions to observed facts and operative ideology. Like the masters, for the most part he did not acknowledge such disparities in the first place.

Lukács's awareness of Marx's terminological indeterminateness did not lead him to concede that Marx and Engels used some key concepts, even that of freedom, as if through the various uses they made of them they were clarifying them systematically. They apparently assumed, but (wisely) never tried to demonstrate, that all variations of these uses added up to a set of mutually reconcilable connotations. Similarly, they were only able to bestow a semblance of credibility upon the central idea of the unity of theory and practice, among other things, by using the term 'class' differently in the contexts of revolutionary militancy, historical dramatization or sociological analysis.[19] Given the postulated relationship between class and ideology, variations in the use of one concept could not fail to reflect themselves in the use of the other. Moreover, Marxist revisionist and bourgeois interpreters have found that, apart from the notion of class, the notion of reality itself remained unsettled by Marx and Engels. As the attempts at further clarification by Lenin and Lukács of this general philosophical issue show, there remained the unsolved problem of avoiding on the one hand the positivist–rationalist assumption of the transcendent character of the object in relation to its sensory apprehension by the subject, and on the other, the idealist – or for that matter the materialist – assumption of the identity of object and subject.[20]

✻

19 Ossowski, *Class Structure in the Social Consciousness*, pp. 71ff.
20 P. Eppstein, 'Die Fragestellung nach der Wirklichkeit im historischen Materialismus', *Archiv für Sozialwissenschaft und Sozialpolitik*, LX, 3 (1928), 449–507.

It is, thus, less surprising than it might seem at first sight that Marx, like the less systematic Pareto after him, did not really face the well-known paradox to which I have drawn attention at the beginning of this study.[21] He assumed the possibility of identifying thought as false, and this assumption implied an initial knowledge of the criteria of correct thought.[22] Yet how could he presume to know the criteria of correct thought and, moreover, claim the creation on his part of an objective theory of social thought, if all social thought is distorted as the result of being dependent on socio-economic conditions, or in Pareto's case, on classifiable 'psychic states'?[23] Marxists cannot resolve this and kindred contradictions in Marx's theory of ideology by insisting that determination, and with it distortion, will cease, according to Marx, when determination becomes rational in the 'historical' period, which is that of the classless and stateless society.[24] If so (to say nothing of the implication that rational determination is non-determination), the question remains precisely: how can we know this in the 'prehistoric' period of non-rational determination?

The paradox was squarely faced by Mannheim in his attempt (published six years after the appearance of Lukács's *History and Class Consciousness*) to work out the first systematic theory of ideology. He built it on Marxian foundations but did not concern himself with relating his agreements with Marx, and more particularly his disagreements, to the shifts and twists within the Marxian and Marxist argumentation itself.

[21] See above, Chapter 1.II.
[22] Geiger, *Ideologie und Wahrheit*, pp. 40ff, 150f, 185ff, 162.
[23] Pareto, *Sociological Writings* (Finer's selection), p. 244.
[24] H. Marcuse, *Reason and Revolution: Hegel and the Rise of Social Theory* (London, New York and Toronto, 1941), p. 319; and Lichtheim, 'The Concept of Ideology', pp. 177–8.

8

THE WAY OUT OF THE VICIOUS CIRCLE: MANNHEIM

i. Conceptions of ideology – Avenues of truth

If it was a 'Copernican revolution' to perceive that 'also the discovery of truth was socially (historically) conditioned',[1] Marxism can claim only qualified credit for the revolution. There are not only the inevitable forerunners,[2] but what Marx has added in depth and sophistication is least helpful when it comes to explaining with any consistency how and to whom the socially conditioned truth can become accessible.

Mannheim addressed himself to the unfinished business and tried to overcome the inference that because the beliefs and insights of a given period or group are determined by the interplay of economic and social conditions, those who are involved in the life of the period and/or group can have no true notion about the situation they live in. One could wish Mannheim to have been more precise about his classification of conceptions of ideologies and about the degrees of equivalence and distinction between categories for analysing ideological thought on the one hand, and categories of ideology as they are professed in the actual party struggle on the other. There is, however, no doubt that his conceptions of ideology are intended not to represent a typology of the collective manifestations of ideological thought but to circumscribe supplementary avenues for the attainment of fuller knowledge about social and political life.

The conception of 'particular' ideology is based on the assumption that political struggles have led to the discovery of the sources of more or less unconscious collective motivations.[3] In their political clashes, class opponents had become aware of one another's distortions of reality and consequently tried to 'unmask' them. Enlarging upon Marx, and at the same time going beyond

---

[1] Merton, *Social Theory and Social Structure*, p. 459.
[2] See the survey in W. Stark, *The Sociology of Knowledge* (London, 1958), Chapter 2.
[3] Mannheim, *Ideology and Utopia*, pp. 39, 81, 40ff.

(or against) him, Mannheim suposed that their different class positions enabled the contestants to perceive that the interests of their opponents forced them to disguise the real nature of the situation. This is why 'conscious lies ... half conscious and unwitting disguises' permeate their ideas and arguments. The supposition is that truth would be derogatory to the interests of the opponent; hence he dupes others; but in the process he dupes himself as well.[4] The conception of 'particular' ideology denotes, then, what one class is capable of perceiving about the thought of another class. It contains two conditions of attaining truth: scepticism about what others believe and the knowledge of what causes distortion in the beliefs of others. Mannheim did not pause to consider how truthful we can be or want to be when we set ourselves to expose the deceptions of political opponents, nor to ask why the knowledge of what falsifies the beliefs of others should not at the same time induce us to apply that knowledge to our own beliefs.

There is, of course, something to be said for the implication that we find it easier to see through others than through ourselves. It is something else to proceed from the extraordinary Marxian supposition that the true appraisal of a situation by one class at least is incompatible with the effective pursuit of the interest of that class, which is to imply that critical introspection is counter-productive. Mannheim modified quite sensibly the presupposition and its implication, since otherwise he could not have gone beyond the 'particular' conception of ideology.

Marx and Engels themselves did not consistently uphold the idea of the distortion of thought through interestedness. Mannheim attenuated his generalizing assumption about the blinding effect of class interests by restricting its manifestation to 'certain conditions' and by arguing moreover that the *élan politique* is capable of being thrown back upon itself, and is therefore susceptible to critical control.[5] He thus came forth with what any moderately intelligent observer of politics has reason to presume, which is that, occasionally at least, politicians are apt to learn from experience. Still, as was not the case in Marx and Engels's theory of ideology, in which the explicit modification of distortion was hamstrung because distortion was attendant upon the division between mental and physical labour, there was nothing in

4 Mannheim, pp. 55–6, 61, 76.
5 Mannheim, pp. 40, 47.

Mannheim's presuppositions which prevented him from abiding by his restriction of distortion to 'certain conditions'. In point of fact, he made the attainment of undistorted knowledge dependent on a specific social position particularly suited to being accounted for in terms of the division between mental and physical labour.

Mannheim's attempt at systematization was perhaps to blame for his restriction of the 'particular' conception of ideology to the awareness of ideological distortion in others only. He reserved the awareness in oneself of such distortion, and the perception of the results of conditioning in general, for the most comprehensive conception of ideology. It is within the reach of a small group only, the intellectuals (who epitomize mental labour), and it no longer belongs to the sphere of ideological thought but to the science of which ideology is the subject matter. In between that highest and the 'particular' conception lies the 'total' conception, which extends the radius of critical analytical perception beyond the specific socio-political views of the opponents to 'the conceptual apparatus' of the thought of an age or a class. To be aware of these deeper recesses and wider confines of ideological thought is expressive of the urge and ability to enlarge the avenues for the attainment of truth. The conception is 'total' in so far as it 'calls into question the opponent's total *Weltanschauung* ... and attempts to understand these concepts as an outgrowth of the collective life of which he partakes'.[6] We are no longer concerned merely with 'a psychology of interests' laying bare the motivations of specific lies and deceptions, but with 'a functional analysis' aiming at 'an objective description of the structural differences in minds operating in different social settings'.[7]

The importance of the 'total' conception does not lie in the assertion that existential conditions, predominantly the social ones, colour 'the conceptual apparatus' and the very categories of thought. Mannheim failed to demonstrate anything in this connection and, as his examples indicate, he had only modes of evaluation in mind. The importance of the 'total' conception consists in the assumption that beyond the mere detection of lies and distortions of other people 'an objective description' is possible. (It hardly needs saying that to uncover lies is the precondition of, but not the same as, uncovering the truth.) Unlike Marx, Mannheim subscribed unambiguously to the belief that

[6] Mannheim, p. 57.
[7] Mannheim, p. 58.

although untruthfulness springs from social conditioning, not all conditioned thought is untrue. Despite being conditioned, our thought and the thought of the opponent are held capable of aiming at an understanding of each other's total belief system. In this way, Mannheim avoided the logical foreclosure by Marx of the possibility of stipulating the objective analysis of ideological thought itself.

The unmasking, in accordance with the 'particular' conception, of the interests which on the psychological level distort the thought of opponents is surpassed and supplemented in the 'total' conception in so far as the forms and contents of thought are related to the social setting in order to reconstruct the whole outlook of a social group or era. Only 'the *general* form of the total conception' includes our own thought and its socio-historical basis in the analysis. It promises objective insights, provided we do not mean by that 'ultimate' or 'absolute' truths, but those only which are 'relational', i.e. which are confined to a given time and situation. Knowledge bound to 'actual life situations, though not absolute, is knowledge nevertheless'.[8]

The progress of increasing knowledge runs the gamut from unmasking deceptions to sorting out in each era and stratum true from untrue, genuine from spurious categories of thought or norms.[9] Mannheim insisted that this 'dynamic relationism' can be meaningfully distinguished from relativism. He did not make good his claim, if for no other reason than that he did not specify the terms on which categories of thought or norms do (and others do not) achieve genuineness and adequacy in the context of their time and class. His reasoning in these crucial matters is assertive rather than demonstrative and thus, in sum, question-begging. Indeed, this is the general weakness of his pioneer study, as has been pointed out many times by his critics. There is no need to

[8] Mannheim, pp. 86 and 61, 80, 86, 79–86, and 100 respectively. Just as there is much in Marx's conception of history which betrays the influence of the historism practised by Ranke, so we find in Mannheim the reflection of the theoretical elaboration and demonstration of the historism defended and practised by Troeltsch and Meinecke. A systematic comparison should be of interest. The evidence adduced in this chapter and the analysis of Marx and Engels's conception of ideology in the preceding chapters show the arbitrariness of the assertion made by Lenk, *Ideologie*, p. 59, that while Marx 'held fast to the possibility that reason is capable of [attaining] the truth', Mannheim's 'total conception of ideology' casts doubt on this assumption.

[9] Mannheim, *Ideology and Utopia*, pp. 94, 107.

go into all this again, but rather to recognize clearly that his classification of conceptions of ideology serves the methodological purpose of grading the range or contexts in which truth inheres in ideological thought and can be ascertained. It must be stressed that this was his purpose, since it has often not been understood that Mannheim suggested a distinction not between 'particular' and 'total' ideologies but between the 'particular' and 'total' approaches to ideological thought. The progression from the 'particular' to the 'total' conception of ideology and from that to 'the general form of the total conception of ideology' – which fuses with the sociology of knowledge – is a progression from the restricted to the optimal understanding of its manifestations and sources. This progression demarcates the path to truth, for it is 'objectivity which comes from the unmasking of ideologies'.[10] In these stages of uncovering the truth about and behind ideologies, the truth-content of ideologies themselves must not be forgotten.

II. The total perspective and the putative Mannheim
     paradox

For Mannheim the achievement of objective insights was connected not with the expectation of the impending millennium but with the mundane assignment of political science. He had no doubt of its feasibility, nor did the belief involve him in the paradox bearing his name.

The demand that 'thought should contain neither less nor more than the reality in whose medium it operates', that 'every idea must be tested by its congruence with reality',[11] was not logically obstructed by his assumption of the dependence of thought upon social conditions. Mannheim did not give cause to attribute to him the view that such dependence excluded the discovery of truth in the here and now. First he did not aim at 'final' or 'absolute', but only at 'relational' truth, at what is valid in the circumstances in which the adequacy of policies and of political orientations have to be tested.[12] Second, the 'quest for reality' requires 'the attempt to escape ideological and utopian *distortion*';[13] it does not require

---

[10] Mannheim, p. 262.
[11] Mannheim, p. 98.
[12] On the partial inconclusiveness of such testing, see above, p. 51.
[13] Mannheim, *Ideology and Utopia*, p. 98; my italics.

us to elude ideological thought altogether. On Mannheim's terms, the end of ideology would not signifiy, as it does in Marxist futurology, the end of distortion and the uncontested reign of reason. He did not play for stakes as high – or for aims as naive – as that. He merely thought that through proper scientific training factual knowledge could be increased and assured a more central place in the orientation of political leaders, and that ideologies could even contribute towards this purpose. Indeed, the inseparability of ideology and politics which Mannheim took for granted, and which I defend elsewhere,[14] does not involve the incompatibility of truth with either politics or ideology.

Irrespective of the dubious conclusion he drew from it, there is much to be said for Mannheim's view that political ideologies themselves contribute an important share in the search for a full picture of reality, because in every political point of view conjoins 'a rather comprehensive *Weltanschauung*' with 'the affirmation or rejection of *an indisputable set of facts*'.[15] It is in the nature of political opinions to be partisan, since each of the different political points of view reflects different class interests. But this key to distortion is also the key to partial truth. Each class view contains, according to Mannheim, fragments of correct insight which are conducive to the interests of that particular class and could be perceived only from its standpoint. Added together, the fragments give the total picture of a given period.[16]

It could be convincingly argued that how accurately one sees things at times depends on whether one is placed on one or the other side of the fence. Also, the truth is often to be pieced together from fragments perceived by differently placed onlookers and participants. It is certainly sensible not to attribute to interest orientation an exclusively falsifying effect. It is, however, an over-simplification to argue that the situation of one class vouchsafes insights which are normally inaccessible from the position of another class. Moreover, if one can put oneself into another

---

[14] See my *Ideology and Politics*.

[15] Mannheim, p. 148; my italics.

[16] Mannheim, p. 149 and *passim*. It seems to have escaped Mannheim's notice that he adapted here to his purpose Aristotle's argument that the sum total of the appreciations of music and poetry (and eventually also of politics) by the many is superior to that of the few. *The Politics of Aristotle*, trans. with an Introduction, notes and appendices by E. Barker (Oxford, 1952), iii, xi, 3 and note Y, pp. 127–8. The objections to Aristotle's argument and to Mannheim's elaboration are the same.

class position, as Mannheim, like Marx, supposed, the cognitive moat is drained of water. Nor is it immediately evident that all available fragments of correct insight form the mutually supplementary components of the whole truth about a given reality. One may well doubt whether the assumption that specific slices of the truth can only be found in specific cakes of class ideology is the proper foundation for asserting, in the spirit of Weber, that because 'our thinking is socially conditioned, [it] is not necessarily a source of error . . . it is often the path to political insight'.[17]

However, Mannheim did provide a sensible foundation for his view that even ideologically committed thinkers are not prevented from succeeding in attempts 'to unify and reconcile', although for the most part they keep to 'those conflicting currents which they encounter in their sphere'.[18] Relying by implication on the division between mental and physical labour (or at least on the division between mental kinds of labour), he assigned to the intelligentsia the task of synthesizing the various aspects of truth contained in competing ideologies. He argued explicitly that the special social standing of the intelligentsia would allow it to adopt a largely unbiased perspective. Already John Stuart Mill had advanced similar views. Julien Benda, who regarded aloofness from the political arena as the precondition of the exclusive commitment of intellectuals to the pursuit of truth, accused them of having betrayed their mission almost at the same time as Mannheim professed his faith in the synthesizing role of the intelligentsia.

Mannheim did not, as is often argued, base his belief in the intellectuals on an idealist suspension of social determination. Neither his explicit modification of the notion of the total falsity of ideologies, nor his awareness of the adoption and/or rejection of some identical principles and tenets in different ideologies,[19] nor his recognition of the possible divergence between ideological outlook and class position in individual cases – none of all these seemed to him to require the abandonment of the basically Marxian principle of the determination of outlooks by social factors. Although he modified the application of the principle considerably, it still made so much sense to him that he retained it as the central hypothesis of the sociology of knowledge. He offered,

---

17 Mannheim, *Ideology and Utopia*, p. 125.
18 Mannheim, p. 163. Marx and Stahl are Mannheim's examples.
19 See below, p. 192.

therefore, a specific version of social determination in order to explain why the intelligentsia was in a position to unify and reconcile the truths inherent in different ideologies.

Well-prepared by Kautsky, Bernstein and Lenin, Mannheim consummated the break with the Marxist mythopoetic idea, not to say slogan, that the proletariat is the embodiment of historical truth and the heir of philosophy. There is therefore no foundation for conceding to Marxist–Leninist theorists that they have assimilated Mannheim's theory of perspectives into their 'dual theory of ideology',[20] since they continue to invest 'the revolutionary classes' with the more 'correct' perspective. To do so is to disfigure Mannheim's views in the spirit of Marx's pronouncements on the eventual achievement of correct insight by the proletariat, and by some parts of the international working classes in the meantime.[21] Mannheim held quite simply that to establish the truth is the business of those who are professionally engaged in the various fields of science, and thus reasserted what a moderate respect for common sense should have prevented anyone from ever obfuscating. At the same time, he conceived the class situation achieved by the intellectuals as being conducive to the pursuit of truth and the synthesizing of the different aspects of truth contained in class ideologies.

As Mannheim explained, the class position of intellectuals had become increasingly removed from the influence of the economic process, that is from the immediate involvement in it, which of necessity entails the divergent outlooks of the other classes and their members. Mannheim was thus in no way illogical in maintaining at one and the same time that the intellectuals can rise above all other class outlooks and that both error and truth are socially conditioned. It was the less illogical to put forward these propositions, since each was reconcilable with retaining the connection between class and economic process, though not exactly in the Marxian sense. In view of the presuppositions Mannheim shared with Marx, he could have called the intellectuals 'a classless class', for according to Marxian presuppositions (and to common sense), it is as much of a contradiction in terms to speak of a social 'stratum' which is largely uninvolved in the process of the production and more particularly the distribution of goods as

---

[20] Jordan, *Philosophy and Ideology*, pp. 496 and 523 n.149, appears to be making the concession.
[21] See above, pp. 47–8, 66.

it is to speak of a 'classless class'. In Mannheim's conception the intellectuals form a class like other classes inasmuch as their outlook is held to be determined by their special relation to the economic process. They form a class which is unlike all other classes in so far as they are not immediately involved in economic production and distribution. Neither their cohesion nor their outlook, therefore, is determined by what determines the outlook of all other – or of proper – classes, but determined by their place in the economic and social structure they are. Mannheim avoided calling them a class because a non-economic class was apparently still anathema to him, and so he defined what Alfred Weber had called 'the socially free-floating intellectuals' (*sozial frei schwebenden Intelektuellen*) as an 'unanchored, relatively classless stratum'. They are 'too differentiated to be regarded as a single class' but 'participation in a common educational heritage progressively tends to suppress differences of birth, status, profession and wealth'.[22]

On Mannheim's own terms there is thus no 'Mannheim paradox',[23] because objective situation-bound knowledge, as distinct from timeless truths, is attainable, according to Mannheim, not despite the social conditioning of the analyst himself (this would be the paradox), but by virtue of his special social conditioning, viz. a socialization by education, without the influence exerted by direct involvement in the economic process. A social determination is seen to be at work which by not being directly related to the production and distribution of material goods is conducive to the objectivity of sociological and political analysis. On these grounds Mannheim postulated that a 'stratum' composed of members of different class origin is unified by becoming immersed in a common heritage and is thus capable of unifying on its part the elements of truth dispersed among the various party ideologies. Mannheim may have been overoptimistic in believing that the 'awakening of class consciousness in all classes' will combine with the intelligentsia's increasing awareness of its special position – whether within or outside the existing parties – so as to

[22] Mannheim, *Ideology and Utopia*, p. 155.
[23] Its existence is asserted, for instance, by Merton, *Social Theory and Social Structure*, p. 507; C. Geertz, 'Ideology as a Cultural System', in Apter, *Ideology and Discontent*, pp. 48–9; J. LaPalombara, 'Decline of Ideology: A Dissent and an Interpretation', *American Political Science Review*, LX, 1 (1966), 5–6; and Harris, *Beliefs in Society*, p. 249.

permit it to carry out the cognitive mission of gaining a 'total perspective' and achieving a 'total orientation and synthesis'.[24] He was perhaps not fundamentally wrong as far as the bulk of the more developed industrial societies and their social sciences is concerned, if we replace the pretentious 'total perspective' (the Marxist residue, that is) by 'more adequate perspective'. One might also object that Mannheim disregarded 'the institutionalization of intellectual life' and the concern of intellectuals, as far as their incomes are in question, with their status in the class structure and their direct connection with the distributive aspects of the economic process. However, none of this necessarily affects cognitive detachment, except on the supposition that the latter is evinced exclusively in criticism of the Establishment[25] – or, for that matter, in its acceptance.

In any event, Mannheim did not let himself become entangled in any contradiction between the propositions of the conditioning of the thinker by his life-situation and of his ability to produce objective insights. He simply believed that what he regarded as the *normal*, i.e. economically based class position and its influence, did not apply to 'a relatively unattached middle stratum which is open to the constant influx of individuals from the most diverse social classes and groups with all possible points of view' and to which we already owe 'the possibility of mutual interpenetration and understanding of existing currents of thought'. In conformity with Marxian ideas, therefore, Mannheim believed that the distortion-cum-irreconcilability of thought processes is mainly attendant upon economically based social determination. In contrast to Marxian doctrine, he did not merely regard intellectuals as free to opt out of the doomed bourgeoisie and throw in their lot with the ascendant class. He considered the intellectuals as a stratum by themselves and supposed education together with the absence of direct involvement in the process of production to constitute that kind of social determination which offsets another kind, i.e. the distorting influence of the economic base.

Like Lukács, Mannheim based the advance towards objectivity upon the transformation of class bounds into those characteristic of a stratum. Mannheim's distinction is more convincing than

---

[24] Mannheim, *Ideology and Utopia*, pp. 160–1.
[25] This appears to be the reason why A. Arblaster, 'Ideology and Intellectuals', in Benewick, Berki and Parekh, *Knowledge and Belief in Politics*, pp. 117–18, in noting Mannheim's two faults of omission, which I have just mentioned, exaggerates their significance.

Lukács's, since it is at least not associated with the general disappearance of classes. Furthermore, he moved towards appraising the relationship between class position and ideological orientation in its complexity by attributing more equal weight than Marx and Marxists do to the adoption by bourgeois intellectuals of the proletarian cause on the one hand, and to the change of the social personality of a proletarian who becomes an intellectual on the other; and he was also aware of the distrust the intellectual aroused as a result of his 'assimilability'.[26] In his treatment of ideology, Mannheim did not consummate the break with the rigid economically based class conception. The role he assigned to 'the more outstanding intellectuals' consisted in the elaboration of a total perspective which should serve as a corrective to class–party ideologies, but not replace them. In fact, since he attached supreme political significance to the total perspective, it remained action-oriented and, therefore, ideological. Those who produce such a corrective of party ideologies, or as I would say such corrective ideology, are also, on Mannheim's terms, not detached from the overall class structure and party struggle, but accorded a special standing within them. Hence I think it wrong to conclude that Mannheim moved from property class systems to meritocratic elite systems;[27] rather, he appended something of the

---

[26] Mannheim, *Ideology and Utopia*, pp. 158–9. Gramsci likewise assumed two-directional assimilation and took it that no immediate relationship existed between 'intellectuals and the world of production' (*The Modern Prince and Other Writings*, p. 124), but he did not share Mannheim's belief that intellectuals could be independent (p. 120).

[27] As T. B. Bottomore, *Elites and Society* (Harmondsworth, 1966), p. 43, and J. H. Meisel, *The Myth of the Ruling Class – Gaetano Mosca and the Elite* (Ann Arbor, 1958), p. 8, maintain. On Weber's taking exception to the Marxist ruling-class/subject-class model, on the ground that 'the means of administration' are of greater importance for political power than 'the means of production', see also below, p. 188, and Bottomore, pp. 83ff, who relies for the distinction on M. Weber, *Politik als Beruf*, 2nd edn (München and Leipzig, 1926), pp. 12–13. Weber stressed there the parallel between the expropriation by the prince of all independent private possessors of administrative power and the gradual expropriation by the capitalist enterprise of the independent producers. Lukács, *Geschichte und Klassenbewusstsein*, p. 107, also referred to this part of Weber's exposition but failed to mention that Weber likewise pointed out that despite far-reaching analogies, capitalist management and political administration follow different rules. For a comprehensive attempt to depict stages of the concentration of 'the instruments of political and administrative action' in pre-modern political systems, see S. N.

latter to the former. As his use of 'stratum' *besides* 'classes' symbolizes, he was not even ready to consider the educational divide generally as the major competitor of the economic divide, and education as being as decisive a determinant in the formation of class and class consciousness as the economic situation, or as influencing decisively the economic and political situation of a class, as Mill held.[28] Mannheim believed, like Mill, in the restraint of the major class perspectives by the perspective of the intellectual elite. Only Mill found that, in order to mitigate the excesses of class legislation, constitutional safeguards were necessary, and he proposed therefore the plural vote,[29] providing thus another example of how much liberals actually distrust 'the invisible hand'.

If there remains a 'Mannheim paradox' at all, then, it exists only as far as the relationship between the 'classless class' *qua* 'middle-stratum' and all other classes is concerned. If the immediate involvement of the worker and the entrepreneur in the economic process determines 'their outlooks and activity directly and exclusively', how can they follow the harmonizing–synthesizing lead of the intellectuals who, 'besides undoubtedly bearing the imprint of their specific class affinity [with the regular classes from which they issue], are also determined in their outlook by this intellectual medium which contains all those contradictory points of view'?[30] The bridgehead is provided by Mannheim's straightforward admission that social conditioning is not only the source of political error, but 'often the path to political insight'. He did not envisage

---

Eisenstadt, *The Political Systems of Empires: The Rise and Fall of the Bureaucratic Empires* (New York and London, 1969), esp. Chapters 2, 6 and 10.

[28] On the competition between the educational and economic divides, see D. G. MacRae, *Ideology and Society* (London, 1961), pp. 63, 66, 69, 72ff. Naturally, better education normally secures economic advantages and is easier to come by for those with a better educational and economic background. According to Mill, the prospects of the working classes for being rational and self-relying depended upon 'spontaneous education' going on in the minds of the multitude, and they were improving by virtue of such 'artificial' aids as newspapers and political tracts, to which school education had to be added (*Principles of Political Economy*, Book IV, Chapter VII, 1, pp. 756–8). Mill was thus aware of the fact that formal education is not the sole indicator of political understanding and involvement.

[29] *Representative Government*, Chapter 8 in J. S. Mill, *Utilitarianism, Liberty and Representative Government*, Everyman's Library (New York and London, 1951).

[30] Mannheim, *Ideology and Utopia*, p. 157.

the walls of party ideologies crumbling at the sound of the pipings of the free-floating intellectuals, but neither did he think that the class-bound remainder of society and its leaders were stone-deaf.

Whatever view one takes of Mannheim's consistency, as he proceeded along the various strands of his argument and adjusted them to one another, he undoubtedly loosened the wedge driven *ab initio* between ideology and factual knowledge by Napoleon's spurious, and Marx and Engels's serious, theoretical treatment of the matter. It therefore seems appropriate at this point to consider briefly to what degree Mannheim's affirmation of the truth-content of ideologies and of the possibility of attaining correct overall assessments of situational contexts can be defended and extended both beyond Marx and Engels's, as well as their successors', deviations from the notion of 'false consciousness' and even beyond Mannheim's own advance over the original and modified Marxist positions.[31]

III. The factual component

The notion of 'false consciousness' is justifiable in so far as the adherence to certain values, which forms an indelible part of social action orientation, is likely to entail biased and unverified, as well as unverifiable, statements in ideologies. When predictions and promises are confuted by events, falsity, however, reveals itself as the result both of disregarding and concealing existing or foreseeable variables (and of other deceptions), and also as the consequence of the intervention of unforeseeable variables which upset the expected results of otherwise well-founded and sincere calculation of action. At one stage or another, premeditated, unconsciously motivated or inadvertent falsification is part of almost any political argument. Yet a statement does not qualify as ideological merely because it is proved false, or because value judgments are disguised as statements of facts,[32] nor do statements distort facts solely because they form part of ideological discourse. When Bernstein argued that an ethical judgment underlies Marx's

---

[31] It is from this specific angle that the following section is different from Chapter v, 2 of my *Ideology and Politics*, although it relies upon material used in it. The treatment is more extensive and bears on the relationship between truth and ideology in general.

[32] Geiger, *Ideologie und Wahrheit*, pp. 139, 141; and E. Topitsch, *Sozialphilosophie zwischen Ideologie und Wissenschaft*, 2nd edn (Neuwied, 1966), p. 32.

interpretation of 'surplus value' in terms of 'relations of exploitation', he did not mean to say, nor did the argument make it incumbent on him to say, that the ethical judgment and its emotional charge prove the falsity of Marx's interpretation.

Neither Marx nor those who have followed him in equating ideological with distorted statements have ever demonstrated that everything said in the context of socio-political belief systems contains nothing that has a claim to validity. Few have claimed, and nobody has proved, the extreme contention that epitomizes the Marxist dogmatic conception of ideology, i.e. that the entire intellectual superstructure prevalent prior to the demise of capitalism is ideological in the sense of being intrinsically false.

True, commitment to values and material interests, as well as being unconsciously influenced by them, invites and makes susceptible the ideologist – or the social scientist – to the manipulation and streamlining of facts and the transgression of available knowledge. Indeed, the problem of the scope and limits of objectivity, or the attainment of truth-contents, is similar in social science or ideology, and to both applies Weber's elaboration of the distinction, originally made by Rickert, between valuation (or value relation) and value relatedness, and the parallel distinction drawn by Weber between 'economically determined' and 'economically related'.[33] Value relatedness means that values are instrumental in choosing the problems for scientific inquiry, but do not necessarily affect its results. Similarly, to regard a subject of inquiry, or a political posture, as 'economically related' does not signify more than that in choosing the one or adopting the other the consideration of the economic aspects of specific problems has

---

[33] H. Rickert, *Die Grenzen der naturwissenschaftlichen Begriffsbildung* (Freiburg and Leipzig, 1896), 4th edn (Tübingen, 1921), pp. 245ff; and Weber, 'Die "Objektivität" sozialwissenschaftlicher und sozialpolitischer Erkenntnis', pp. 162, 165. The first part of the essay (pp. 146–61) expresses the views shared by Edgar Jaffée, Werner Sombart and Max Weber as the new editors of the *Archiv für Sozialwissenschaft und Sozialpolitik*. For the more salient points concerning the problem of objectivity in general, see pp. 155–8, and esp. pp. 158–9, 162ff, 170. Weber also connected the selection of subjects of inquiry according to changing 'value-ideas' (*Wertideen*) (pp. 179–85, 192–3, 209ff) with his conception of 'ideal-types', in both the logical and the practical paradigmatic senses of the concept (p. 198). He insisted also on 'scholarly self-control', in order to keep the two aspects apart from each other (p. 200), but confessed that science and belief are often divided by no more than a hair's breadth (p. 212).

been decisive, while the scholarly conclusions reached with regard to these problems are not preempted by the conditions reflected in such perspectives. Only if they were thus preempted could the problem and the solution or conclusion qualify as being 'economically determined', that is, the range of alternatives would be prescribed solely or decisively by material conditions and interests.

With respect to the transcendence of available knowledge: by itself this is the aim of science as well as of ideology. Simplification that is conducive to the manipulation of facts is exercised in the course of all systematization of knowledge. Simplification is a corollary of the exercise of rationality and a prerequisite of both science and ideology inasmuch as there is no other way to order the multifarious variety of facts. Although the exercise of rationality, and what it entails for such elementary purposes and others, is subject in science and ideology to different objectives and different methodological and axiological presuppositions, reliance on rationality does not for this reason cease to provide a link between, and constitute a cause of the likeness of, ideology and science. In effect, it is safe to assume that Marx could not abide by his dogmatic conception of ideology, because he believed in the possibility of an adequate social science, his social science, and thus found it difficult to judge all existing social science, let alone the natural sciences, in terms of a falsified and falsifying superstructure. However, even if Marx and Engels had wished to argue consistently that correct insights about human existence, and to a lesser degree about the natural world, are unattainable prior to 'the reign of reason' (and to this proposition they have been shown to stand logically committed), one wonders how they could have demonstrated that the quest for some certain knowledge – pursued on the basis of the age-old awareness of the possible uncertainty of knowledge, or of some kinds of knowledge – has remained entirely unfulfilled. Understandably, Marx and Engels made no serious effort to refute the proposition that some knowledge at least has proved testable inasmuch as it has withstood profound cultural, social and technological change.

The founding fathers of Marxism themselves used actual occurrences and existing institutions as the testing-ground of bourgeois ideology, to demonstrate the falsity of the claims. When it came to the non-compliance of proletarians, and hypothetically even of the entire proletariat, with their dispensation, Marx and Engels rejected actual behaviour as evidence and resorted on the level of fundamentals to historicist derivation.[34] In other words, they accepted and evaded, as a matter of ideological convenience, the testing of ideological claims. Marx might be supposed to have denied such an accusation since he allowed for the coincidence of false consciousness and distorted social relations. But this is not only to stipulate the congruence of thought with facts, but to do so on implicitly normative grounds.[35]

What is likewise implicit in, and tainted by, Marx and Engels's dogmatic conception of ideology is the insight that the facts relied upon to verify or falsify propositions forming part of ideological, philosophical and scientific argument are not accessible, even for the purpose of articulate description, until after they have been given propositional form. To be aware that only in this form can facts serve us to test propositions according to the principle of 'correspondence' (with facts), besides testing according to the principle of 'coherence' (between statements), is not to solve the problem of the immediate perception of facts, but to come to terms with it within manageable limits. This means to accept Kant's self-denying ordinance in respect of *das Ding an sich* and to confine ourselves within the limits of verifiable experience delimited, or circumscribed, by the transcendental categories of apperception and its unity. While in the original Marxian theory of ideology this relationship between objects and categories of perception was not only reversed, but the categories of apperception were invested with the property of falsification, Mannheim reverted to Kantian epistemology in so far as he believed in the attainability of non-absolute truth as mediated by the total perspective of politically minded intellectuals on the one hand and systematized in the sociology of knowledge on the other.

Within these briefly sketched confines of philosophical criteria for seizing facts as against the commonsense notion of the testability of political promises and predictions, it can safely be stated that in the absence of any congruence with facts no political doctrine has any chance of gaining credence. No important social theory or doctrine can be identified with, because it simply cannot afford, totally false consciousness, if one agrees, as Marx and Engels did at least indirectly in regard to themselves, that some people are available who are capable (and are given the opportunity) of exposing falsity and deception. If Marx and Engels

[34] See above, for instance, pp. 47–8, 64–5, 72–3.
[35] See above, pp. 38–40.

really believed that such an undertaking was useless, they ought to have regarded their lifelong preoccupations as senseless. Normally, belief systems are adapted to the audience to which they are designed to appeal, and this is unlikely to succeed if the propagated beliefs do not correspond, or cannot be sensibly related, to a minimum of incontestable facts, the minimum varying from case to case. That this requirement must be met is particularly true of a Western-type society where, notwithstanding Marcuse's half truths,[36] competing mass media can be counted upon to pounce on contestable evidence, if for no other reason than that they make a living out of mutual unmasking, and thus help the common run of men to gain or confirm knowledge of facts no less than to confuse them about their nature and significance. In fact, what could be rather arbitrarily construed into being the (sensible) substance of Marx's pronouncements on proletarian understanding coincides with a conclusion to be reached by speculation about commonsense observation and derivable from survey data. It is the conclusion that mass publics reveal contextual judgment, if not in coherent argument, then in their behavioural reaction to events and situations.[37] Their capability of articulating correct assessments of causes and consequences of social action is not really refuted by the data adduced by researchers who are concerned with the differences of 'constraint' (or coherence) between belief elements in the belief systems of mass publics and elite publics respectively. Precisely because the judgment of mass publics cannot be evaluated correctly on the strength alone of what they say but of their actual attitudes as well, and since therefore a discrepancy between the two is likely to emerge, it is only too easy is misconstrue survey data and underestimate the contextual grasp of mass publics and their sensitiveness to what is actually going on. This is all the more likely when questions are formulated in disregard of the generally prevailing discrepancies between the official ideologies of parties and their public policies, or in my terminology, between their fundamental and operative ideologies.[38]

[36] See my 'Herbert Marcuse's One-dimensionality – The Old Style of the New Left', esp. pp. 202ff.

[37] Gramsci, *The Modern Prince and Other Writings*, p. 61, also makes such a distinction. A subordinate group, he says, 'has its own conception of the world, even though embryonic (which shows itself in actions, and so only spasmodically . . .)', but 'it affirms in words a . . . borrowed conception', that of the ruling groups.

[38] See my *Ideology and Politics*, pp. 160–1, 245–7.

As I have said, a strain in Marx and Engels's teachings affirms the capability of mass publics to achieve contextual understanding. We have also seen that the most important successors of Marx and Engels have explicitly played down the notion of 'false consciousness', and that on these grounds Mannheim made his more systematic attempt to bridge the gap between ideology and truth. Nevertheless, it is the dogmatic kernel of the Marxian theory of ideology, the emphasis on the contrast between ideology and truth, rather than Mannheim's gradual or 'relational' approach, which reverberates in present-day distinctions, drawn almost exclusively by opponents of Marxism, between ideological and pragmatic politics, between an opinionated and prejudiced and a matter-of-fact approach. This Marxist residue is not the only one to be found in modern political theory and science. To highlight such residues and what has become of them is not, as should be clear at the outset, to presuppose that all that which is parallel in Marxian and modern theories and belief systems originated in Marxism. The concern with class conflict, for instance, and, in connection with it, the ascription to classes of more or less structured belief systems – and generally the habit of speaking of classes as if they were action units – though highly characteristic of Marxism and transmitted particularly through it to modern political science and sociology, are of long standing and can be found also in John Stuart Mill. He took no note of his only-twelve-years-younger contemporary Karl Marx, but spoke of classes in reifying fashion like him, just as he was as concerned as Marx with class conflict and its influence on society and politics.

I propose, then, to examine in Part Three first the reverberations in modern behavioural political theory and science of approaches and notions that have been central to the Marxist conception of ideology. To begin with, some comments are offered on the conceptual confusion involved in speaking of classes as if they were united by belief systems and characterized by the properties of action units. Marx's recognition of the *differentia specifica* and its disregard by him is particularly instructive here. I proceed then to the demonstration of the extent to which Marxist and behavioural conceptions coincide with, and cut across, one another in respect of the juxtaposition of factual and ideological orientations in the context of the presumed relationship between class-bound beliefs and what according to each conception is understood by ideology. The clarification of the degree of both similarity and dissimilarity between basically opposed approaches brings us to the subject with which it seems most appropriate to conclude this critical study: the phenomenon of ideological pluralism. For agreement or analogy between the contents of ideologies, as exemplified with particular reference to Marxism, obviously requires the severe limitation of the Marxist claim that the economic and social conditions of an era determine the nature of ideological principles and goals.

PART THREE

PERSPECTIVES, CHANGING AND PERSISTING

9
CLASS AND IDEOLOGY

1. Class: Category of classification or action unit

The manner of speaking of classes, even with some reservation (for the most part soon forgotten), as if they shared interests, systems of values and hence ideologies in the same way as action units do, reflects the influence of historism, often associated with historical and ethical relativism, inasmuch as according to historism standards of judgment and methods of argumentation in general are unique to an epoch. Historism is thus implicit in Marxism (but not *vice versa*), since the latter's determinism underlies a theory of historical development in economically, socially, politically, and culturally distinct stages. In other words, to attribute certain interests, systems of values and ideologies to social classes in a certain stage of historical development is a corollary of the historist attribution of unique characteristics to a given era. The question is, then, why do such ascriptions more often than not amount to an illicit reification and create conceptual confusion?

The criteria according to which an investigator classifies people as a group in order to analyse what they have in common (or not) are one thing; the criteria applicable to action units are another. While the second kind of criteria always presupposes the first, the first kind must often be used without even implying the second. The reason is quite simply that, as Max Weber said, 'the growth of socialization, or even of community action [*Gemeinschaftshandeln*]' is 'by no means . . . a universal phenomenon'. The effect of a common class situation might consist in no other 'mass action' than identical reaction, even though this is not invariably the case and what often occurs is 'amorphous community action', like 'the grumbling of workers known in ancient oriental ethics and probably similar in its practical significance to a typical phenomenon of precisely the newest professional development: "braking" [go slow]'. For a class 'is not in itself a community', as

Weber said in taking up literally a criterion used by Marx.[1] In other words, an entire social class is not an action unit. It is by no means unavoidable that the fact be obscured by semantic inexactness, as some of those scholars argue who are aware at all of the problem.[2]

A group of persons within a given society, or a group composed of persons dispersed all over the world, represents a 'class' in so far as these persons share certain occupational or other characteristics by virtue of which they can be included in one category by an investigator or even by one or more observers who themselves belong to one such category. Unless, however, any number of people so classified are joined together in one organization, they are not an action unit; they remain a group or class in a purely classificatory sense. The difference also needs to be kept in mind when we refer to the interests and beliefs of such groups.

Again, it is one thing for outside, or inside, observers to specify the common interests of such a group. It is something quite different to suppose that the people included in such a group, whether associating for the purpose of common action or joined together in one organization by constraint, will evaluate their common interests or wish them to be pursued and protected in the ways a relatively objective investigator or an ideologist may find to be most suitable. The difference between classificatory and action units is immediately evident if we just consider that, while events have occurred in an era or happened within and to a class, no class as a whole, let alone an era, has ever been directly responsible for any such event. No social class in its entirety, or even its overwhelming majority, has ever formed one organization and functioned like a club, a church, a trade union, an army, a party or a state.

Although Marx often invested 'class' with the meaning of an action unit, he occasionally showed awareness of the fact that neither the bourgeoisie nor the proletariat were united by the same beliefs or could be induced to act in unison. This was one reason, as I have suggested in Chapter 4, why Marx's deviations from his belief in determinism always led him back to it, an attitude for which Lukács sought to provide the theoretical under-

---

[1] Weber, *Wirtschaft und Gesellschaft*, p. 633. For Marx's use of 'community' in this context, see below, text to note 3.
[2] R. Bendix, *Work and Authority in Industry: Ideologies of Management in the Course of Industrialization* (New York and London, 1956), pp. 13–14 nn.3–4, 199.

pinning in his distinction between subjective and objective class consciousness. What is more, in some instances Marx referred to the criterion of organization when he spoke of class or called for class action. 'The organization of the proletarians into a class and political party forthwith' was the aim proclaimed in the *Manifesto* (MEGA, vi, 534). In accordance with the acceptance of organization as the criterion of class action, he explained that the French *Parzellenbauern* (holders of small lots), 'these sixteen million troglodytes', were not genuinely a class, because during the reign of Napoleon III they were still isolated and extremely poor, being, therefore, more engaged in exchange with nature than with society. In these conditions, they formed a merely additive entity, like 'potatoes adding up to a sack of potatoes'. They were no real class, concluded Marx, in the sense of 'community [*Gemeinsamkeit*] . . . national interdependence and . . . political organization'.[3] Yet although Marx insisted here, as in the *Manifesto*, on organization as a decisive constituent of class, he immediately contradicted himself in saying that 'the troglodytes' were 'the most numerous class'.

In some other contexts, too, Marx insisted on the organized pursuit of common interests as the hallmark of a real class, that is, of 'a class for itself'.[4] Obviously, one can hardly expect Marx to have been consistent on this point, for this would have led him to the self-contradictory admission that even the 'pure' classes, the bourgeoisie and the proletariat, were no real classes, because, as he could scarcely deny, neither class had ever been united in a single political organization, nor even been represented by one. Yet one must not forget either that Marx knew that his theory of classes awaited completion and systematization.

Mannheim did not avoid the confusion we have just noted in Marx when it came to the beliefs characteristic of an action unit or attributable to a whole class or an era. He used the notion of 'the total conception of ideology' not only as a category of perception but also as that which is perceived, that is, as the 'total' ideology of a class or an era, or the total structure of the mind of either. In proceeding from the 'total' to the 'special' and 'general' formulation of 'the total conception of ideology', Mannheim

---

[3] *Der 18. Brumaire des Louis Bonaparte*, pp. 201, 198.
[4] See the references adduced and commented upon by R. Bendix and S. M. Lipset, 'Karl Marx's Theory of Class', in their collection *Class, Status and Power* (New York, 1953), pp. 30ff.

intended the first to refer to the more or less structured belief system of our opponents, not merely to the sum total of opinions held by persons who are included by an observer in a class, nor to the elements common to the different ideological perspectives found among such people. In his notion of 'the general form of the total conception of ideology', which includes both our own views and those of our opponents, he likewise did not have in mind an additive totality. He presumed that this general form, or perspective, would provide us with the views of an age, or 'of the whole historical process'. Such totalities of beliefs ascribed to a class or an era were conceived by him as enlarged versions, as it were, of the structured systems of belief characterizing organized groups like those forming what he called 'the intellectual armament of a party'.[5]

Mannheim knew, of course, that the belief system attributed to an age could only be a reduction of 'the multiplicity of the conceptions of reality' to 'different modes of experiencing "the same thing"'.[6] Yet while he understood the totality in this reduced sense also as merely additive, Mannheim leaned, I think, under the influence of Marxism, historism and the organic conception of social entities, all of which met at this point, towards conceiving the totality of norms and views of a class or an era as 'an articulated structure' which is 'integrated materially'.[7]

To confound what is merely additive and what is both additive and structured in regard to a multiplicity of beliefs is evidently the correlate of confounding in respect of classes of people the criteria of mere classification and analysis and the criteria defining an action unit. Beliefs may be shared by many people without uniting them in action, but sharing a more or less coherent belief system, or parts of it, is a necessary condition for turning a class or classes of people into an action unit. In each historical period shared and somehow interconnected belief elements provide a common basis for the conflicting trends and tendencies of most action units. Similarly, belief elements which are shared alongside those that divide a 'state nation' into conflicting (and cooperating) action units are a necessary condition for its existence.[8] The belief

---

[5] Mannheim, *Ideology and Utopia*, pp. 56, 77, 78 respectively.
[6] Mannheim, p. 99.
[7] Mannheim, pp. 149, 138, 58 respectively. See also pp. 93, 104.
[8] I use 'state nation' (the English for *Staatsnation*) advisedly, since 'nation state' (*Nationalstaat*) implies the maximal congruence between state and nation, the latter being understood largely in the ethnical

elements which characterize an historical period or a state nation naturally differ from each other in the same point as a class differs from a state nation. Unlike an historical era, a state nation is an action unit by virtue of its political system, and normally the most typical and powerful action unit of all.

As the pluralist would have it, the state is an association (or organization) of associations. It has specific functions like any other organized group, and these are carried out in the light of moral and technical norms which in a state are embodied in a general obligatory legal framework, or held to be enforceable on all citizens on other grounds, such as deeply rooted and widely shared habits and conventions, and by means other than coercion by law. These norms do not constitute a 'total' ideology in the sense of an all-inclusive system of values,[9] but they add up to a body of belief elements which in a Western-type democracy is not identical with the belief system of any one political party; it is an aggregate of values endorsed and changed by increase and deletion through the rule of successive parties or coalitions. This aggregate is therefore on the whole more general, although not less specific and asymmetrical, than a party ideology at any given time. The institutional and value system prevalent in a polity bears the imprint of the ideological platforms of the successive ruling parties but never reflects such platforms fully. Since only part of the ideological demands of parties is implemented through law and policies, the aggregate of prevalent belief elements is at once more specific and less comprehensive and systematic than a party ideology (itself no model of symmetry). The substratum of prevalent belief elements also forms a configuration of specific and by and large mutually adjusted elements because any party in power must let itself be guided by those beliefs which are required to safeguard the maintenance of the political system as a functioning action unit.

For these reasons such a configuration of norms is not a merely additive entity, but neither does is represent a structured 'totality' in any of the senses in which Mannheim, and for that matter Marxists, uses the term. First of all and above all, it is a structured

sense, that is to say, as characterized by the sharing of a language and a culture. A 'state nation' may be composed of several such ethnical units, which share values that commit them to a state of which they form part.

[9] For a convincing refutation of the assumption, see e.g. R. Dahrendorf, *Gesellschaft und Freiheit* (München, 1962), pp. 95ff.

frame of reference, a prevalent and yet ever-changing normative infrastructure with which accretion and deletion have to be harmonized so as to preserve the polity as a functioning action unit. Since what in a broad sweep is usually called a social class has never displayed the properties of an action unit, no class so far could ever boast, as any state can, of a functionally structured core configuration of belief elements in the light of which most of its members can be induced to regulate a decisive part of their behaviour and to be engaged or acquiesce in concerted action.

It is needless to say that because no class is an action unit, it follows that class interests in the broad sense in which we still use that notion do not weigh with people in the formation and adoption of beliefs. However, although it certainly makes sense to speak of class-conditioned or class-bound beliefs, it makes no sense to uphold the proposition that in the final analysis all beliefs are so determined and bound.[10] We have already encountered in Marxist theory itself a separation of ideology from the economic class base. One such separation is implicit in Lukács's juxtaposition of subjective and objective class consciousness, the consciousness entertained despite class condition and the consciousness consonant with that condition, but often not exhibited by most members of that class. The other separation also indicated by Lukács, and current in official communist ideology, is part of acknowledging the persistence of ideology, together with class differentiation, euphemistically called status differentiation, in post-capitalist society, although it is postulated that the socialization of the means of production and distribution has changed or even obviated the divisive effects of the relations of production. Mannheim performed another dissociation of ideology from economic causation. As has likewise been shown already, the economic determinant of class remains for him decisive, but a small stratum is removed from direct involvement in the economic process. Hence its outlook is supposed to be independent of economic determination, but not of social determination exercised by the unifying character of the intelligentsia's education. In addition, a contemporary behavioural separation of ideology from class is being made. Incorporating a Marxist tenet into a non-Marxist approach, this dissociation represents a partial corrective of Marxist theory.

[10] See below, Chapter 9.ii and pp. 202–4, 206–7.

II. Ideology and class consciousness

a. *Juxtaposition*

Many modern political scientists and sociologists who regard it as normal, not to say healthy, that politics be centred in the pursuit of chiefly material interests, adopt a basically Marxian perspective. Even when they turn this upside down, they have a precedent, especially for detaching ideology from its class base, in Marx and Engels's own deviations from their main position, as well as in later Marxist theories. Still, except within the context of specifically Leninist militancy against the sole preoccupation with trade unionism (*nur Gewerkschaftlerei*), interest orientation for Marxists is the mainspring of ideology and class enmity. This view is contradicted even by those modern behavioural scholars who do not deny that, besides pragmatic *qua* non-ideological considerations, there is room within the framework of the liberal-democratic Establishment for the influence of ideology on party politics and political behaviour. For in contrast to Marxists, these scholars distinguish political behaviour motivated by material interests from political behaviour motivated by ideology.

According to Alford, voting which is related to one's class position and which reflects class loyalty and class consciousness is also rational, because to vote in this way is not considered as a hindrance to the politics of compromise but rather as its precondition. The implicit assumption, regarded as self-evident, is that the more clearly voting can be related to class, the less ideological it is. In maintaining that group affiliation according to interests is the mainstay of party loyalty in English-speaking countries, Alford assumes a contrast between ideological voting and class voting, since he argues that religious loyalties are 'ideological and value-laden' inasmuch as they are most likely to conflict with class loyalties.[11] On this view, ideological loyalties are, then, all those which do not emanate directly or indirectly from class loyalties. Casting one's vote for the British Liberal Party is ideological,[12] presumably because the platform of and support for Labour and the Conservatives are more distinctly class-based than the Liberal vote and programme. Dahl likewise identifies an ideological

[11] R. R. Alford, *Party and Society: The Anglo-American Democracies* (London, 1964), pp. 249, 165–6, 365–6, 326 respectively.
[12] Alford, pp. 156, 305, 2.

attitude as one which cuts across socio-economic motivation. The same distinction is implied when more intense commitment is seen to follow from the coincidence of ideological and interest orientation.[13] The rather widespread distinction between the two among American and other behavioural political scientists is not always rigorously upheld. This is the less surprising, since its corollary, the identification of only 'extremist' (Marxist or fascist) with ideological belief systems, cannot be consistently maintained either.[14]

In any event, the modern opposition of ideology to the pursuit of mainly material interests retains on the one hand the connotation of 'unrealistic' in the Napoleonic use of the word 'ideology' and on the other also corresponds quite specifically to what Marx apparently regarded as a logical extension of his theory of ideology, but which in fact provided a precedent for the behavioural reversal of the dogmatic Marxian position. Mannheim followed Marx when he designated as 'merely ideological' what Marx had called Kant's 'purely ideological conceptualization', i.e. the adoption of the liberal ideas of the French Revolution in Germany. Like Marx, Mannheim meant that these ideas did not correspond to the reality (*Realfaktoren*) obtaining at that time in Germany.[15] Yet, much as Marx and Mannheim stretched the causal tie between the economic base and ideology in this specific case, as in other cases, they did not for a moment consider it as normal that ideology be entertained and pursued in contrast to class interests, however false or dysfunctional the ideology might turn out to be, become or cease to be.

In opposing ideological and factual orientation, modern behavioural theorists adopt the Napoleonic stance enlarged upon by Marx. The original Marxist and the behavioural approaches under discussion also resemble each other inasmuch as in both the

---

13 See respectively, R. A. Dahl, 'The American Opposition: Affirmation and Denial', in Dahl (ed.), *Political Opposition in Western Democracies* (New Haven and London, 1966), p. 68; and H. McClosky, P. J. Hoffman and R. O'Hara, 'Issue Conflict and Consensus among Party Leaders and Followers', *American Political Science Review*, LIV, 2 (1960), 407, 410, 415, 418.

14 See my *Ideology and Politics*, Chapters I, II.

15 K. Mannheim, 'Das konservative Denken (I–II), Soziologische Beiträge zum Werden des politisch-historischen Denkens in Deutschland', *Archiv für Sozialwissenschaft und Sozialopilitik*, LVII, 1 and 2 (1927), 80, 108–9. It will be remembered that Lukács also used 'mere ideology', but in order to denote unprincipled tactics. See above, p. 76. For Marx, see above, p. 124.

socio-economic interests of a class constitute the objective matrix and determinant of social action and political orientation with which ideology is, and policy may be, at variance. In the behavioural approach, however, ideology does not, as it does in Marxism, compromise all political orientations and reflect itself in all institutions prevailing in a class society; and ideology is entirely external and impervious to class interest. The clash of ideology with class loyalty, and hence also with normally prevailing party loyalty, does not, therefore, as in Marxism, cause any difficulty or contradiction in the behavioural approach, because all this is seen as characteristic of what is understood by ideology.

Apart from what is implicit in the founders' deviations from the position to which they must be held programmatically committed, there exists, then, an explicit Marxist, post-capitalist, yet ante-millennial detachment of ideology from the socio-economic base, and an anti-millennial separation of the two by Mannheim and the behaviourists. In each case the separation rests on different premises and has different implications. According to Lukács (and this applies generally to official communism), the dissociation of ideology from economic determination is taken to have occurred in post-capitalist classless but not stratumless society. It is assumed actually that ideology continues to exist in two contrary forms (whose irreconcilability attests the arbitrariness of the 'dual' conception): the officially sanctioned beliefs and insights and the residues of 'false consciousness'.

Mannheim believed that the factual insights contained in class ideologies can be synthesized from a higher vantage point. The 'total perspective' (which despite its high truth value remains ideological inasmuch as it remains action-oriented) can be attained by a small stratum alone for whom education has the same class-forming effect as the more immediately economic conditions have for the 'normal' classes. According to the behavioural approach exemplified by Alford and others, the overcoming of the determining power of economic interests is also an exception, but it occurs in all classes and is an important factor in the day-to-day life of pluralistic politics, rendering it not more rational, as in Lukács's and Mannheim's conceptions, but less rational. From data of voting behaviour it is inferred that since people engaged in similar occupations often reveal a similar political orientation, voting in accordance with the occupational or class position presents the rational norm of political behaviour. To behave ideologically is, therefore, to deviate from the rational norm of class-determined or class-oriented political behaviour.

The behavioural approach we are discussing is thus in agreement with Marx and Mannheim about the alignment of prevalent norms of political behaviour with material interests, as well as about the conflict of ideology with such interests. In the behavioural approach, however, ideology is not in any way causally related, but is actually in principle opposed, to material interests. Yet this juxtaposition provides the basis for the similarity between the behavioural assumption of a cleavage between the matter-of-fact attitude and ideology on the one hand and Marx's dogmatic assertions about the falsity of ideology, together with the simple-mindedness of the Napoleonic precedent, on the other. The socio-philosophical ground on which Marx performed his shifts is as absent in the behavioural approach as it was in the Napoleonic verdict. None the less, since the orthodox Marxist conception of ideology invites shifts of position and the taking of liberties with the concept of reality itself, the behavioural distinction between political motivations deriving from class position and those independent of or opposed to material interest seems to be a partial corrective of Marxism, particularly in so far as the opposition of categories of beliefs to material interests involves the frank recognition that political standpoints are largely a matter of choice. Yet since in both approaches (though on vastly different premises) objective material interests and ideology are opposed to each other and the rational norm of political behaviour is associated with the material conditions of life, the behavioural approach is open to the same objection which Bernstein had levelled against historical materialism. This objection is that in postulating the dependence of political postures on objective class interests, we cannot presume their disconnection in group action from moral judgments,[16] that is from values embodied in an ideology.

Indeed, interest-based beliefs are the same as all other political beliefs, if for no other reason than that the organized pursuit of socially important interests, their satisfaction and their integration with other interests require in any regime public justification and adjudication and therefore the eventual resort to ethical norms. Moreover, irrespective of whether they embody material or spiritual aspirations, political demands are metafactual, since to meet them is not only to pursue objectives on the ground of moral

[16] See above, p. 100.

judgments but to initiate action leading beyond given facts, whether the aim is to change the *status quo* or fortify it against change. In this respect too, the political pursuit of material class interests cannot be set over and against, or even apart from, the adoption or support of policies that run counter to one's class interests or have no connection with them.

b. *Equivalence*

It is, of course, sensible to assume that to base a decision on the material interests one has in common with other people is a rational way of acting, and that such action is not, as Marxist theory presumes, performed for the most part unconsciously or even against our intentions. It is reasonable to assume that people act in many instances with a considerable degree of familiarity with the facts they create and encounter, as well as in the knowledge of what they wish and can expect to achieve in certain circumstances. The Marxist argument according to which people, or a whole class, inevitably misappraise the trend of things, including the more far-reaching consequences of their own actions, because they pursue of necessity the interests determined by their class position, represents as lopsided a view of human nature (and abstraction from observable facts) as the Benthamist axiom that everybody knows best where his interests lie. The untenability of the Marxist assumption also shows in the fact that Marx and Engels were unable to uphold it consistently and that their most important immediate successors explicitly modified it.

No doubt, people's judgments are susceptible to being influenced adversely by their interests; but appropriate judgments, like misjudgments, are as much a matter of intelligence, resourcefulness and the nature of the case as they are of class consciousness. This latter, together with the preference of immediate over future material gain, seems to deflect intelligent working-class youth from continuing with higher education, and thus contributes to the disproportion between working-class and middle-class students. On the other hand, neither the histories of successful individuals in various walks of life, nor the history of bourgeois or social-democratic welfare societies, of international corporations and reformist labour organizations, so far confirm the contention as to the constant self-delusion of individuals and collectivities about the true nature of their interests and the implications of their pursuit, about what is conducive to the promotion of their interests both in the short and in the long run. To say this is neither to exclude nor minimize error, ill-concealed perplexity and brinkmanship, but to allow for rationally purposeful (*zweckrational*) choice as well.

It would likewise be wrong to conclude that the adequate awareness of interests and of how to promote them politically renders the political choices of similarly situated people predictable. Even in situations where one course of action could be said to serve the interest of a group best, a member could still for perfectly rational reasons decide to favour another course. He might have made up his mind to be disloyal to his professional group, social class or political party and support the interests of the class into which he wants or hopes that he or his children will rise. Asymmetry between class position and political posture is also caused by the decision of middle-class intellectuals to throw in their lot with the less privileged classes for reasons of justice and the advancement of society. Not only might (and actually do) members of these classes vote for other than workers' parties because they find it just and/or expedient that the national leaders should come from a class materially and/or intellectually superior to their own, but class-conscious workers who support a workers' party also adopt on average a more moderate attitude than either some of their leaders or members of the (middle-class) intelligentsia in general. The attitude towards the students' revolts in the 1960s seems to be a case in point – and not the only one.

It can be likewise observed, and is rationally and morally defensible, that according to what people believe to be in the public interest, they alternate between supporting and not supporting the interests of their professional group or social class. Indeed, what is best for one's class, whether judged in connection with the public good or not, is more often than not a matter of dispute. This is the main reason why class cannot serve as an unequivocal indicator of political orientation. This observation, which clearly guided Lenin as well as communist leaders after him, tends to be neglected in non-Marxist sociology of knowledge also, at least in its initial stage. Mannheim took the nexus between class and political opinion so much for granted that he referred to Burke's thought as an example of how 'immediately evident' its roots are, and identified these with the dominant class.[17] Yet neither Burke's social roots nor his actual 'life situa-

[17] Mannheim, *Ideology and Utopia*, p. 120.

tion' were aristocratic, and he suffered from this as a disability which hampered his career. Not only for a few individuals but also, as studies of voting behaviour and public opinion show, for relatively large sections of various classes, class identification and class loyalty are adopted and changed like all other social and political beliefs. Besides the fact that class membership is not the exclusive matrix or determinant of political attitudes, behavioural studies demonstrate in addition that while nationalism, regionalism and religion are important factors in the formation of political allegiances, class consciousness in the sense of class-oriented political solidarities is still a particularly strong belief element, though not equally in all classes. In England, class loyalty continues to unite the working classes less than the middle classes, and this was probably a secular reason for Marx's determinism[18] – and rejection of political democracy.

To some extent the vote of the working classes in England bears out rather Marx's view of the tendency of the proletariat to support their class opponents than his claim that the class consciousness of the proletariat could already be seen to have progressed towards 'complete clarity'.[19] Broadly defined, the British working classes can be presumed to comprise from 1884 onwards roughly two-thirds of the electorate.[20] Yet the Labour Party, like the Conservative Party, cannot count upon more than one-third of the entire vote. It is seldom that more than 20 per cent of the middle-class vote goes to Labour, whereas it is rare that less than 40 per cent of the votes of the working classes should be cast for a party other than Labour, and in most elections a third of the middle-class vote represents about half of the Conservatives' electoral support.[21]

18 See above, pp. 70–4, 113.
19 See above, pp. 125, 66 respectively.
20 R. T. McKenzie and A. Silver, 'Conservatism, Industrialism and the Working Class Tory in England', in R. Rose (ed.), *Studies in British Politics* (London, 1966; repr. New York, 1967), p. 24. As to self-classification of the population as working-class the percentage was 60 in 1948, the same as in Norway. America comes second among the nine nations studied, with 51 per cent. This contradicts the assumption that most Americans think of themselves as middle-class (W. Buchanan and H. Cantril, *How Nations See Each Other* [Urbana, 1953], p. 13) – or indicates nuances in the evaluation of class categories.
21 M. Abrams, 'Party Politics after the End of Ideology', in Allardt and Littunen, *Cleavages, Ideologies and Party Systems*, pp. 57ff; and McKenzie and Silver, 'Conservativism, Industrialism and the Working Class Tory', who try to explain on historical grounds, as well as by relying on contemporary survey data (25ff), the phenomenon of 'the

To go by voting behaviour, the middle classes continue to exhibit class consciousness to a greater degree than the working classes, a fact which at his time Marx seems to have taken for granted. Similarly, just as there is no stringent correlation between the self-identification of people with social class and what might sensibly be regarded as class voting (also where this is less easy to define than in England), the centrality of issues which at first sight make for divisiveness along class lines does not preclude a considerable degree of inter-class consensus. For example, data of the Michigan Survey Research Center show that in 1956 the percentage in America of those who supported greater government responsibility for measures dealing with unemployment, education, housing and other welfare problems was the largest in all occupational sectors, varying from 40 per cent among professionals to 68 per cent among unskilled workers.[22] If, then, the proletariat on the whole continues, as Engels lamented, 'to discredit itself terribly', the reason is that, particularly on issues of social welfare, the correlation between occupation (or class) and political opinions has become (or remained) severely limited, though by no means irrelevant.

Awareness of considerable asymmetry between class membership and ideological commitment and its concomitant, ideological consensus beyond class confines, is the essence of the most sensible implication of Lukács's semantically confusing but in its substance genuinely Marxian distinction between subjective and objective class consciousness. It is the point stressed likewise by Kautsky, Bernstein and Lenin that political working-class consciousness has to be brought to the workers 'from without', because they cannot produce it consciously themselves, nor can it emerge spontaneously in the working class. The necessity to teach and cultivate

proletariat "discrediting itself terribly"' (Engels on the elections of 1886) from that time onwards. On the differences in party preferences of people in manual and non-manual occupations in the United States, Great Britain, Australia and Canada, see Alford, *Party and Society*, and on the division of votes of the same class among different parties in Italy, for instance, see S. H. Barnes, 'Italy; Opposition on Left, Right and Centre', in Dahl, *Political Opposition*, pp. 318–22.
Cherished assumptions about the parallelism between sociological and ideological differentiations have been dispelled in S. M. Lipset, 'Working Class Authoritarianism' (1955), repr. in *Political Man* (New York, 1960), Chapter IV; see also Chapter V, 'Fascism Left, Right and Centre'.
22 V. O. Key, jun., *Public Opinion and American Democracy* (New York, 1961), p. 124.

class consciousness, however, is neither characteristic of the proletariat alone nor is it attributable to specific conditions, such as the absence in America of the feudal tradition.[23] It is universally borne out by experience that the masses, as well as elite publics, have been taught whatever class consciousness, or, for that matter, whatever other beliefs they have. Parents, priests and political leaders of any period have needed no sophisticated opinion surveys to make them aware of the need for direct and/or indirect education for certain kinds of behaviour to be observed or for any kind of organization to retain or gain members. On these grounds, one also can assume, as Marx and Engels did, that in certain circumstances class consciousness might cease to be a necessary (or desirable) aim of social and political education. Moreover, education might help to bring about the circumstances permitting, or requiring, the forgoing of instruction in class consciousness.

Since the beliefs which are assumed to tally with class position are not held by all who are in that position, and since, like any kind of social and political belief, class-based beliefs are permeated by values and must be imparted to be upheld, the behavioural setting of class-bound beliefs apart from ideological beliefs is as inadmissible as the Marxist dogma that all political beliefs and attitudes are explicable in terms of class membership.

The necessity of teaching social and political beliefs and of engaging in propaganda also limits the validity of the dogma of the unmitigated falsity of ideological thought. The propagation of beliefs invites the public scrutiny of ideological assertions either from within or from without a given political culture, depending on whether it is a genuinely pluralist and competitive democratic system, or one in which the hegemonic position of a party and its leaders (or leader) cannot legally be challenged. In either case, a modicum (though of quite different proportions) of verified and verifiable propositions needs to form part of an ideological argument, since sooner or later a point is reached where blatant offences against common sense and well-known facts will impugn the credibility of any political ideology.

That it is not natural for political ideologies to be impervious to facts, because this is also not conducive to their propagative purpose, is one reason why ideologies share propositions about

[23] As asserted by S. M. Lipset, 'Political Cleavages in "Developed" and "Emerging" Polities', in Allardt and Littunen, *Cleavages, Ideologies and Party Systems*, p. 25.

facts. They also are not totally divided over the evaluation of facts, or even over value judgments. The sharing of assumptions in all systems of thought I propose to call 'propositional pluralism', and one of its variants, therefore is 'ideological pluralism'. According to this, the sharing of propositions can extend to any constituent component of ideological thought, that is, to description, analysis, moral and technical prescriptions, rejections of beliefs (or disbeliefs) and the broadly conceived ways and means of the implementation of an ideology. Overlapping of the specific contents of ideologies in any one or more of these components of ideological argumentation, that is, ideological pluralism, affords further proof of the severely limited validity of the contention that ideologies are linked in every respect to a certain social class structure and a given historical period and are explicable only in reference to them.

10

IDEOLOGICAL PLURALISM

1. Contemporaneous contexts

Ideologies, like political philosophies, share assumptions, whether they confront each other in the same epoch or are separated by time and country. Let us begin with some examples of the sharing of ideas between contemporaneous ideologies.

Ideologies are far less divided than they are made out to be over the perception of phenomena, the interpretation of the causal nexus between them and the evaluation of their significance. There are no great differences in ideologies of the Right, Centre and Left, for instance, in respect of the emergence of industrial society, the ways in which it operates and its structural characteristics. Or, differences of opinion in these matters divide ideologies as they divide historians and sociologists irrespective of their ideological persuasion. The main controversial question for both ideology and social science is whether in the long run the market economy (or some part of it) can promise, and which kind of socio-economic structure can contribute to, both maximal production and an allocation of benefits morally acceptable to the majority and favourable to their well-being. To accept or reject certain criteria for answering this question is the ideologically controversial issue, not the inquiry into the degree of their realization in the past, whereas to pronounce on the possibility of their applicability in the more distant future is likely to be again, though not necessarily, more a matter of ideological controversy. Similarly, disagreement does not bear on the fact but on the nature of redistributive taxation and the just order of redistribution. From lasting disagreement on these lines it does not follow, therefore, that the notion of 'false consciousness' prevailed because it was believed that standpoints were both inadequate and incompatible.[1] Neither Marx nor his bourgeois predecessors or contemporaries, nor his successors, confirm this view. None of

---

[1] Lichtheim, 'The Concept of Ideology', p. 193.

them had the slightest hesitation about the adequacy of his standpoints, and not all of their standpoints were incompatible.

The analyses of bourgeois society by Marx on the one hand and by Guizot, Tocqueville, Mill and Spencer on the other were by no means entirely different from one another. Unlike Marx, the others owed nothing to Hegel in this respect, but, like Hegel himself, they were indebted to a tradition of thought which *via* the classical economists led back to Hobbes and Locke. And, as we have already noted, Marx did not shun acknowledging his indebtedness for insights and even evaluations to British government officials and commissions and the classical economists.[2] The recognition of the compatibility of some insights implies the recognition of their adequacy. Moreover, although in view of their deviations from the dogmatic conception of ideology it may be said that what Marx and Engels's notion of 'false consciousness' amounted to concerned the interpretation rather than the immediate perception of facts, they also shared with bourgeois thinkers interpretative assumptions. Marx was apparently entirely unaware of how much his rejection of industrial civilization had in common with Tocqueville's astute criticism of it, and in his predictions he ignored the central socio-political trends outlined by Tocqueville for the development of modern mass society. Yet like Tocqueville, Marx belonged to 'a movement of rebellion more than a hundred years old against the dehumanization of man in industrial society', a movement from which eventually existentialism emerged.[3] But Marx also was aware, and ready to acknowledge, that in his interpretations he relied on those advanced by thinkers of the bourgeoisie who remained dedicated to its cause. It is obviously for polemical purposes, but in harmony with historical record, that he made it a point to insist on the fact that it was not communists like him who had introduced the idea of class war. He cited as his immediate predecessors the French liberal historians, especially Augustin Thierry and François Guizot. In a polemic with the *Débat Social* Marx asked:

[2] See above, p. 53. One of the main and timely concerns of the series *The Making of Sociology* (2 vols., London, 1971), ed. R. Fletcher, is to show how much the social theories of the nineteenth century and the early twentieth century have in common. Although the other concern is to make up for the neglect of British sociology, the enlightening comparisons extend across the Channel and, therefore, also include Marx.

[3] P. Tillich, *Der Mensch im Christentum und im Marxismus* (Düsseldorf, 1953), p. 4.

Does the *Débat* understand by communism the emphasis on class contrasts and class war? If so, it is not communism which is communist, but political economy, bourgeois society. We know that Robert Peel has prophesied that the class contrast of modern society will burst forth in a terrible crisis. We know that in his *History of [European] Civilization* Guizot believes himself to present nothing except certain forms of the class war.[4]

In his speech on the occasion of the second anniversary of the Polish Revolution, Marx pointed out that the feudal and royalist opponents of the French Revolution, de Bonald and de Maistre, had correctly recognized that 'in order to bring back good politics, one has to reinstate good property' (MEGA, vi, 410–11).

Naturally, Marx was far from hiding his light under a bushel. Thus, while he referred to Thierry as 'the father of class war in French historiography', he conceitedly remarked, after having attributed to Thierry dissatisfaction with innovators who went beyond him: 'if Thierry had read our things, he would have known better'. Both these assertions were unfounded.[5] At any rate, in his political polemics, that is when his ideological involvement was palpably evident, Marx gave the lie to his overstatements on the exclusive falsity of bourgeois ideological thought, just as he did in his deviations from the dogmatic position in the more theoretical contexts of his teachings. The deviations are not dialectically or otherwise related by him to that position, but he conceded in all contexts, his assertions on principle notwithstanding, that even fundamental notions of evaluation and causal interpretation, besides being expressive of time and class, also transcend the two. In this way, Marx himself provided inadvertent support for a major objection against Marxist determinism. This is the view

[4] Reported in *Deutsche Brüsseler Zeitung*, 13 February 1848, MEGA, vi, 407–8. See also letter to Weydemayer (5 March 1852), *Selected Correspondence*, pp. 56–7. Lenin drew the practical lesson. He said in 1917 that resistance to the Bolshevik Revolution had to be repressed 'by the same methods by which the propertied classes suppressed the proletariat. New methods have not yet been invented'. Quoted in E. H. Carr, *The Bolshevik Revolution* (London, 1950–3), i, 113.

[5] MEGA, iii, 46. In his *Considérations sur l'histoire de France*, vol. i (Paris, 1840), A. Thierry himself correctly traced the conception of French history in terms of class war back to Hotman's *Franco-Gallia* (1573). And, for Thierry, *le tiers état* always remained identical with the whole nation, while 1848 meant for him the negation of the principles of 1789 and 1791. Hence there was little chance that reading Marx would have changed his mind.

that, whatever the extent we can attribute to the influence of social conditions on people's attitudes and ideas, in a relatively developed society it does not of necessity prevent consensus or cause dissensus on the interpretation, and much less the establishment, of facts. This conclusion is at once the premise of 'the great books' of political philosophy and historiography, and is confirmed by them, as it is by almost any kind of book or document, by daily experience and modern empirical research.

Ideological pluralism furnishes additional proof against Marxist economic and social determinism inasmuch as besides agreement in the description, analysis and evaluation of the significance of facts, agreement is also found in what distinguishes ideologies most from one another: the moral norms which underlie their fundamental principles, prescriptions and goals. Socialism opposes capitalism in order to supersede it. Nineteenth-century conservatism and twentieth-century fascism wished to contain it. Hence a distinctly reserved or emphatic anti-capitalist strain, and with it a qualified evaluation, or rejection, of values of industrial civilization, permeates these ideologies. As Mannheim has pointed out, nineteenth-century conservatism and Marxism share the same preoccupation with collectivities,[6] their preordained destiny or historical mission to which individual will is (or ought to be) subordinate, although these postulates rest on radically different premises and serve no less different goals in these two kinds of ideologies. Divergent premises and postulates may, as in the case of Maurice Barrès, be telescoped in the outlook of one ideologue and not necessarily all follow one another in a sequence in which no standpoint leaves a permanent trace.[7]

Central values of liberalism are rejected by the Right and Left, while étatism has found itself under fire from feudalism, liberalism and Marxism. Although the rejection of social determinism is natural in liberalism and unorthodox in Leninism, in both we find determinism severely qualified. Mill disagreed with the view that 'the greater political phenomena...are not amenable to the

[6] Mannheim, 'Das konservative Denken', p. 84, also speaks of the contact between the opposition from the Right and Left in respect of 'the concrete'. See also below, p. 192. Despite his awareness of the phenomenon of ideological pluralism, Mannheim neither used the term nor considered the significance of the phenomenon for a theory of ideology.
[7] See the intellectual biography by Z. Sternhell, *Maurice Barrès et le nationalisme français* (Paris, 1972).

direction of politicians and philosophers', and he adduced examples to prove that 'mere physical and economic power' is by no means 'the whole of social power'. Mill's explicit exceptions to the conservative 'naturalistic theory of politics' reverberate in Lenin's rejection of the Economists' actually orthodox standpoint that it is beyond the ability of the 'inspired ideologist' to overcome attitudes 'determined by the interaction of the material elements and the material environment'.[8]

Communist China maintains an official '"populist" hostility to formal state administration'.[9] At least semantically, we find taken up the precommunist distinction between state and society which the pluralists (Barker, Lindsay and the early Laski) made in the spirit of Tocqueville and Mill's quest for associations as the bulwark against the omnipotence of state organization. In a similar vein, a Polish scholar, Wiatr, identifies the formal existence of several parties in his country with a kind of corporative representation of different groups and strata.[10] Since the political independence and rivalry of these parties is practically nil, for they are not 'to undermine the position of the "hegemonial" party', and since it is likewise admitted that there is no 'legalized form of the struggle for power',[11] the practical significance in communist Poland of the representation of corporate interests is essentially the same as in fascist Spain and Titoist Yugoslavia. In these systems the adoption or modification of certain policies can be influenced by pressure groups, whether or not they are called 'parties'. According to Wiatr, the Roman Catholic Church is the strongest and best-organized pressure group. Taking his cue from the situation in his country, the Yugoslav scholar Lukić even envisages that in a fully communist society the participation and mobilization of 'free individuals, politically active' will assume the form of the 'non-ideological' activity of American pressure groups.[12] The evaluation as non-ideological by a considerable number of American political scientists of one of the most vaunted

---

[8] *Representative Government*, pp. 242, 244–5, 247. For Lenin, see above, p. 89.
[9] F. Schurmann, *Ideology and Organization in Communist China* (Berkeley and Los Angeles, 1966), pp. 97, 111ff.
[10] J. J. Wiatr, 'One-party Systems – The Concept and Issue for Comparative Studies', in Allardt and Littunen, *Cleavages, Ideologies and Party Systems*, p. 283.
[11] Wiatr, p. 287.
[12] R. D. Lukić, 'Political Ideology and Social Development', in Allardt and Littunen, *Cleavages, Ideologies and Party Systems*, pp. 67–9.

characteristics of the prototype of advanced capitalist polities is seized upon in order to make good the claim that this particular piece of capitalist political organization augurs what a central feature of the future full-fledged communist society will be like.

The ideological cross-cutting just mentioned is less astonishing if we consider that ideologies are also asymmetrical because, in the attempt to realize principles they share with one another – in this case the maximization of freedom through multiple associations in the context of liberalism and communism – or even in the attempt to implement diametrically opposed aims, organizational devices which are common to all or to several forms of political and social systems cannot be dispensed with. A similar or even identical piece of organization, however, will assume a different complexion in accordance with the overall nature of the belief and institutional system of which it forms part.[13] This is immediately evident if we consider how differently operate in West and East even formally and functionally similar institutions dealing with policy-making, legislation and law-enforcement, or if we compare the role of trade unions and, indeed, of pressure groups in pluralist and other systems. It is likewise true that in the absence of democratic devices in modern society, such as the plurality of freely competing parties, part of their function is fulfilled by the age-old substitute of informal though highly efficacious groupings of power holders. Where the hegemonial party is unchangeable such nationally influential groupings are emulated by, and often also connected with, what practically amounts to pressure groups, formed on less elevated layers of the socio-economic and political structure, or otherwise situated at the periphery of the system.

Although formally similar institutions or their substitutes can be incorporated into different systems without effacing the distinctive institutional and ideological character of these systems, assimilatory tendencies, once tolerated, are not always easy to contain. The intention in the early twenties to achieve 'communist Americanism' in the Soviet Union and the corollary of state capitalism and NEP are a case in point. Indeed, particularly in industrial organization, similarities may develop to a degree which casts doubt on the will or ability to preserve fundamental principles

[13] See R. Aron, *Dix-huit Leçons sur la société industrielle* (Paris, 1962), for critical exemplifications. For the problem of ideological asymmetry, see my *Ideology and Politics*, pp. 102–4.

and goals.[14] If neither failure nor ideological change is admitted, the similarities must be shown to be, or dressed up as, dissimilar in their function.

Soviet sociological research and theory ritually affirm that nationalization has put their system in an ideal position to use science and technology in order to overcome technical–economic and subjective aspects of alienation, which are admitted still to exist in the factory. The means recommended for the purpose recall less Marx's theory of conflict than elements of Western 'structural–functional' theories of social equilibrium.[15] Stress is laid on the subjective role of the participants in work teams and on all-round diversification, which should not so much replace specialization as alleviate its narrowness and monotony, and eventually lead to suspending even the division between mental and physical labour, as witnessed in attempts to fuse manual and intellectual efforts. Incentives, too, are offered to workers for suggestions for improvements. These means are all declared to lead towards the total disappearance of classes. Actually they serve, for the time being at least, the same purpose as in the West: to reduce conflict in order to meet the functional requirements of the large factory system by job satisfaction, control and working discipline. Yet, although ideological regimentation interferes with following up operational research of such problems,[16] there remains an important similarity between East and West: in industrial organization the ideological commitment to egalitarian ideals is interpreted much more differently than it is implemented.

Another example, closely related to the previous one, of interpreting structural and functional equivalences as having different effects and different overall significance is the acknowledgment in the Stalinist era of the existence in precommunist socialist society of a class divide. The divide was claimed to be horizontal, i.e. in

---

14 See Bendix, *Work and Authority in Industry*, p. 209 and Chapter 4, for 'communist Americanism' and a comprehensive comparison of Soviet with American managerial ideologies and their relation to the ideological fundamentals proclaimed in the two regimes. Schurmann, *Ideology and Organization in Communist China*, pp. 298ff, comments perceptively on the degree of relevance of the managerial practices of General Motors for communist China and those of Ford for the USSR – and the ensuing dilemmas and confusion in both instances.

15 G. Fischer, 'Sociology', in Fischer (ed.), *Science and Ideology in Soviet Society* (New York, 1967), pp. 41–3.

16 L. S. Feuer, 'Problems and Unproblems in Soviet Social Theory', *Slavic Review*, xxiii, 1 (1964), 119.

the main functional and meritocratic, and not vertical, as is the case when one class is placed above another. In accordance with the contention that social relations generally lag for some time behind the relations of production, it could be argued that the vestiges of class differentiation that survived the suspension of the private ownership of the means of production accounted for conflicts[17] but could no longer reflect class exploitation, because that suspension had removed the foundations for an antagonistic vertical class structure.[18] As Ossowski points out, in Soviet ideology Marx's militant conception of class relations – the vertical class structure – was said to exist only in the capitalist countries, and what amounted to Adam Smith's horizontal conception of class structure, a conception which Marx also used, was claimed to exist in Soviet socialist society. Given the intimate relationship in Marxism between class and ideology, it is not surprising that a parallel should reveal itself between the two conceptions of class structure and the 'dual' conception of ideology developed in latter-day official Marxism–Leninism according to which the pejorative connotation is attached to the ideology of the opponent and the positive connotation to Marxism.[19] A somewhat similar distinction exists in the West. For an important body of political scientists and sociologists, it is only Marxism and extremist political belief systems that are ideologies, but not those that prevail in a Western-type parliamentary democracy and affirm its political structure.

Now, according to Western opinion, the vertical class structure (and with it ideology) exists in the USSR, and the horizontal structure (and with it pragmatic *qua* non-ideological give-and-take) in the West. Those who believe in the ideologically most explosive of Marx's theories about classes thus see it borne out by the society of those who for the most part do not believe in that theory. For their part, the latter judge Marxism to be disproved by identifying as vertical the class structure of the society whose ideologists proclaim it already to have reached the socialist stage and hence to be horizontal. Since all-too-prominent differences in income and status have made it impossible for communist ideolo-

---

[17] Thus, for instance, Lange and Malewski, the Polish Marxists in following the official lead. Jordan, *Philosophy and Ideology*, p. 463.
[18] Ossowski, *Class Structure in the Social Consciousness*, p. 113. See also R. Aron, *La Lutte des classes: Nouvelles leçons sur la société industrielle* (Paris, 1964), pp. 125ff.
[19] Jordan, *Philosophy and Ideology*, pp. 452, 424, 426.

gists to maintain that classlessness has been achieved in the socialist stage, they resort to a concept of bourgeois provenance, the 'horizontal' divide, in order to draw the line between the class structure of capitalist and of post-capitalist society.

These exercises in ideological polemic are revealing inasmuch as both sides obfuscate the obvious. The principle 'to each according to his merit' does not cease to be a principle of liberalism after it has been espoused as the principle of post-capitalist distribution. Surely there is not much sense in even asking why the application of the same principle of distribution should not have the same social effects, irrespective of who is the legal owner of the means of production and distribution. By itself the legal formality has no bearing on distribution, and as long as merit remains the yardstick and is connected with the inequality of functions and capabilities, the allocation of benefits must remain differential. Marx, like Mill, know this only too well – and both made suggestion for remedying this situation, though by different means.[20] Furthermore, even the communist ideal of 'an association in which the free development of each is the condition of the free development of all' is nothing but an apt epitome of liberal values.[21]

Ideological pluralism is neither new, nor, as some examples I have already adduced intimate, is it manifest only in the relationship between the belief systems of one and the same era and country. Ideological pluralism exists at one and the same time both between such contemporaneous belief systems and between those of other epochs. Similarity and dissimilarity coexist in the epoch-bound as well as in the epoch-transcending relationships between ideologies.

II. Epoch-transcending comparability

In responding to the challenges of their time, political belief systems face problems of a perennial nature besides problems specific to a given time and situation. These latter may be a more

---

20 *Critique of the Gotha Programme*, in K. Marx, *Selected Works*, ed. V. Adoratskij (2 vols., London, 1942), pp. 564–6; and Mill, *Principles of Political Economy*, Book II, Chapter I, 1, p. 212.

21 Stadler, *Karl Marx: Ideologie und Politik*, p. 70, points out this affinity. But I do not see why Stadler considers these values to emerge as from 1789, when they found their most influential though not their first expression in Locke.

or less direct reflection, or variation, of perennial problems and persistent aspirations for their solution, ranging from the defence of the *status quo* to its replacement by the ideal city, and giving rise to similar kinds of controversies about these aspirations. The most enduring problem, so far, of social structure, which is also the most crucial one, the cleavage between poor and rich, has evoked radically egalitarian proposals and these in turn have occasioned successful endeavours to prevent their realization. While there have been partial reforms, and even incisive ones, neither the fundamental problem nor similar kinds of panaceas have ceased to exercise men and societies for many centuries.[22] This continuity attests the independence, so far, from modes of production and levels of technology of social problems, mental predispositions, conscious attitudes, feelings and, above all, traditions of thought and behaviour. In point of fact, the prime importance of the stage of technology and modes of production for the explanation of specific social phenomena and developments, and ideas about them, was undermined by Marx himself in his attempt to account in terms of his theory of economic causation for the persistence of both social phenomena and ethical norms, that is, for ideological pluralism in its epoch-transcending variety.

In accordance with the opening sentence of the first part of the *Manifesto* ('The history of all hitherto existing society is the history of class struggles'), Marx argued that the impression is created of the existence of eternal truths and (ethical) norms because 'in all past centuries' the diverse forms of class conflict consisted in the exploitation of one part of society by another. 'No wonder that despite all varieties and variations, social consciousness has assumed certain forms which will dissolve only with the total disappearance of class conflict' (MEGA, vi, 544). Logically, this explanation reduces to the point of obliterating it the relevance throughout known history of the modes of production for the fundamental problem of social structure and human existence. What significance in terms of the quality of life of the masses can we attribute even to the prodigious changes in the modes of production, and to the vicissitudes of the class struggles forming 'the history of all hitherto existing society' in general, if the most crucial of all social problems, the exploitation of the many by the few, has existed 'in all past centuries'? The only logical answer is that changes in what in Marxism is claimed to be the most potent

[22] R. Mucchielli, *Le Mythe de la cité idéale* (Paris, 1960).

determinant of social life and human consciousness engender a
result essentially the same, though with an accumulative effect in
the form of progressive dehumanization. Exploitation of the many
by the few is the concomitant of all known history; it changes its
form but not its essential nature. The hitherto persisting forms of
social consciousness, like the likewise persisting forms of class
conflict they accompany, must, then, be variations of what has
been experienced at all times.

Placed in the context of his assumptions about the difference
between socialism and capitalism, Marx's admission that the
nature of class conflict and class exploitation has stayed essentially
the same during all known history, entails the conclusion that
changes in modes of production, and those which they have
triggered off in the sphere of social relations and the superstructure, cannot be supposed to have affected the fundamental problem of human existence, nor can we expect this in the future
unless and until the modes of production and the level of technology make possible the substitution of socialism for capitalism.
One might as well go one step further and ask: does Marx not
invite here the query whether class conflict and class exploitation
as such have hitherto had anything to do at all, or at least in a
specific sense, and one existentially meaningful to him, with
changes in the modes of production and technological conditions?

We cannot consider the query to arise from a rhetorical slip, if
for no other reason than that Kautsky had to return to the problem, and while he was aware of the implications, he was not able
to solve it any better than Marx and Engels did. Kautsky admitted
straightforwardly that the same tools were used in different stages
of social development and concluded explicitly that the state of
technology was not the sole key to historical interpretation.[23] His
diversification of causal factors, however, did not lead him either
to specific propositions which would have permitted the claim
that to the extent that historical materialism is useful in accounting
for specific historical modalities, it is not confuted by the coexistence of basically similar social relations with changing technological conditions. Like Marx, Kautsky related time-transcending
similarities of ideals to time-transcending properties of the social
structure, and in the process he lifted the two not only above
technological change but also above the impact of the forces of
production. The social ideal, he acknowledged, appears to be

[23] Kautsky, *Ethik und materialistische Geschichtsauffassung*, p. 117.

always the same. After insisting on the importance of the different attitudes that Christianity, the French Revolution and social-democracy exhibited towards property and production, Kautsky explained that ethical ideals of different times and countries betray an 'external' likeness, because despite all social differences 'the fundamental lines of class rule in human society have always remained the same'.[24] With the possible exception of the deliverance of women from the bondage of private household duties, Kautsky's understanding of the abolition of classes testifies to more than a merely external similarity of the egalitarian ideals of different times. The abolition of 'the differences between poor and rich, exploited and exploiters, the knowledgeable and the ignorant', as well as the end of war, are, on the whole, time-honoured ideals.

The attempt of Marx and Kautsky to relate recurrent ideas and ideals to social relations led them to admit that the basic problem of social structure, which overshadows all others and is at the root of all evil, has so far persisted through history. They did not draw the inescapable conclusion which impairs the core of Marx's theory of economic causation: that what in his view constituted the most important problems of hitherto known social relations, the existence of class differentiation and class exploitation, as well as the ideals to which they give rise, are unaffected in their core by all the changes that since the division of mental and physical labour have occurred in the modes of production. Moreover, this division of labour itself is no indicator of a specific stage of technology; it takes us right back from our times to the stage of tribal societies and these are comparable in important respects to European feudal societies.[25]

The way in which Marx and Kautsky tried to meet the challenge to historical materialism posed by trans-epochal ideological pluralism, that is to say, their explanation of the persistence in time of social problems and thoughts about their solution, amounts to all intents and purposes to acknowledging important evidence of the relative independence of specific social problems from the nature of the forces and relations of production, as well as of feelings and ideas about assessing and dealing with such problems. This inadvertent admission corresponds to Marx and Engels's pro-

[24] Kautsky, pp. 136, 137–8.
[25] M. Gluckman, *Politics, Law and Ritual in Tribal Societies*, 2nd impr. (Oxford, 1967), pp. 40, 139, 136.

ceeding in various contexts of their writings according to the presupposition that the perception and explanation of facts and the adoption of political attitudes are not related to and conditioned by the place individuals and groups occupy in the economic process and the social structure. These concessions, which remain unreconciled to Marxian theory, strengthen the likewise inadvertent admission of the part played by ideas and feelings in their own right, through admitting that perennial problems and similar reactions to them are reflected in and underlie diverse forms of social relations and reactions to them.

Indeed, the transgression of socio-economic conditions by ideas and political attitudes is also evinced in those characteristics which tie them to their time and culture and create a common denominator. In their immense variety, material factors, such as the technological peculiarities of processes of production and their tools, or the instrumentalities of medicine, certainly account a good deal for the distinctive complexion and complexity of the social problems and solutions that are (or can be) envisaged. Yet time-bound distinctiveness reflects itself also on the spiritual plane in the shared presuppositions of conflicting political and other belief systems. Mental predispositions and metaphysical–methodological presuppositions contribute to both epoch-transcending similarity and epoch-bound distinctiveness.

Socialist and liberal claims have confronted each other, particularly since the end of the eighteenth century, on the basis of a number of shared assumptions which, like their divergent assumptions and conclusions, rest on a secular rationalism. It set socialism, democratism, and liberalism apart from rightist ideologies but provided quite generally the grounds for the refutation and substantiation of claims, since the protagonists of anti-rationalist traditionalism, for instance, cannot ward off their opponents without engaging in rational refutation and justification. In their clashes over similar problems, the Hebrew prophets, the critics of society, and the priests, the habitual defenders of the Establishment, like later rebellious monastic movements on one side and the Church on the other, appealed to the same authority for their opposing standpoints. For them this authority was not reason but divine revelation. Assumptions were also shared between the sixteenth and eighteenth centuries when reason and religion were relied upon at the same time, though to varying degrees, and the shifts between them marked off from each other the Christian-inspired metaphysics of order and Baconian empiricism. Even the systems of thinkers who did not fall neatly into either of the two patterns were not unrelated to these two traditions, nor were they at variance with one another in all their major assumptions and propositions.[26] Hobbes and Locke embraced the notion of the social compact but drew different conclusions from it. Locke grafted his theory of consent on far-reaching concessions to Filmer's patriarchalism, while in his justification of revolt, he looked for support against Filmer to the teachings of the traditional school of absolutists.[27]

The centrality of moral prescriptions in the composition of secular and religious political philosophies and ideologies vividly highlights the coexistence of era-bound and era-transcending propositional pluralism and its variants, ideological pluralism, inasmuch as neither ends nor means follow of necessity from the nature of the underlying ethical premises.[28] Hobbes opposed utilitarian norms to traditional absolute norms on the ground that these had proved inapplicable. On this fundamental issue he diverged from the political theory of traditional absolutists while he shared with them, like Machiavelli on a secular basis, the intrinsically Christian scepticism about human nature and, therefore, a belief in the inevitability of authoritarian rule, also basing his scepticism, however, on his acid dissection of modern *homo economicus*. While Aristotle shared Plato's conception of ethics, he took exception to Plato's vision of the best state. Furthermore, as in the cases of prophets and priests, rising monastic orders and the Church, the Anabaptists and Luther etc., conflicting moral and political principles have often been derived from identical theological and metaphysical premises, just as similar moral and political principles have been based upon divergent metaphysical premises. Liberalism, democracy and democratic socialism on the one hand and various forms and degrees of autocracy or totalitarianism on the other have been justified as the functionally and/or morally most adequate political systems, on the grounds of rationalist deductive or empirical inductive reasoning, of a rationalist or irrational reliance on immutable laws of history or tran-

---

[26] W. H. Greenleaf, *Order, Empiricism and Politics: Two Traditions of English Political Thought* (London, New York and Toronto, 1964), pp. 10ff.

[27] M. Seliger, *The Liberal Politics of John Locke* (London and New York, 1968–9), Chapter vii and pp. 254ff, respectively.

[28] See Seliger, pp. 46ff, for this point and the following examples.

scendent values and authorities. Conversely, as Marxists also recognize, the identical function of moulding and preserving the faith of the masses is performed on different grounds of belief by religious organizations (past and present) on the one hand and modern political parties on the other.[29]

The following are the main reasons why ideological pluralism characterizes the relationship between the belief systems of one time and country and of various times and countries. Firstly, in political theories and ideologies, ends and means do not of necessity follow from the ethical norms that are adopted, nor do different political ways and means reflect unequivocally the differences between ends. Persuasion bolstered by force or persuasion where freedom of dissent is part of the rules of the game may both serve to secure legitimating consensus. A core of organizational ends and means is common to all political systems; in the main it is the precondition for their existence as such systems. Secondly, in conjunction with specific time-bound problems, similar problems of social existence persist and so does similarity in the appraisals of both kinds of problems and the controversies about their solutions. Thirdly, while basic features of solutions and the differences of opinion about them persist, yet situations change, particular aspects of political belief systems are enlarged upon, and in the process also previously held ideals are transformed and become differently based. As a result belief systems of the same and different times continue to share assumptions and postulates in regard to what they affirm and reject.

I propose now to give some indication with special reference to Marxism of the recurrence in differently based (religious or secular) and differently oriented (individualist or collectivist) belief systems of themes, principles, presuppositions and approaches. This will enable us the better to gauge the extent, depth and finally the significance of propositional interpenetration, especially with respect to the tenability of Marxist tenets.

[29] Thus, Gramsci, *The Modern Prince and other Writings*, pp. 65, 91–2, 73.

11

THE RANGE AND DEPTH OF ANALOGY

1. The vision of the good order

One of the more persistent variations of the same theme in different times and contexts is that of a Kingdom of Heaven on earth. The urge to 'build Jerusalem' (Blake) reflects the refusal to live with imperfections as best one can. The various attempts to set up the perfect city have always been disappointing. Or, as Kautsky prosaically remarked, having most probably the latest, i.e. the Bolshevik, experiment in mind, 'the ideal . . . hitherto has always ended with a hangover'.[1]

True, the vision of a perfect order is a natural defence mechanism (for some people), but to assert that it is needed because relatively modest improvements require an extraordinary amount of collective means is to posit a false alternative.[2] If Kolakowski's assertion were true, together with his additional contention to the effect that 'through the accretion of reforms no revolutionary aim is attainable',[3] one would have to conclude that the cost of satisfactorily incisive reform is prohibitive. If a revolutionary aim, that is a radical change (reform), is desirable, and, as it would follow as well, if revolution (which on this reasoning certainly aims at perfection, or at least radical break) is cheaper, why do we need the revolutionary vision as a defence mechanism and not as a mechanism of ignition instead?[4] It would seem that the costs of reform are often high, because the call for modest and immediate improvements is likely to elicit wider support than the demand for radical and in their realizable entirety remote ones, as Lenin

[1] Kautsky, *Ethik und materialistische Geschichtsauffassung*, p. 134. He appended the threadbare and essentially question-begging admonition of the necessary coincidence of the ideal and the conditions required for its realization.

[2] As L. Kolakowski, *Der Mensch ohne Alternative*, rev. edn (München, 1967), p. 112, does.

[3] Kolakowski, p. 129.

[4] Kolakowski's redefinition of the Left as 'permanent revisionism' (p. 134) adds to the confusion in which the issues of reformism and revolutionism are shrouded in his collection of essays.

knew and communists to this day have no reason to gainsay. Hence modest reformers have frequently encountered more serious opposition from the powers-that-be than radical utopists. The politics of genuinely democratic meliorism is difficult to sustain over a prolonged period, since it requires, above all, a considerable amount of widespread political maturity, so that the utopian vision of a rationally defensible and continuously debatable just order can be invoked to ensure that the strategy of gradualism and expedient tactics remain subservient to the vision and to the respect for the uniqueness of human life and intellectual honesty which motivate the inception of the more ultimate goals in the first place. So far, in any extremist revolution, the betrayal of precisely these two fundamental values has been legitimated with reference to the ultimate goals of the utopian vision.

Utopianism provides the fuel for uncompromising extremism and mediating reformism, as well as for both conservative and revolutionary escapism. Just as reformism is not simply a device to take the wind out of the sails of extremism, conservatism is not always engaged in a rear-guard battle to halt changes, but also justifies radical changes to implement the utopian vision of reviving a good old order. In point of fact, the utopia of a good new order may take its cue from the assumption of a good old one. Innovating radicalism more often than not harks farther back for legitimation or demonstration of realizability than any real conservatism.

The utopian theme most deeply engrained in Western culture revolves around 'the community of all things' as the correlate of the perfect primeval order (or non-order).[5] The idea was fully developed and occasionally also practised in ancient Greece, though not necessarily in alliance with the ideal of generally applicable equality. In the Judeo-Christian culture the egalitarian state of equality and propertylessness was supposed to have

---

[5] On Pufendorf's logically still valid distinction between the absence of any property − 'negative community' − and common ownership − 'positive community' − see Seliger, *The Liberal Politics of John Locke*, pp. 180ff. The distinction reappears without reference to Pufendorf and his terms in Marx's manuscript 'Private Property and Communism', MEGA, III, 109. For Marx and Engels's belief in the historicity of original 'natural common ownership', see Marx, *Zur Kritik der politischen Ökonomie*, pp. xix, 9; Engels's note at the beginning of the *Manifesto's* English edition of 1888; and F. Engels, *Der Ursprung der Familie, des Privateigentums und des Staates*, 2nd edn (Stuttgart, 1886).

existed *ante peccatum* and original equality was thought to have been revived by the Essenes and early Christians in conjunction with communal property. The ideal never disappeared from European political thought and aspirations, as Marx himself was well aware. Yet notions associated with the various religious and secular conceptions of the ideal and of manifestations in its spirit reappeared, albeit transformed, in Marx's unique version, to an extent that he did not acknowledge, and most probably was not aware of, when he admitted the persistence through all past eras of the basic conflict between the exploited and the exploiters.

Marx took it as much for granted that there would be abundance for all under communism as Christian theologians did in respect of paradise.[6] Then there is an obvious parallel between the values on which his condemnation of the capitalist order is based and those embodied in the protests of the Hebrew prophets. His calling the proletariat 'the universal class' on account of its 'universal suffering' and the role he assigned to it at the end of days (of prehistory, that is) have a precedent in the teachings of Jesus, who proclaimed the meek and oppressed to be the salt of the earth, the last who would be the first on the Day of Judgment – when the first would be the last. Indeed, 'the proletarian' as depicted by Marx could be said to retain essential traits of Jesus himself. Calvez singles out the intrinsic humanity attributed to both; their suffering and humiliation preceding their elevation; their being conceived as individuals and as universal categories. Thus the '"proletarian" saviour of Christians' is an atheistic duplicate of what the Incarnation means to Christians.[7] These are some elements of the platforms proclaimed by the mass movements which militated in the Middle Ages and the Reformation under the banner of the elitism of the oppressed.[8] Just as the division of labour, entailing alienated existence, has the same significance in Marx's theory as has the Fall in Christian theology, the idea of this-worldly regeneration of man in a communist society has retained the meaning of the recapture through atonement of the paradise lost through sin. As Sombart opined, this myth has recurred in all proletarian movements.[9]

6 Tucker, *Philosophy and Myth in Karl Marx*, p. 151; Sombart, *Der proletarische Sozialismus*, i, pp. 325–30, who also pointed out that at times Marx was inclined to more sober thoughts.
7 Calvez, *La Pensée de Karl Marx*, pp. 596, 599, 622.
8 N. Cohn, *The Pursuit of the Millennium* (London, 1957).
9 Sombart, *Der proletarische Sozialismus*, i, 317. Likewise and more

In view of the secularization of religious themes in Marx's teachings, it is perhaps not without significance that there is a foundation for what communists and their clerical partners engaged in Marxist–Christian bridge-building, and also neo-Marxists,

recently, from a Marxist perspective, E. J. Hobsbawm, *Primitive Rebels: Studies in Archaic Forms of Social Movement in the Nineteenth and Twentieth Centuries* (Manchester, 1959), comments on the presence of millenarianism in all revolutionary movements. On Marx's profession of 'a secularized Jewish Christian conception', see Barth, *Wahrheit und Ideologie*, p. 114. Similarly, MacIntyre, *Marxism*, p. 63; Tillich, *Der Mensch im Christentum und Marxismus*, pp. 9, 13; and Tucker, *Philosophy and Myth in Karl Marx*, p. 23. As Sombart's *Der proletarische Sozialismus* shows (the work which grew out of *Sozialismus und Soziale Frage* [1896] 143 pp., into two volumes [488 pp. and 523 pp.] in the 10th edition of 1924) the awareness of the connections between Marxism and Christianity is not new, nor is it confined to works wholly dedicated to the subject. Sombart dealt with it specifically in the context of the chapters 'The Mythical Foundation' and 'The Ideological Origin'. *Inter alia* he showed the wide ramification in the religions and sagas of various cultures of the belief in the recapture of paradise, and traced the outline of its development up to Engels, together with the belief in the eventual prevalence of inexhaustible abundance (pp. 317–30). Sombart also stressed that Marx filled the previous class-war theories 'to saturation with ethical and mythical content' (p. 382).

The bibliographical indications given by E. Demaitre, 'An Inconclusive Dialogue', *Problems of Communism*, xx (Sept.–Oct. 1971), 41–7, contain the major works dealing with the relationship between Marxism and Christianity. Special mention is deserved by the survey of their parallel teachings by C. W. Lowry, *Communism and Christ* (London, 1954), and the treatment of the theme from various aspects in some of the volumes of *Marxismusstudien*, ed. E. Metzge and I. Fetscher (Tübingen, 1953). G. Wetter, *Dialectical Materialism: A Historical and Systematic Survey of Philosophy in the Soviet Union*, trans. from the German by P. Heath (London, 1958), also discusses parallels in method and substance between Catholic scholasticism and Soviet philosophy.

MacIntyre's books, although they are not as comprehensive as Tucker's work, are representative of those personally involved in the problems of the connection. He deals in *Marxism* with differences and parallels as one who aspired to be at once Marxist and Christian and who in the revised and enlarged version, *Marxism and Christianity* (London, 1968), has become more sceptical of both. MacIntyre also refers to some earlier manifestations of the awareness of the relationship. He quotes Spengler: 'Christianity is the grandmother of Bolshevism', and Tawney: 'The true descendant of Aquinas is the labour theory of value. The last of the Schoolmen was Karl Marx.' He might have added that the similarities between puritanism and communism had already been noted by E. Bernstein, *Sozialismus und Demokratie in der grossen englischen Revolution*, 3rd edn (Stuttgart, 1919) trans. into English as *Cromwell and Communism: Socialism and Democracy in the Great English Revolution* (London, 1930); L. D. Trotsky, *Whither England?* (New York, 1925). Gramsci, *The*

contend, namely that Marx's most famous remarks on religion convey a wrong impression since for the most part they are quoted out of context. The full passage reflects not so much disparagement of religion as an explanation of that which requires its opiate effect:

> The *religious* misery is on the one hand the *expression* of the real misery and on the other the *protest* against the real misery. Religion is the sigh of the hard-pressed creature, the feeling of a heartless world, just as it is the spirit of spiritless situations. It is the *opium* of the people.[10]

It is certainly not derogatory to Marx's understanding of the function of religious motivations, hopes and consolations that, being convinced that ultimately 'the religious reflex' would vanish, he more or less inadvertently, but nevertheless quite clearly, secularized its contents and function.

Indeed, Marx's onslaught upon the capitalist system incorporated the premise of the duality of a perfect and an imperfect world which Christianity had inherited from Judaism and

Modern Prince and Other Writings, frequently draws parallels between the Catholic Church and religion on the one hand and the function of communist politics in Italy, if not also of ideology, on the other. H. J. Laski continued the comparison between puritanism and communism in *Reflections on the Revolution of Our Time* (New York, 1943), and A. G. Meyer, *Communism,* 4th impr. (New York, 1962), pp. 4–7, offers a brief summary of the similarities.

It is of particular interest, at least in the present context, that according to MacIntyre, *Marxism,* p. 87, Marx adopted *via* Hegel the Christian idea of the unifying historical pattern of conflict and reconciliation while at the same time inheriting from Christianity the temptation to corrupt the gospel, so that the worst in Marxism is still Christian (p. 77). MacIntyre does not substantiate his claim that Marx was more biblical than Hegel (p. 57) and seems to go wrong in saying that Marx was at one with St John in his prophecy of the irreligious character of the good society, because, according to St John, it has no temple. Surely, it is the immediacy of the connection with God that renders the temple redundant. The differences from a Christian point of view are well brought out by Calvez, *La Pensée de Karl Marx,* pp. 530ff, 628ff, who concludes neatly that Marxism represents 'des vérités chrétiennes devenues folles' (p. 602). However, a French sociologist has found that communism is 'l'Islam du vingtième siècle' (J. Monnerot, *Sociologie du communisme* [Paris, 1949]), which in respect of its territorial conquest Soviet communism certainly is. Last and by no means least, most of the parallels mentioned, and a few more to boot, have been drawn by A. J. Toynbee. For a sample, see his *A Study of History – Abridgment of Volumes* i–vi by D. C. Somervell (New York and London, 1947), pp. 204, 368f, 399–400.

10 *Zur Kritik der Hegelschen Rechtsphilosophie,* MEGA, i, i, 607–8.

developed further.[11] In Kant's distinction between the phenomenal and the noumenal world, the world of appearances and the world of reality inaccessible immediately by cognition, the duality had been secularized while finding philosophical expression. An unwitting rebellion against religious tradition was thus implied. Marx strove to reveal the real focus of the duality and thereby the inevitability of its solution, by reversing the gist of Hegel's reinterpretation and solution of the conflict. Hegel had brought the philosophical rebellion begun by Kant to a head. He posited an epistemological totalist dynamism which removed the separation between the object of knowledge and the knowing subject.[12] However, in terms of social existence, Hegel's 'megalomaniacal' world-conquering spirit (Tucker) was supposed to find its adequate universalistic expression in the existing state which laid no claim to overcome, but rather to restrain in authoritarian fashion, the conflicting tendencies of particularist civic society. Marx's announcement that its immanent conflicts were propelling bourgeois society towards the turbulent *dénouement* reflected what Buber called 'a socialist secularization of eschatology'.[13]

No doubt, Marx joined issue with the contents and categories of the great religious conceptions of Western culture. He also followed Feuerbach's critique of Hegelianism, in so far as Feuerbach had linked Hegelianism, like all speculative philosophy, to theology. 'The nature of speculative philosophy is nothing else than the rationalized, realized and substantiated nature of God. Speculative philosophy is true, consistent, rational theology.' 'Whosoever does not give up Hegelian philosophy, does not give up theology.'[14] This was true of Marx himself, who rather transformed

---

[11] Tucker, *Philosophy and Myth in Marx*, pp. 32ff.

[12] Tucker, p. 59. See also pp. 54, 63. For the relationship between philosophy and religion in reference to Marx, my presentation is in many respects indebted to Tucker's work. I use 'totalist' where Tucker uses 'totalitarian', since the latter term is better reserved for political regimes and action-oriented belief systems. See C. J. Friedrich and Z. K. Brzezinski, *Totalitarian Dictatorship and Autocracy*, 2nd edn (Cambridge, Mass., 1965), pp. 15ff. There is, of course, a further affinity between Kant and Marx, the nexus between Kantian ethics and the aims of socialism which has occupied German scholars like Hermann Cohen, Stammler, Natorp, Staudinger and Vorländer. One might add Max Adler's attempt to establish a connection between Kant's theory of knowledge and Marxism *qua* social science. See especially his last work, *Das Rätsel der Gesellschaft* (Wien, 1936).

[13] M. Buber, *Paths in Utopia* (London, 1944), p. 10.

[14] L. Feuerbach, *Grundsätze der Philosophie der Zukunft* (1843) and *Vorläufige Thesen zur Reform der Philosophie* (1842), in *Kleine*

than replaced either Hegelian or religious contents and categories. This is strikingly evident in his pairing of the unmitigated condemnation of capitalist society as the epitome of dehumanization with the promise of complete redemption in the impending realm of freedom and equality. As against apocalyptic imagery or the down-to-earth reformist liberalism of a Mill, Marx did not match his certainty of the coming redemption by clarity about its nature. Was it to be something beyond communism, as the *Manuscripts* assert (MEGA, III, 126), or a higher stage of communism, as *The German Ideology* (MEGA, V, 22, 66ff) and the *Critique of the Gotha Programme* appear to indicate?[15] Would it mean anarchy (no state, no classes, no family) or a centrally conducted association of cooperative societies, as *Kapital* seems to envisage (*Kapital*, III, I, 96–7, 167, 373–4, 431; III, II, 354, 355)? Neither in the *Manifesto*, where Marx announced the substitution of the administration of things for the administration of men, nor elsewhere, did he foresee what Max Weber stated in 1918: first, that bureaucracy under capitalism would increase faster than the workers; second, that under communism 'the dictatorship of the official, not of the worker, is, for the time being at least, pushing forward'.[16] Despite the vagueness of Marx's vision of redeemed humanity, it is safe to argue that what it adds up to is a phantasmagoria of a secularized (and mechanized) version of St Augustine's City of God, accommodating within itself the liberal commitment to individual liberty and the allied apprehension of the abuse of state power, and carrying both to a hopelessly naive extreme. Though for this reason no less potent, the ideal cast its spell not so much on the masses whom it was to benefit most as on the intellectuals and others who arrogated to themselves the right to speak and act in their name. The ideal caused sharp conflict and splits among its adherents and eventually served as the excuse first for Lenin's

philosophische Schriften (1842–5), ed. H. G. Lange (Leipzig, 1950), pp. 87–8 and 72 respectively. See Tucker, *Philosophy and Myth in Karl Marx*, pp. 95ff, on Feuerbach and Marx; MacIntyre, *Marxism*, pp. 30ff and *Marxism and Christianity*, Chapters III, IV.

15 *Selected Works*, I, 565–6. For Mill's detailed outline of the transition to the eventual realization of a socialist organization within and besides an economy based on private property and competition, see his *Principles of Political Economy*, Book II, Chapters I, II and Book IV, Chapter VII.

16 M. Weber, 'Der Sozialismus – Rede zur allgemeinen Orientierung von österreichischen Offizieren in Wien (1918)', in *Gesammelte Aufsätze zur Soziologie und Sozialpolitik* (Tübingen, 1924), pp. 507–8.

disciplined *avant-gardism* and then for the unprecedented application of state power for the purpose of achieving faraway state-
lessness. If this dichotomy between ideal and means is explicable
in terms of dialectics, then these, too, are evidence of ideological
pluralism.

It is in the spirit of the romantic preoccupation with contrasts,
permeating both Hegelian and Marxian dialectics, that Marx
matched ultimate peacefulness with present contentiousness,
preaching class-militarism instead of state-militarism. Since revolution was his life-long preoccupation, he viewed war as an opportunity, and increasingly as the only opportunity, to bring the
revolution about. It is perhaps not overstating the case when
Feuer says that 'a kind of historical militarism tended to supersede
historical materialism'.[17] The fusion of the two can also be seen
to follow from joining the contrasts of the 'real positive science'
and apocalyptic imagery in the conception of how the plot of
world history – paradise *qua* communism lost and regained – will
be consummated.[18] Whether or not the final battle which, together
with its outcome, Marx's 'positive science' permits us to predict,
will be a walk-over or a savage reckoning, or both, men must still
pass through a debasing purgatory after that battle is won. A
secularized version of what precedes the Second Coming clearly
reverberates in the notion of 'crude and thoughtless communism'
found in the *Economic and Philosophical Manuscripts* of 1844.[19]
In the last scene but one of the scientifically predictable and
dialectically unfolding drama of world history, the sequestration
of private property and the dissolution of the family lead to the
loss of all self-restraint, to viciousness and vileness. As in Christian
mythology, and again in the teachings of the 'false Messiah'
Sabbetai Zvi, a last bout of the rule of Satan precedes salvation,
which in Marx's terms means the cessation of man's self-alienation.

[17] L. S. Feuer, 'Karl Marx and the Promethean Complex', *Encounter*,
xxxi, 6 (December 1968), 18. 'Historical militarism' seems to be in
elaboration of Weber's 'military materialism'. See above, p. 111.
[18] Tucker, *Philosophy and Myth in Karl Marx*, p. 23.
[19] MEGA, iii, 111–13; Tucker, *Philosophy and Myth in Karl Marx*,
p. 154; and L. J. Halle, 'Marx's Religious Drama', *Encounter*, xxv,
4 (October 1965), 35–6, and his reference to *Revelations* 20: 7–10.
Marx here followed Proudhon, whom he mentioned, and Lorenz von
Stein – whom he did not mention – and both of whom he outdoes, as
Tucker remarks.

II. Blends and lineages

Marx's message of this-worldly salvation has an individualistic ring but, like its religious forebears, it harbours the ominous tendency to transfer the responsibility for sin and retribution from individuals to collectivities. Some scholars have seen a sudden transition in Marx's work from alienation in the personality to alienation between collective bodies. To the extent that it can be argued that Marx unaccountably equated the split in the individual with the split between classes,[20] he assimilated for inverse moral and political purposes Plato's mistaken identification of the structure of the soul with the class structure. Whether or not we attach more significance than that of a thematic shift to the fact that in his mature writings Marx gave less prominence to the problem of personal alienation than in his earlier work, it appears a well-founded conclusion that there is a noticeable quantitative and substantive shift away from describing the subjective world in subjective terms to a depersonalized version of Marxism.[21] Or, conversely, as Barth put it, as a result of Marx's personification of economic forces, his 'history-making man is turned into an entirely illusory personality'.[22]

Moreover, at the very least, the equation of individual and collective concerns, and much more the absorption of the former in the latter, is already strikingly apparent in the young Marx's preoccupation with the truly human existence of man in terms of a 'species being' (*Gattungswesen*). This concern absorbs the individualistic in the collectivist perspective. In the wake of Hegel's overcoming of the romanticist oscillation between an irresponsible individualism and a mystic collectivism, Marx equated in the *Economic and Philosophical Manuscripts* the

[20] Tucker, pp. 146ff, regards this as the decisive step from philosophy to myth, the criterion being that something internal is presented as external (p. 219). The view of the equation has been challenged but seems to be confirmed by the evidence adduced in the passages that follow, since it bears on what can be said to follow from the equation; and this Tucker himself does not note.

[21] Tucker, pp. 160, 220 respectively. See also pp. 176, 165, 185. In Tucker's interpretation the collectivist implications are missing. MacIntyre, *Marxism and Christianity*, pp. 50–1, unlike Tucker and others, does not note any shift, but refers to the sacrifice of the individual for eternal purposes as being carried over into Marxism from Christianity (p. 113).

[22] Barth, *Wahrheit und Ideologie*, p. 199.

distinctiveness of the individual with that which makes him 'into the real *individual* community being [*Gemeinwesen*]'. This he is to the same extent as he is 'the subjective existence in thought and feeling of society by itself' (MEGA, I, I, 117). The intention would seem to be what Plato, Rousseau and Hegel demanded in their different ways, namely that in the relationship between the individual and the community no important difference between private and general interest is admissible. It is as characteristic of the young Marx's conception of the relationship between individual and society as it is of his adaptation of religious concepts and themes to his purposes that he should have said that in the democratic state man lives a 'heavenly' life in the political sphere, because there he regards himself as 'a community being', whereas in civic or bourgeois society he leads a 'terrestrial' life, because there he is a private being who regards himself and others as a means, as subject to the play of 'alien forces'.[23]

The immersion of the individual in community life as the norm by virtue of which he evades subjection to 'alien forces' also accounts for Marx's opinion that in bourgeois society the fullest realization of political emancipation occurs only in the transient moments when that society produces its 'political state' by revolutionary force. When, at the height of the French Revolution, religion was destroyed by the state, the *maximum* (the Acts of Price Control of 1793 and 1794, which extended eventually to wages also), requisitions and progressive taxation suspended private property, just as the guillotine dissolved life. In these

> moments of its specific self-consciousness, political life seeks to crush its conditions [viz.], bourgeois society and its elements, and to constitute itself as the real, contradictionless species life [*Gattungsleben*] of man ... the political revolution ... broke bourgeois society into its simple components ... unchained the political spirit ... assembled it ... freed it from its intermingling with bourgeois [civil] life and constituted it [the political spirit] as the sphere of community, of the universal interests of the people in ideal independence of those specific elements of bourgeois [civil] life.[24]

23 Marx, *Zur Judenfrage*, MEGA, I, I, 584. He uses *Gemeinwesen* (community being) both for the individual and the community.
24 Marx, p. 586. Marx's enthusiastic evaluation of the Jacobin revolution deserves particular attention in view of the attempts to present him only as a critic of Jacobinism and to make him out as a

In this connection too Marx himself drew a parallel between religious and secular conceptions in considering that Christianity and political democracy both create the illusion of overcoming alienation, so that political democracy is Christian in a secularized form. The point here is that Marx's almost lyrical enthusiasm for Jacobin revolutionism is a further indication of the fact that, much as he went politically and socially beyond and against Hegel, he appears to have taken over right from the beginning the basically anti-individualist intent of Hegel's view of 'the destiny of . . . individuals to lead a common [universal] life'.[25] The two thinkers adopted a self-transcending conception of freedom in the sense that freedom lies in the self-willed identification with the requirements of a common life and its universal values. This would mean a non-individualist individualism, if there were such a thing, just as to call this 'positive' freedom, as is frequently done, is to commit the illogicality of equating prescriptive with free choice. At any rate, Marx envisaged the reconciliation of self-regarding and other-regarding concerns in a classless and stateless society, rather than taking it, like Hegel, to be already manifest in the political sphere of the existing modern (Prussian) state.

The assumptions Marx shared with Hegel connected him with traditional conservative thought also. As Mannheim put it, 'the thousandfold-repeated stress on the abstract character of human relationship in the capitalist world goes back to the thought of the old estates [*altständisches Denken*]', which meets with socialist thought also because for it, too, the true object of history is not the individual but collective entities in the 'historic life-space'.[26] Hegel and Marx opposed to individualist 'civic' or 'bourgeois' society an order of relationships rooted in the Platonic subjugation of conflict-ridden plurality to harmonious unity. Only Marx, who preceded Popper in denouncing the *Politeia* as an apologia for a caste system, envisaged, unlike Plato and Hegel, the emergence of one all-embracing, undifferentiated and therefore harmonious City of Man. In it, as distinct from St Augustine's City of God, self-regarding mundane interests, while not ceasing to exist, would cease to be divisive.

To the extent to which it can be said that the empirico-rational

true and pure humanist whose teachings have nothing to do with the terror perpetrated in their name.

[25] G. W. F. Hegel, *Grundlinien der Philosophie des Rechts*, ed. J. Hoffmeister, 4th edn (Hamburg, 1955), para. 258.

[26] Mannheim, 'Das konservative Denken', pp. 101, 106.

tradition deriving from Bacon's theory of idols intertwined in Marx with the tradition which led *via* Hegel back to the Church Fathers of Swabian pietism, neo-platonic gnostic, cabbalistic and kindred sources, the connection is recognized as being at once precariously and contradictorily reflected in Marx and, of course, not acknowledged by him.[27] I have sketched this genealogy back to St Augustine, Plato and the Hebrew prophets, as well as extended it across to traditional conservatism and liberalism. Yet although it would not be difficult to buttress it further, it is easier still to make dents in this ramified genealogy, if one asks, as one is bound to, whether the differences do not outweigh the similarities. There is no quantifiable answer to that question, but it stands to reason to suggest that we must answer it in the affirmative. There is no denying the overall distinctiveness of political ideologies and other belief systems, whether we view them in contemporaneous or era-transcending contexts. The fact of analogy, however, does not admit of any doubt either. Indeed, it is so conspicuous that even Marx and Marxist cannot deny it, although it derogates decisively from the pertinence of Marxist fundamental principles. Nevertheless, Marx not only admitted the recurrence of ideas and social problems and used religious concepts and parallels, but also agreed methodologically with Feuerbach's 'reformational criticism', which was taken over by the latter from the philosophy of religion and is tantamount to 'transformational criticism'.[28]

Analogy is not invalidated by dialectical inversion, for analogy presupposes difference, or would otherwise mean identity. Thus, for instance, Marx transferred the attribute of creative activity from God to man. One might say even that in engaging in the secularization of religious belief, he ascribed to man (as a 'species being') the will to be like God but not to acknowledge God.[29] Needless to say, the transference makes a profound difference precisely because it leaves the centrality of creativity untouched.

---

[27] Topitsch, *Sozialphilosophie zwischen Ideologie und Wissenschaft*, pp. 16, 326. See also pp. 36–7, and for greater detail, pp. 261 *passim*.

[28] The term used by Tucker, *Philosophy and Myth in Karl Marx*, pp. 97, 103, 171. For Feuerbach, see *Kleine philosophische Schriften*, p. 89: 'Die Methode der reformatorischen Kritik der spekulativen Philosophie' (The method of reformational criticism of speculative philosophy), which is not different from the one applied already in the philosophy of religion.

[29] As Calvez, *La Pensée de Karl Marx*, p. 593, put it. Actually, however, Marx resecularized a religious belief, since he could be said to have reverted to Protagoras and Xenophanes.

It furnishes a striking expression of Marx's intention to break with religion, though not, as is often argued, only to end up with a secular religion. In more than a strictly formal sense, it is a contradiction in terms to talk about certain ideologies as 'secular religions'. It might be more appropriate to speak of *Religionsersatz*, as Sombart did, who argued that 'the emptier the mind of the proletarian socialist became of genuinely religious ideas', the more it imposed upon itself the belief in the coming of socialism.[30] Religion is based upon the belief in Gods or gods, while the ideologies which have come to be called 'secular religions' are atheist either in principle or in actual fact. This difference is of importance although it does not obliterate functional and substantive analogies between religious and secular belief systems.

As Mme de Staël and other contemporaries of the French Revolution had noted, political and religious fanaticism are indistinguishable. The Terror, she explained, throve upon the hatred between those on top and those at the bottom of the political ladder. 'The germs of this sentiment have existed at all times' and fed upon the hatred of the poor for the rich, inciting the same fanaticism. Although she showed no sympathy for 'this insane hope' of the working classes 'that the yoke of the disparity of fortunes would eventually cease to weigh upon them', a hope which she thought had played a part in the advent of the Reign of Terror between 1793 and 1794, she insisted that massacres no less atrocious than those perpetrated by the Jacobins had been committed in the name of religion.[31] On this showing, the analogy between religious and political fanaticism comprises, besides motivations, the intensity of commitment and its practical consequences. Indeed, variously founded and oriented fanatical commitments are analogous inasmuch as the fanatic more than anybody else is committed to one authority to the exclusion of all others and exhibits what Rokeach calls 'the closed mind'.[32] This reveals itself also in the consciousness of an unbridgeable gulf between the reality the fanatic condemns and the vision he espouses, or between the visions he rejects and the reality he defends, depending on whether he is a revolutionary or a conservative. Analogy here encompasses not merely the manner of

[30] Sombart, *Der proletarische Sozialismus*, pp. 225, 317 respectively.
[31] Mme de Staël, *Considérations sur les principaux événements de la Révolution Française* (1818), new edn (Paris 1842), pp. 287, 297, 289.
[32] M. Rokeach, *The Open and the Closed Mind – Investigations into the Nature of Belief Systems and Personality Systems* (New York, 1960).

believing but also aspects of the nature and contents of beliefs themselves.

The coexistence of analogy and disparity, of imitation and rejection, in the relationship between religious and other kinds of thought is not surprising. As Marxist philosophers themselves have become aware, branches of philosophy like metaphysics, ethics and even epistemology have never freed themselves entirely from the inheritance of both speculative and mythical theology, which in turn took over fundamental questions of human existence and of proper knowledge about it from pre-theological magical thought.[33] The inheritance comprises, for example, the ascription of significance to an event which stands in no apparent relation to its empirically observed effects; the presuppositions of knowledge, the quest for knowledge about an immanent order of the world and of man's place in it; the questions of progress, determination and responsibility in history, and so forth.[34]

Analogy between religious and secular belief systems extends beyond the preconditions of human knowledge, its objects and actual contents, to presuppositions and methods of demonstration of statements and modes of argumentation as well. As Kolakowski points out, in these respects the directives issued in communist systems for writers bear comparison with decrees adopted by the Council of Trent (1545–7, 1551–2, 1562–4), which under Jesuit guidance reformed the Catholic Church during the Counter-Reformation. Embedded in religious thought we also find the use of the dialectical method, the ideas of the unity of theory and practice (reappearing in romanticism),[35] the *negatio negationis* (Meister Eckhart), not to forget alienation in connection with the

---

[33] Kolakowski, *Der Mensch ohne Alternative*, pp. 224ff. In this context there seems to be a recognizable reverberation of the theories of Lévi-Strauss, who acclaims Marxism as one of the influences on his structuralism. See E. Leach, *Lévi-Strauss* (London, 1970). Gramsci, *The Modern Prince and Other Writings*, p. 79, commented critically on the survival of theology and metaphysics in the notion of 'what man is'. He also related the return by orthodox Marxists to philosophical materialism to the closeness of a materialistic conception to the masses, as evinced in their 'beliefs and prejudices' and 'nearly all popular superstitions (sorcery, ghosts, etc.)', to which 'the crassly materialistic' popular versions of Catholicism and Greek Orthodoxy respond (pp. 87–8).

[34] Kolakowski, *Der Mensch ohne Alternative*, pp. 229–31.

[35] Topitsch, *Sozialphilosophie zwischen Ideologie und Wissenschaft*, p. 37; Tucker, *Philosophy and Myth in Karl Marx*, pp. 25, 229 (and for other parallels, pp. 23ff); and Mannheim, 'Das konservative Denken', p. 493, respectively.

knowability of truth.[36] According to the Marxist philosopher Lucien Goldmann, Marx and Pascal did not only share awareness of the struggle between the stronger and the weaker and of 'the ropes of necessity' that cause 'the ropes of imagination', viz. ideology. The idea of *credo ut intelligam* provided common ground for the epistemology of St Augustine, Pascal and Marx. Even though the attitude towards faith in the systems of the three was of a very different kind, it could be said that Marx's socialist society had a function analogous to 'the highest good' and 'the Kingdom of God' in other philosophical systems.[37]

In point of fact, the analogy between ideology and 'the ropes of imagination' suggests the more fundamental one between the Marxian theory of ideology and the religious teachings about the effects of the Fall. Marx not only used 'ideological' thought in the sense in which Hegel used 'alienated' [*entfremdet*] thought,[38] but he took 'the extreme step of objecting to alienation' as 'a distortion of man's essence'.[39] Apart from identifying ideological with distorted thought, he postulated, therefore, in accordance with the assumed determination of consciousness by social being, the congruence between ideological thought and alienated existence.[40] Thus ideology in the dogmatic Marxist sense is the necessary false consciousness of man alienated from himself by the division of labour. In Christian theology the Fall hindered the soul from imbibing the truths of salvation. Notwithstanding the Fall of Christian theology and false consciousness in Marxism, in the teachings of both a few are presumed to be able to conceive through reason the fundamental truths of either natural theology (Thomas Aquinas) or of the laws of historical development

36 Topitsch, *Sozialphilosophie zwischen Ideologie und Wissenschaft*, pp. 274 n.38, 282.
37 Goldmann, *The Hidden God*, pp. 278, 94–5, and *Recherches dialectiques*, p. 18.
38 For Hegel this was empirico-rational thought, and while Feuerbach considered Hegel's philosophy 'alienated' in this sense, Marx held that both Hegel and Feuerbach remained ensnared in 'alienated', i.e. ideological thought (Topitsch, *Sozialphilosophie zwischen Ideologie und Wissenschaft*, pp. 312–16). In his *Vom Ursprung und Ende der Metaphysik, Eine Studie zur Weltanschauungskritik* (Wien, 1958), Topitsch analyses in terms of a historizing sociology of knowledge models of world views, beginning with original myth and progressing *via* the developed mythology of ancient 'high cultures' to philosophy terminating as ideology.
39 Rotenstreich, *Basic Problems of Marx's Philosophy*, p. 157. Cp. also pp. 159–60.
40 See above, pp. 38–9.

(Bossuet, Marx). The few can enlighten those worthy of and destined for salvation or the restoration of their humanity.[41] Thus, as we have already noted, Gramsci was of the opinion that 'the determinist, fatalist mechanist element has been an immediate ideological "aroma" of Marxism', particularly in times of defeat. Then 'real will is disguised as an act of faith . . . a primitive and empirical form of impassioned finalism which appears as a substitute for the predestination, providence etc., of the confessional religions'.[42]

Ideology as false consciousness also serves as the counterpart of idolatry, the attempt of man to disguise his and some of his world's finiteness,[43] while ideology purged from its pejorative meaning fulfils the function of theodicy. Theodicy justifies by God's infinite wisdom that which appears in the finite perception of man as the shortcomings of the world. Ideology justifies the undeniable evil in revolutionary methods and the visible imperfections of a long-established regime or of revolutionary achievements. It does so in reference to the wisdom and goodness either inherent in the existing order as a whole or in the one yet to materialize fully.

It stands to reason that without the range and depth of such parallels the traditional attempts to reconcile philosophy and religion could never have been so much as broached. Nor has the Enlightenment put an end to them. While the Catholic Church, like the Establishment of Judaism and Islam, remains opposed to Marxism as a world view, Pope John XXIII's *Pacem in terris* (1963) gave some official sanction to the endeavours of priests and others to seek more than ever before to establish common ground between Marxism and Christianity in matters of social policy and philosophy.[44] For all we know, Teilhard de Chardin may, after all,

---

[41] Cp. Topitsch, *Sozialphilosophie zwischen Ideologie und Wissenschaft*, pp. 288 n.80, 306; and Kolakowski, *Der Mensch ohne Alternative*, pp. 227–8. E. Grünwald, *Das Problem der Soziologie des Wissens* (Wien, 1934), who had already pointed out that one of the sources of Marx's theory of ideology, German metaphysics, was, as Feuerbach had maintained, secularized theology and suggested that Marxian ways of argumentation run parallel to the view that God has inflicted 'false consciousness' on man in order to realize his plan of salvation (p. 24n4).

[42] Gramsci, *The Modern Prince and Other Writings*, p. 69.

[43] Tillich, *Der Mensch im Christentum und im Marxismus*, p. 14.

[44] This is done on various levels and in different contexts and also in varied degrees of avowed non-conformity with official doctrine. For some samples on a none-too-exalted intellectual level, see J. Klugmann and P. Oestreicher (eds.), *What Kind of Revolution? – A Christian–*

have pointed the way to achieving again something as comprehensive and far-reaching as Thomas Aquinas's authorized adaptation of Aristotelianism to Catholicism, which was preceded by the adaptations of Greek philosophy to Judaism by Philo Judaeus and of Platonism to Islam by Muslim philosophers.[45] That no synthesis of a comparable philosophical significance between Marxism and one of the major religions has so far been achieved might well be due not just to the pronounced atheism of Marxism but, above all, to the fact that the development of Marxism was paralysed even before it had become the official belief system of a state. For all too long before and after that there was no substitute available in international communism for the duality between Church and State to afford some safeguard for manoeuvrability within the camp but beyond the narrowly drawn (though not unchanging) official line.

The institutionalized duality between Church and State enforced upon Christianity some latitude for dissent and development. In the first place, the duality as such constituted a problem which exercised the minds of priest and layman, statesman and thinker. Furthermore, it was not necessarily with closed ranks that State and Church faced each other, nor did they always confront schisms, heresies and challenges to reform as allies. Hence there was a chance and often a necessity of coming to terms with opposition from within and not only of crushing it. To do the latter was possible in any case only with the combined force of the two power factors, the *imperium* and *sacerdotium*, which ultimately had to rely on each other. The existence of this duality has certainly been an important factor in preventing Christianity

---

Communist Dialogue (London, 1968). Of a different calibre is R. Garaudy, *De l'anathème au dialogue* (Paris, 1965). For a succinct survey article and a relevant choice from the voluminous literature, see Demaitre, 'An Inconclusive Dialogue'. For a Protestant position, see Tillich, *Der Mensch im Christentum und im Marxismus.* The Jesuit Naphtha in Thomas Mann's *Der Zauberberg* reveals Mann's awareness of the possible fusion of communism and Catholicism. That, as Mann said in 1949, Lukács failed to recognize himself in Naphtha (K. Kerény, *Zauberberg–Figuren,* in *Tessiner Schreibtisch* [Stuttgart, 1963], reported in A. MacIntyre, 'Marxist Mask and Romantic Face: Lukács on Thomas Mann', *Encounter,* xxiv [April 1965], 64), was perhaps not so strange.

[45] Cp. J. Guttman, *Philosophies of Judaism* (New York, Chicago and San Francisco, 1964); L. Strauss, *Persecution and the Art of Writing* (New York, 1952); and E. I. J. Rosenthal, *Political Thought in Medieval Islam* (Cambridge, 1958).

from exercising in the long run the fossilizing influence, particularly on the humanities, which official Marxism has had, not only where its alternating authorized versions were imposed directly by state power, but also where their acceptance was demanded as a condition of party membership. Almost from the beginning lasting genuine compromises in the Marxist camp were the exception; their reversals and splits were the rule. The schisms in Marxism have been part of genuine doctrinal controversies, political calculations and power struggles. If intellectually significant, further development occurred with few exceptions outside organized orthodoxy, and were rather sooner than later stamped as deviations. In any event they did not have the effect of raising the stature of Marxism as an integrated system. More often than not such attempts to revitalize Marxism enlarged upon some Marxian or Leninist ideas, while modifying or relinquishing others. These attempts did not contribute to tightening the original framework, since they thrived on its inconsistencies and lacunas in the first place. The result was either a *pars pro toto*, and in any case a divergent, version (Rosa Luxemburg or the Frankfurt School), or engulfment in essentially non-Marxist systems of thought, like existentialism (Sartre) or various branches of mostly Weberian-inspired sociology.

The less-engaging features of philosophy and theology rapidly came to the fore in official Marxism. Some of its methods of argumentation bear comparison with Platonic and ecclesiastical procedures. As a critical Marxist (who has experienced communist rule) points out, this shows in daily experience in the derivation of 'public opinion' from the normative construction of 'the consciousness of the masses'.[46] We have already encountered the construct in Lukács's 'objective class consciousness'. What the press presents as public opinion is not the true reaction of society but what the reaction would be if it were what it ought to be in the light of the exegesis of Marxist principles sanctioned at the moment. Editors who must aim at presenting public opinion as the power holders wish it to be, thus learn to behave like Platonists, inasmuch as they describe a concrete event not by way of factual analysis but by deducing the analysis from what they have reason to believe is the normative model. 'They likewise describe the social institutions in deriving . . . [their descriptions] from the "essence" of socialist society . . . In this way an unconscious

[46] Kolakowski, *Der Mensch ohne Alternative*, pp. 193–4.

Platonism underlies the embellishment and schematism of press and literature: the derivation of actual *being* from the general *essence* of the matter.' The real reactions of public opinion which do not fit such mystification are either not reported or stigmatized as perversions. This Platonic pattern of conveying information which has served the historians of the Church for centuries, underlies 'the pseudo-Marxist platonizing historiography ... sociology ... political economy ... [and] politics',[47] not to mention, of course, the overweening didacticism (and in Mao's case didactic repetitiveness),[48] the ferocious intolerance and the presumptuous denigration of all kinds of holders of opinions different from theirs by the founders and their ruling successors themselves.

Lastly, in addition to the overlapping of categories and themes of thought, of criteria of moral judgments and their implementation and methods of argumentation, there is also some agreement on the criteria used in the mutual 'unmasking' of ideologies. Besides belief systems which conflict within the same time and culture, those of various times are likely to share criteria by which truth and error are distinguished from each other. Such agreement narrows the gap between science and ideology in general and between specific ideologies, and between them and other belief systems. Agreement on means of eliminating error and demonstrating truth is a prerequisite of any vindication of beliefs in a basically rational culture – as all modern cultures are. If within one, or between several such cultures, belief systems compete, controversy will not extend to all propositions. Logical consistency, correspondence of statements with commonsense observation and the findings of science (or its substitute, magic, in not yet literally rational cultures) are normally accepted as the grounds of refutability; so is the correspondence between principles, predictions and promises of a doctrine with the degrees to which its implementation is evaded or effected.

What I have called propositional pluralism, which within the context of action-oriented belief systems becomes ideological pluralism, comprises, then, the appearance of analogous contents, criteria of thought and modes of demonstration and argumenta-

---

47 Kolakowski, pp. 196, 197.
48 Gramsci, *The Modern Prince and Other Writings*, p. 73, regarded repetitive argument as a tool, taken over by political from religious *cadres*, for mass indoctrination.

tion in different systems of thought developed at the same time and in different periods. Aspects of the phenomenon have been frequently commented upon in philosophical inquiry and in the history of ideas, social beliefs and movements.[49] As far as I know, the term 'propositional pluralism' has hardly ever been used and 'ideological pluralism' only seldom otherwise than cursorily.[50] Far from sufficient importance has been attached to ideological pluralism for judging the validity of theories about the relationship between thought and other existential factors in general, and of the Marxist conception of this relationship in particular.

[49] Apart from the works referred to already in the course of this chapter, and studies of thinkers and movements, see, for instance, J. Touchard in his Preface to Touchard *et al.* (eds.), *Histoire des idées politiques* (2 vols., Paris, 1959), I, viii, for pointing to the recurrence and eventual secularization of themes in social belief systems and movements in different times and contexts. Harris, *Beliefs in Society*, shows a constant preoccupation with such continuities, as well as with culture-transcending similarities and contemporaneous overlapping of ideologies, though in a perspective at once rather too restricted and too generally expressed.

[50] Exceptions are M. Leroy, *Histoire des idées sociales en France*, 3rd edn (3 vols., Paris, 1946–54), II (1950), p. 124; and among political scientists, J. Meynaud, *Destin des idéologies* (Lausanne, 1961), uses the term frequently to designate the points which traditional and present-day 'isms' have in common (pp. 12, 43–5).

CONCLUSION

In my comments on the unadjusted ramifications of the orthodox Marxist theory of ideology I have already indicated that its action-orientation drove it, like all other ideologies, towards asymmetry – one side of a coin of which ideological pluralism is the other side. Indeed, asymmetry is as much inherent in ideologies as ideological pluralism is the inescapable corollary of the endeavour to realize an ideology. In the process, asymmetry as evinced in ideological pluralism grows to the point of dividing an ideology into a fundamental and an operative dimension of argumentation.[1] On these grounds, it therefore seems appropriate by way of concluding the present study to sum up the significance of ideological pluralism for assessing the gist of the Marxist theory of ideology, which embodies the central hypotheses offered by Marxism for the understanding of social life. I propose to do so by elaborating briefly on two intertwined conclusions which I have already demonstrated.

Firstly, since ideological pluralism attests that disagreement between ideologies is far from being total, it calls in question the assumption that the contents and categories of thought can be unequivocally related to a specific class structure and the specific conditions of an epoch. More particularly, the fact that agreement on a number of propositions exists between ideologies contending in the same political arena, or between ideologies of different times, requires a severe qualification of the notion that each ideological claim is class-bound and time-bound. Conversely, to the extent that ideologies can be distinguished by reference to time and class, they are not necessarily on this count incompatible with one another in all major aspects. Secondly, whatever the degree of the dependence of thought on class conditions (and on what determines them), ideological pluralism furnishes an important part of the evidence which invalidates the thesis that the

[1] See above, pp. 4–5.

ineluctable effect of such dependence is the distortion of thought. Agreement between ideologies does not disprove falsity, but it is a necessary condition of correctness, and at any rate of agreement between persons who possess both a sufficient measure of familiarity (however unquantifiable that measure may be) with a given matter and competence to judge it.

If, then, the dependence of thought on class and time is held to be the cause of the incompatibility of ideologies as well as of their falsity, evidence of the overlapping and recurrence of ideological propositions refutes these claims, particularly the Marxist thesis that all socially relevant thought of people is exclusively determined by their place in a given class structure. The bond between class and ideology is further loosened by the fact that, besides agreement between ideologies, there exists agreement between members of different classes as to the same ideology, as shown in their common preference of the same political party over another.[2] The exception to Marxist (and other) sociological conditioning applies to psychological conditions as well. Neither one's place in the social structure nor one's personality can be shown to cause the adoption of any set of opinions or, for that matter, to entail only interest-oriented or pathological distortion. History provides no ground for imagining any kind of viable political system in which people with different social backgrounds (and different personality structures) cannot agree amongst themselves on anything of political and social importance.

It is thus not astonishing that by now there exists relatively widespread consensus to the effect that the most fundamental proposition of Marxist social theory, namely that any superstructure of ideas and institutions is unequivocally derivable from prevailing social relations (and their relation to the economic matrix), is too sweeping to be of much use for the interpretation of specific events or their anticipation. Rather, it is surprising that the proposition should be retained as a basic hypothesis not only by Marxism, together with the imputation of false consciousness, but also by those dedicated to the sociology of knowledge, even without that imputation. Although qualified in either case, the causal hypothesis has preserved much of its original centrality, while at best it can serve only as a point of departure for constructing more detailed and complex hypotheses for historical and sociological research. This conclusion is implicit in the fact that

2 See above, pp. 161–4.

Marx and Engels could not disavow the existence of agreement between members of different classes upon the same ideology, demonstrated in the founders' acknowledgment of the unproletarian outlook, including the voting habits, of the working classes. Moreover, particularly as a result of acknowledging era-transcending ideological pluralism, Marx and Kautsky were forced to rescue the applicability of the principle of the social determination of ideas at the price of diminishing, if not jeopardizing, its explanatory value in regard to specific events and circumstances and, above all, its derivation from the array of the forces of production.

Marx and Kautsky explained the phenomenon of the continual belief in the same truths, ethical norms and ideals as the reflection in the consciousness of men of the constancy of the fundamental nature of class conflict. Thus, when relied upon to meet the challenge of ideological pluralism, one central thesis of the Marxist philosophy of history restated with force and brevity at the opening of the *Manifesto* ('The history of all hitherto existing society is the history of class struggles') revealed itself as dwarfing another central thesis: the much-advertised causal primacy of the modes of production and forms of technology. For their change obviously could not be said to have affected the perenniality (hitherto) of class exploitation and the class struggle, which on Marx's own showing mattered most, if it was maintained at the same time that no change could render existence human unless it obviated the exploitation of man by man; and this was to be the corollary of the demise of capitalism. The unwitting but thoroughly logical implication of insisting on the permanence of class exploitation and hence class war during all known history is to reduce to nil the explanatory value (which Marx claimed for it) of the resort to economic–technological conditions, in relation to the most incisive fact of known human existence. This logical inference leaves us not only with the causal framework reduced to the relationship between social conditions and the superstructure as the explanatory key to the vicissitudes of hitherto known history, but with as much importance attached to these vicissitudes as Ecclesiastes ascribes to them. Marx's acknowledgment of the persistence in time of the pivotal social problem, and the ideas related to it, is all the more significant since his awareness of it, i.e. of ideological pluralism, was not accidental. He returned to the subject and commented on it in general terms to the effect that we can isolate by way of comparison that which is common to different epochs and which in its overall complexion is multifariously structured. Some components belong to all periods and others only to some. Yet over the unity one must not forget 'the essential difference' and its roots in 'specific historical conditions'.[3]

This admirable declaration of principle notwithstanding, it may be doubted whether in dealing with specific historical events Marx supplied models either for the documented delineation of really specific historical conditions or for what on the grounds of historical and sociological evidence can be ascribed to those conditions, in conformity with the general principles of his theory of history and society.[4] As Max Weber remarked, despite praising the *Manifesto* as 'a scholarly achievement of the first order',[5]

> if anything has so far damaged . . . [methodical] research, then it is the imagination of eager dilettantes that they can achieve something specifically different . . . from expanding the possibility of assured ascription of single *concrete* cultural events of historical reality to *concrete* historically given causes by way of gathering *exact* material of observation according to specific aspects.[6]

Thus, at the first meeting of the German Sociological Association in 1910, Weber rejected as 'completely finished as a scientific proposition' mono-causality in general and the Marxist variant in particular.[7] The existence of propositional and ideological pluralism in fact buttresses Weber's notion of 'elective affinities'.[8] In Weber's use the notion means that ideas are created or adopted by

---

[3] *Zur Kritik der politischen Ökonomie*, pp. xvi, xli.
[4] The example cited most by Marx's critics for his failure in this respect is *Der 18. Brumaire des Louis Bonaparte*. See above, pp. 68–9, 124–5.
[5] 'Der Sozialismus', pp. 504–5.
[6] 'Die "Objektivität" sozialwissenschaftlicher Erkenntnis', p. 168.
[7] Roth, 'Critique and Adaptation', in Bendix and Roth, *Scholarship and Partisanship*, p. 242. Similarly, W. J. Ashley in his Introduction (1909) to Mill's *Principles of Political Economy*. Ashley said that the 'abstract socialist doctrine, the creation largely of Marx, has meantime waxed and waned' (p. xxiv).
[8] Gerth and Mills, *From Max Weber*, p. 62. See also Bendix, *Max Weber*, p. 64 n.27, for Weber's frequent use of the term, which is taken from Goethe's novel *Die Wahlverwandtschaften*. Weber elaborated on the relationship between ideas and other existential factors in his sociology of religion in particular. Bendix, pp. 258ff, appraises Weber's combination of the three objectives: to examine the effect of religious ideas on economic activity; to analyse the relation between social stratification and religious ideas; and to establish the distinguishing marks of Western civilization.

men and often tally with their material interests. The assumption of automatic or necessary correspondence of ideal and material factors or the mere reflection of the latter by the former is thus denied, while neither correspondence nor reflection is excluded as such, nor are tensions between ideal and material factors.

In their own right, though not solely of themselves, propositional and ideological pluralism make it incumbent on us that, in the attempt at ascertaining with some certainty the extent of determination exercised on thought and beliefs by class and historical epoch, we explore which beliefs and disbeliefs can be attributed to most members of a society in a given period and which ones are shared by the majority (absolute or relative) of the members of distinct classes of people. Once established, differential sociological ascription of this kind (which by virtue of sampling has become more precisely verifiable) does not in fact normally constitute proof that all the important beliefs and disbeliefs shared by most contemporaries can be directly related to the general characteristics distinguishing one historical epoch from another and indirectly to its socio-economic structure. Nor can we relate all different beliefs directly and exclusively to that structure. Usually, 'inherited' beliefs and attitudes are being maintained, those, that is, which persist irrespective of, though to some extent assimilated to, decisive changes in the socio-economic structure that have occurred since the inception of these beliefs.

It is arguable, for instance, that a considerable part even of the more prosperous members of the working classes in Great Britain exhibit a working-class consciousness which in the not too distant past was relatively new, particularly in its political significance, and most importantly, was predicated upon existential conditions very different from, and vastly inferior to, those obtaining today. The *embourgeoisement* of relatively large sections of the British working classes thus has not obliterated the persistence of a traditional class perspective among many of its members.[9] Rather con-

[9] J. H. Goldthorpe and D. Lockwood *et al.*, *The Affluent Worker: Political Attitudes and Behaviour* (Cambridge, 1968), esp. Chapters 3, 4; T. B. Bottomore, *Classes in Modern Society* (London, 1965), pp. 29–30; and Runciman, *Social Science and Political Theory*, pp. 142 and *passim*. Although it is widely agreed that working-class consciousness prevails despite rising living standards, evaluations of its nature and political significance tend to vary. For a most instructive study of the problem in immediate post-war West Germany, see H. Popitz, H. P. Bahrdt, E. A. Jüres and H. Kesting, *Das Gesellschaftsbild des Arbeiters, soziologische Untersuchungen in der*

spicuous differences in the style of life as expressed even in dress and speech seem to be conducive to perpetuating feelings of status deprivation.[10] Hardly less important for a persisting proletarian outlook may be the existence in Britain of the Labour Party, a party which has been responsible for important changes of social policy and has remained committed to democratic socialism. What seems to weigh even more is that, somewhat contrary to Lenin's judgment, the trade unionism of the workers' parties (including large communist parties, as those in France and Italy) is wedded not just to a continuous emphasis of class perspective but also to political class militancy. Such militant working-class consciousness in developed welfarist democracies seems to be sustained by the combined rise in the living standards and growth of expectations in the better-off strata of the working classes on the one hand and by the consciousness of a continuing, if not widening, gap in the distribution of material advantages and all they can procure on the other. It seems to be felt, and seems true, that the corollary of the general upward movement of the bulk of a mobile society is accompanied by cleavages becoming at once wider and more rigid. These appear to have been the reasons for much of the industrial unrest rampant in Britain and elsewhere in the West during the last few years. Of late, stagnation, inflation and growing unemployment have befallen Western-type economies, all of which the energy crisis has rendered more severe, but not created. Nevertheless the prospect still would seem to be that it is the trade unionism of the better-off, rather than what is left in the more developed industrial societies of Marx's 'dehumanized' proletarians, that will be imbued anew with revolutionary radicalism, though of a short-term Bakuninian-cum-Sorelian brand, certainly not intended to usher in an egalitarian and/or stateless millennium. However, these developments in the West, and not entirely dissimilar processes in the industrially more advanced communist societies, again appear to confirm a prediction of Weber, who said that 'each working class will be again and again socialist in some way or other'.[11]

Thus, just as a configuration of attitudes and ideas that were

---

Hüttenindustrie (Tübingen, 1947); and, more generally,
R. Dahrendorf, *Class and Class Conflict in Industrial Society*, 2nd edn (Stanford and London, 1961), who refers *inter alia* to the aforementioned study.

[10] Runciman, *Social Science and Political Theory*, p. 143.

[11] Weber, 'Der Sozialismus', p. 517.

once new is likely to persist in changed conditions, as other habits do, on its part this once-new configuration may have come about through the adaptation to new circumstances and premises of traditional beliefs and thoughts about the age-old conflict between rich and poor, or rather the privileged, the less privileged and the underprivileged. Otherwise it would be impossible to explain the striking similarities in the interpretation of social structure extending from folklore and myth to theologies and philosophies, down to the interwarring ideologies of our time.[12]

To emphasize the observable persistence in time and changing circumstances of social problems, of their interpretation and of the alternative patterns of their solution, or to stress the sharing of assumptions between contemporary ideologies – all this does not mean to deprecate ideological accretion and development. Neither does it mean to affirm that, because innovation and differentiation do not efface the analogies, the similarities are therefore more important than the differences. On this, too, far-reaching agreement is likely. One may easily agree that in decisive aspects pre-Marxist (e.g. Babouvist) and Marxist communism, or developed communist and welfarist societies, resemble each other. All the same, in both instances, the differences will weigh heavier with most people than the similarities, no matter what their personal preferences are. If, then, ideological pluralism does not afford grounds for minimizing the importance of the differences between the analogous and the different, its existence impairs the validity of the Marxist assumption that the socio-political thought and attitudes of people, as well as of the belief systems which they are asked to adopt, are exclusively determined by class, and by economic conditions above all. Ideological pluralism, like data about the political beliefs and behaviour of elites and mass publics, permits us to infer that to the extent that beliefs and postures can be related to economic and social conditions, this does not exclude, as a codeterminant of varying importance, beliefs and disbeliefs in their own right.

Ideological pluralism and the findings of empirical research support the proposition that it is chiefly in responding to the challenges of given circumstances that political philosophies and the less systematic belief systems of any time are conditioned by these circumstances, in so far as these comprise both material and mental factors. In other words, the potentialities and barriers

[12] Ossowski, *Class Structure in the Social Consciousness*, p. 178.

which the purveyors of a socio-political belief system have to reckon with include, besides the natural resources, the state of technology, the existing social structure and external relations (a much-neglected variable in this context despite Marx and Kautsky's reference to it), also the patterns of thought, belief and disbelief, both as they are articulated in speech and writing and as they manifest themselves in the attitudes and patterns of behaviour obtaining in a given society at a given time. Ideological pluralism and observation of political behaviour point not in the direction of a hierarchical order of causal factors, as postulated in Marxist economic reductionism or in ideational reductionism, but in the direction of a more egalitarian, and in any case fluctuating pluralist order of causal factors. Ideological pluralism, like behavioural political science, suggests the assumption of the competitive interaction of a plurality of causal factors whose import varies in different contexts.

'Pluralistic causation' may be particularly 'serviceable to a liberal politics of "piecemeal" reform'.[13] This does not disprove the adequacy of 'pluralistic causation', nor confute its having been in actual fact 'serviceable' to communist politics since Lenin's NEP. It goes without saying that 'principled pluralism' can be as dogmatically used as 'principled monism'. It does not follow, however, that the two are equally adequate instruments of interpretation, nor that causal pluralism is an obstacle to structural change and that 'revolutionary dislocation' does not stand in need of being supplemented by reformist incrementalism or, for that matter, that it cannot serve to achieve structural change.[14]

The fate of influential ideologies, and none more than that of Marxism, shows that they are limited by material conditions only in the sense that they have to cope with certain material conditions and not with others. This difference does not make all the difference; it does not alone explain the success or failure of an ideology. To the extent that ideologies are limited by specific material conditions, because they have to deal with them, they are in the same manner limited in what they can hope to achieve by the existing configurations of beliefs and disbeliefs. These too have a conditioning effect. They determine, though to varying degrees,

[13] C. W. Mills, *The Sociological Imagination*, paperback edn (New York, 1967), p. 85.
[14] Mills, p. 86. Some of these qualifications are implicit in what Mills says on pp. 11, 91ff, 96ff, 115–16, 146ff, 181–8, 192–3.

the susceptibility of their holders to the ideologist's evaluations of a situation and his projects of action and therefore are bound to affect the propagation, if they do not entail the modification, of the objectives of an ideology and more particularly of the ways and degrees proposed, or followed, for their realization. The fate of Marxism, inside and outside the communist orbit, furnishes a singularly instructive confirmation of this rule; which is to say that no exception from it can be claimed for any ideology – and that in this its central point, as in those related to it, Marxist theory falls to the ground or, to put it in Marxist fashion, points beyond itself.

BIBLIOGRAPHY

I have not listed separately here all publications by Marx and Engels or Lenin referred to in the text and the notes, but only the collections of their works which contain these publications.

Collections of essays are listed separately with place and date of publication only when more than one essay of a collection has been used.

Abrams, M. 'Party Politics after the End of Ideology', in Allardt and Littunen (eds.) *Cleavages, Ideologies and Party Systems.*

Acton, H. B. *The Illusion of the Epoch: Marxism–Leninism as a Philosophical Creed.* London, 1955.

Adler, M. *Das Rätsel der Gesellschaft.* Wien, 1936.

Alford, R. R. *Party and Society: The Anglo-American Democracies.* London, 1964.

Allardt, E. 'Finland: Institutionalized Radicalism', in Rejai (ed.) *Decline of Ideology?*

Allardt, E. 'Patterns of Class Conflict and Class Consciousness in Finnish Politics', in Allardt and Littunen (eds.) *Cleavages, Ideologies and Party Systems.*

Allardt, E. and Littunen, Y. (eds.) *Cleavages, Ideologies and Party Systems.* Helsinki, 1964.

Althusser, L. *For Marx.* Trans. B. Brewster. London, 1969.

Althusser, L. and Balibar, E. *Reading Capital.* Trans. B. Brewster. London, 1970.

Angel, P. *Eduard Bernstein et l'évolution du socialisme allemand.* Paris, 1961.

Apter, D. E. (ed.) *Ideology and Discontent.* London and New York, 1964.

Arblaster, A. 'Ideology and Intellectuals', in Benewick, Berki and Parekh (eds.) *Knowledge and Belief in Politics.*

Aristotle, *The Politics.* Trans. with an Introduction, notes and appendices by E. Barker. Corrected repr. Oxford, 1952.

Aron, R. *Dix-huit Leçons sur la société industrielle.* Paris, 1962.

Aron, R. *La Lutte des classes: Nouvelles leçons sur la société industrielle.* Paris, 1964.

Avineri, S. 'Marx and the Intellectuals', *Journal of the History of Ideas*, xxviii, 2 (1967).

Avineri, S. *The Social and Political Thought of Karl Marx.* Cambridge, 1968.

Barnes, S. H. 'Italy: Opposition on Left, Right and Centre', in Dahl (ed.) *Political Opposition in Western Democracies.*

Barnes, S. H. 'Political Ideology and Political Behaviour', in Cox (ed.) *Ideology, Politics and Political Theory.*

Barth, H. *Wahrheit und Ideologie*. Zürich, 1945.

Bell, D. *The End of Ideology – On the Exhaustion of Political Ideas in the Fifties*. New York, 1960. Rev. edn Colliers. New York, 1961.

Bell, D. 'Ideology and Soviet Politics', *Slavic Review*, xxiv, 4 (1965).

Bendix, R. *Work and Authority in Industry: Ideologies of Management in the Course of Industrialization*. New York and London, 1956.

Bendix, R. *Max Weber: An Intellectual Portrait*. New York, 1960.

Bendix, R. 'The Age of Ideology: Persistent and Changing', in Apter (ed.) *Ideology and Discontent*.

Bendix, R. and Lipset, S. M. 'Karl Marx's Theory of Class', in Bendix and Lipset (eds.) *Class, Status and Power*. New York, 1953.

Benewick, R., Berki, R. N., and Parekh, B. (eds.) *Knowledge and Belief in Politics: The Problem of Ideology*. London, 1973.

Berki, R. N. 'On Marxian Thought and the Problem of International Relations', *World Politics*, xxiv, 1 (1971).

Berki, R. N. 'Georg Lukács in Retrospect', *Problems of Communism*, xxi (Nov.–Dec. 1972).

Berki, R. N. 'The Marxian Conception of Bourgeois Ideology: Some Aspects and Perspectives', in Benewick, Berki and Parekh (eds.) *Knowledge and Belief in Politics*.

Bernstein, E. *Die Voraussetzungen des Sozialismus und die Aufgaben der Sozialdemokratie*. Stuttgart, 1899.

Bernstein, E. 'Das realistische und das ideologische Moment im Sozialismus', in *Die Neue Zeit* (1897–8). Repr. in *Zur Geschichte und Theorie des Sozialismus*. 2nd edn. Berlin and Bern, 1901.

Bernstein, E. *Sozialismus und Demokratie in der grossen englischen Revolution*. 3rd edn. Stuttgart, 1919. Eng. trans. *Cromwell and Communism: Socialism and Democracy in the Great English Revolution*. London, 1930.

Best, G. *Mid-Victorian Britain, 1815–75*. London, 1971.

Beyme, K. von. *Ökonomie und Politik im Sozialismus: Ein Vergleich der Entwicklung in den sozialistischen Ländern*. München and Zürich, 1975.

Bottomore, T. B. *Classes in Modern Society*. London, 1965.

Bottomore, T. B. *Elites and Society*. Harmondsworth, 1966.

Bottomore, T. B. *Critics of Society: Radical Thought in America*. London, 1967.

Bottomore, T. B. 'Class Structure and Social Consciousness', in Mészáros (ed.) *Aspects of History and Class Consciousness*.

Buchanan, W. and Cantril, H. *How Nations See Each Other*. Urbana, 1953.

Buber, M. *Paths in Utopia*. London, 1944.

Calvez, J. Y. *La Pensée de Karl Marx*. Paris, 1956.

Campbell, A., Converse, P. E., Miller, W. E. and Stokes, D. E. (eds.) *Elections and the Political Order*. New York, London and Sydney, 1966.

Carr, E. H. *The Bolshevik Revolution*. 2 vols. London, 1950–3.

Carr, E. H. *What Is History?* London, 1962.

Cohn, N. *The Pursuit of the Millennium*. London, 1957.

Cole, G. D. H. *A History of Socialist Thought*. 4 vols. London and New York, 1959–60.

Cox, R. H. (ed.) *Ideology, Politics and Theory*. Belmont, Cal., 1969.

Dahl, R. A. 'The American Opposition, Affirmation and Denial', in Dahl (ed.) *Political Opposition in Western Democracies*.

Dahl, R. A. (ed.) *Political Opposition in Western Democracies*. New Haven and London, 1966.

Dahrendorf, R. *Class and Class Conflict in Industrial Society*. 2nd edn. Stanford and London, 1961.

Dahrendorf, R. *Gesellschaft und Freiheit*. München, 1962.

Delany, W. 'Ideology – A Debate', in C. I. Waxman (ed.) *The End of Ideology Debate*. New York, 1968.

Demaitre, E. 'An Inconclusive Dialogue', *Problems of Communism*, xx (Sept.–Oct. 1971).

Dictionnaire classique de la langue française avec des exemples tirés des meilleurs auteurs français et des notes puisées dans les manuscrits de Rivarol. Par quatre professeurs de l'université. Paris, 1827.

Dion, L. 'An Hypothesis Concerning Structure and Function of Ideology', in Cox (ed.) *Ideology, Politics and Political Theory*.

Drucker, H. M. *The Political Uses of Ideology*. London, 1974.

Duncan, G. *Marx and Mill*. Cambridge, 1973.

Eisenstadt, S. N. *The Political Systems of Empires: The Rise and Fall of the Bureaucratic Empires*. New York and London, 1969.

Encyclopédie ou Dictionnaire raisonné des sciences, des arts et des métiers. Vols. v, viii. Neufchâtel, 1765.

Engels, F. *Der Ursprung der Familie, des Privateigentums und des Staates*. 2nd edn. Stuttgart, 1886.

Eppstein, P. 'Die Fragestellung nach der Wirklichkeit im historischen Materialismus', *Archiv für Sozialwissenschaft und Sozialpolitik*, lx, 3 (1928).

Feuer, L. S. 'Problems and Unproblems in Soviet Social Theory', *Slavic Review*, xxiii, 1 (1964).

Feuer, L. S. 'Karl Marx and the Promethean Complex', *Encounter*, xxxi (December 1968).

Feuerbach, L. *Kleine philosophische Schriften (1842–5)*, ed. H. G. Lange. Leipzig, 1950.

Finer, S. E. 'Pareto and Pluto-Democracy: The Retreat to Galapagos', *American Political Science Review*, lxii, 2 (1968).

Finer, S. E. (ed.) *Vilfredo Pareto – Sociological Writings*. Trans. D. Mirfin. London, 1966.

Fischer, G. 'Sociology', in Fischer (ed.) *Science and Ideology in Soviet Society*. New York, 1967.

Fletcher, R. (ed.) *The Making of Sociology*. 2 vols. London, 1971.

Friedrich, C. J. *Constitutional Government and Politics*. New York and London, 1937.

Friedrich, C. J. *Man and His Government*. New York, San Francisco, Toronto and London, 1963.

Friedrich, C. J., and Brezezinski, Z. K. *Totalitarian Dictatorship and Autocracy*. 2nd edn. Rev. by C. J. Friedrich. New York, Washington and London, 1965. Paperback, 1966.

Garaudy, R. *De l'anathème au dialogue*. Paris, 1965.

Gay, P. *The Dilemma of Democratic Socialism: Eduard Bernstein's Challenge to Marx*. New York, 1952.

Geertz, C. 'Ideology as a Cultural System', in Apter (ed.) *Ideology and Discontent.*

Geiger, T. *Ideologie und Wahrheit, Eine soziologische Kritik des Denkens.* Stuttgart and Wien, 1953.

Gerth, H. H. and Mills, C. W. *From Max Weber: Essays in Sociology.* Repr. New York, 1969.

Gluckman, M. *Politics, Law and Ritual in Tribal Society.* 2nd impr. Oxford, 1967.

Goldmann, L. *Recherches dialectiques.* 3rd edn. Paris, 1959.

Goldmann, L. *The Hidden God.* Trans. P. Thody. London, 1964.

Goldmann, L. 'Reflections on History and Class Consciousness', in Mészáros (ed.) *Aspects of History and Class Consciousness.*

Goldthorpe, J. H. and Lockwood, L. *et al. The Affluent Worker: Political Attitudes and Behaviour.* Cambridge, 1968.

Gramsci, A. *The Modern Prince and Other Writings,* ed. and Introduction by L. Marks. 4th impr. New York, 1970.

Gramsci, A. *Selections from Prison Notebooks,* ed. Q. Hoare and G. N. Smith. London, 1971.

Greenleaf, W. H. *Order, Empiricism and Politics: Two Traditions of English Political Thought.* London, New York and Toronto, 1964.

Grünwald, E. *Das Problem der Soziologie des Wissens.* Wien, 1934.

Gurvitch, G. *Le Concept des classes sociales de Marx à nos jours.* Centre de documentation universitaire. Paris, 1954.

Guttman, J. *Philosophies of Judaism.* New York, Chicago and San Francisco, 1964.

Halle, L. J. 'Marx's Religious Drama', *Encounter,* xxv (October 1965).

Harris, N. *Beliefs in Society: The Problem of Ideology.* London, 1968.

Hegel, G. W. F. *Grundlinien der Philosophie des Rechts,* ed. J. Hoffmeister. 4th edn. Hamburg, 1955.

Hobsbawm, E. J. *Primitive Rebels: Studies in Archaic Forms of Social Movement in the Nineteenth and Twentieth Centuries.* Manchester, 1959.

Hölzle, E. *Idee und Ideologie: Eine Zeitkritik aus universalhistorischer Sicht.* Bern and München, 1969.

Ionescu, G. *The Politics of the European Communist States.* New York, 1967.

Ionescu, G. 'Lenin, the Commune and the State – Thoughts for a Centenary', *Government and Opposition,* v, 2 (1970).

Jordan, Z. A. *Philosophy and Ideology: The Development of Philosophy and Marxism–Leninism in Poland since the Second World War.* Dordrecht, 1963.

Jordan, Z. A. *The Evolution of Dialectical Materialism.* New York, 1967.

Kautsky, K. *Bernstein und das sozialdemokratische Programm. Eine Antikritik.* Stuttgart, 1899.

Kautsky, K. 'Die Revision des Programmes der sozialdemokratischen Partei in Österreich', *Die Neue Zeit,* 20 Jahrg., i, 3 (1901–2).

Kautsky, K. *Ethik und materialistische Geschichtsauffassung.* Stuttgart, 1906. Repr. Berlin and Stuttgart, 1922.

Kautsky, K. *Die proletarische Revolution und ihr Programm.* Stuttgart and Berlin, 1922.

Kautsky, K. *The Dictatorship of the Proletariat.* Ann Arbor, 1964.

Kerény, K. *Zauberberg-Figuren*, in *Tessiner Schreibtisch*. Stuttgart, 1963.

Key, V. O. jun. *Public Opinion and American Democracy*. New York, 1961.

Klugmann, J. and Oestreicher, P. (eds.) *What Kind of Revolution? – A Christian–Communist Dialogue*. London, 1968.

Kolakowski, L. *Der Mensch ohne Alternative*. Rev. edn. München, 1967.

Labedz, L. *Revisionism: Essays on the History of Marxist Ideas*. London, 1962.

LaPalombara, J. 'Decline of Ideology: A Dissent and an Interpretation', *American Political Science Review*, LX, 1 (1966).

Larousse, *Grand Dictionnaire universal du* XIXe *siècle*. Vol. IX. Paris, 1873.

Laski, H. J. *Reflections on the Revolution of Our Time*. New York, 1943.

Leach, E. *Lévi-Strauss*. London, 1970.

Lefebvre, H. *The Sociology of Marx*. Trans. N. Guterman. London, 1968.

Lenin, V. I. *Selected Works*. 2 vols. Moscow, 1946.

Lenk, K. *Ideologie, Ideologiekritik und Wissenssoziologie*. Neuwied and Berlin, 1961, repr. 1967.

Leroy, H. *Histoire des idées sociales en France*. 3rd edn. 3 vols. Paris, 1946–54.

Lichtheim, G. *Marxism: An Historical and Critical Study*. London, 1961.

Lichtheim, G. 'The Concept of Ideology', *History and Theory*, VI, 2 (1965).

Lichtheim, G. 'Comments', *Slavic Review*, XXIV, 4 (1965).

Lichtheim, G. *Lukács*. London, 1970.

Lipset, S. M. *Political Man*. New York, 1960.

Lipset, S. M. 'Political Cleavages in "Developed" and "Emerging" Polities', in Allardt and Littunen (eds.) *Cleavages, Ideologies and Party Systems*.

Loewenstein, K. 'Political Systems, Ideologies and Institutions: The Problem of their Circulation', *Western Political Quarterly*, VI, 4 (1953).

Lowry, C. W. *Communism and Christ*. London, 1954.

Lukács, G. *Geschichte und Klassenbewusstsein, Studien über Marxistische Dialektik*. Berlin, 1923.

Lukács, G. *Schriften zur Ideologie und Politik*. Soziologische Texte, vol. 51, ed. with Introduction by P. Ludz. Neuwied and Berlin, 1967.

Lukács, G. *History and Class Consciousness: Studies in Marxist Dialectics*. Trans. R. Livingstone. London, 1971.

Lukić, R. D. 'Political Ideology and Social Development', in Allardt and Littunen (eds.) *Cleavages, Ideologies and Party Systems*.

McClosky, H., Hoffman, P. J. and O'Hara, R. 'Issue Conflict and Consensus among Party Leaders and Followers', *American Political Science Review*, LIV, 2 (1960).

MacIntyre, A. *Marxism*. London, 1953.

MacIntyre, A. 'Marxist Mask and Romantic Face: Lukács on Thomas Mann', *Encounter*, XXIV (April 1965).

MacIntyre, A. *Marxism and Christianity*. London, 1968.

McKenzie, R. T. and Silver, A. 'Conservatism, Industrialism and the Working Class Tory in England', in R. Rose (ed.) *Studies in British Politics*. London, 1966. Repr. New York, 1967.

McLellan, D. *Marx's Grundrisse*. Selections, trans. with Introduction. London, 1971.

MacRae, D. G. *Ideology and Society*. London, 1961.

Mannheim, K. 'Das konservative Denken (i–ii), Soziologische Beiträge zum Werden des politisch-historischen Denkens in Deutschland', *Archiv für Sozialwissenschaft und Sozialpolitik*, lvii, 1 and 2 (1927).

Mannheim, K. *Ideology and Utopia – An Introduction to the Sociology of Knowledge.* Trans. L. Wirth and E. A. Shils. Harvest Book. New York, n.d.

Marcuse, H. *Reason and Revolution: Hegel and the Rise of Social Theory.* London, New York and Toronto, 1941.

Marx, K. *Selected Works*, ed. V. Adoratskij. 2 vols. London, n.d.

Marx, K. *Zur Kritik der politischen Ökonomie*, ed. K. Kautsky. 7th edn. Stuttgart, 1907.

Marx, K. *Grundrisse der Kritik der politischen Ökonomie.* Rohentwurf, 1857–8. Anhang, 1850–9. Berlin, 1953.

Marx, K. *Das Kapital: Kritik der politischen Ökonomie*, ed. F. Engels. Vol. i, 4th edn. Hamburg, 1890. Vol. ii, 2nd edn. 1893. Vol. iii, in 2 vols. 1894.

Marx, K. *Das Kapital: Kritik der politischen Ökonomie*, ed. F. Engels. Marx–Engels–Lenin Institut, Moscow. 4 vols. Wien and Berlin, 1933.

Marx, K. *Der 18. Brumaire des Louis Bonaparte*, in K. Marx and F. Engels, *Werke.* Vol. viii. Berlin, 1960.

Marx, K. and Engels, F. *Historisch–kritische Gesamtausgabe*, eds. D. Rjazanov and V. Adoratskij. Frankfurt, Moscow and Leningrad, 1927–32.

Marx, K. and Engels, F. *Selected Correspondence.* Repr. London, 1943.

Marxismusstudien, ed. E. Metzge and I. Fetscher. Tübingen, 1953.

Meisel, J. H. *The Myth of the Ruling Class – Gaetano Mosca and the Elite.* Ann Arbor, 1958.

Mepham, J. 'The Theory of Ideology in Capital', *Radical Philosophy*, ii, 2 (1972).

Merton, R. K. *Social Theory and Social Structure.* Rev. edn. New York, 1957.

Mészáros, J. 'Contingent and Necessary Class Consciousness', in Mészáros (ed.) *Aspects of History and Class Consciousness.*

Mészáros, J. (ed.) *Aspects of History and Class Consciousness.* London, 1971.

Meyer, A. G. *Communism.* 4th impr. New York, 1962.

Meyer, A. G. *Leninism.* 6th impr. Cambridge, Mass., 1971.

Meynaud, J. *Destin des idéologies.* Lausanne, 1961.

Mignet, F. *Portraits et notes historiques et littéraires.* 2nd edn. 2 vols. Paris, 1852.

Mill, J. S. *Principles of Political Economy.* 7th edn. 1871. Re-issued with Introduction by W. J. A. Ashley. London, 1909, repr. 1917.

Mill, J. S. *Utilitarianism, Liberty and Representative Government.* Everyman's Library. New York and London, 1951.

Mills, C. W. *The Sociological Imagination.* Paperback edn. New York, 1967.

Monnerot, J. *Sociologie du communisme.* Paris, 1949.

Montesquieu, C. L. de Secondat de. *Grandeur et décadence des Romains, Lettres persanes, Politique des Romains*, ed. and Introduction by E. Faguet. Paris, 1946.

Montesquieu, C. L. de Secondat de. *De l'esprit des lois.* 2 vols. Paris, 1949.

Mucchielli, R. *Le Mythe de la cité idéale.* Paris, 1960.

Naess, A. *et al. Democracy, Ideology and Objectivity.* Oslo and Oxford, 1956.

Nietzsche, F. *Jenseits von Gut und Böse. Werke. Taschenausgabe.* 10 vols. Leipzig, 1906.

Ollman, B. *Alienation: Marx's Conception of Man in Capitalist Society*. Cambridge, 1971.

Ossowski, S. *Class Structure in the Social Consciousness*. London, 1963.

Picavet, F. C. *Les Idéologues: Essai sur l'histoire des idées et des théories scientifiques, philosophiques, religieuses etc., en France depuis 1789*. Paris, 1891.

Plamenatz, J. *Ideology*. London, 1970.

Plekhanov, G. V. *In Defence of Materialism: The Development of the Monist View of History*. 1895. Trans. A. Rothstein. London, 1947.

Popitz, H., Bahrdt, H. P., Jüres, E. A. and Kesting, H. *Das Gesellschaftsbild des Arbeiters, soziologische Untersuchungen in der Hüttenindustrie*. Tübingen, 1947.

Popper, K. *The Poverty of Historicism*. London, 1957.

Reyman, K. and Singer, H. 'The Origin and Significance of East European Revisionism', in Labedz (ed.) *Revisionism*.

Rickert, H. *Die Grenzen der naturwissenschaftlichen Begriffsbildung*. Freiburg and Leipzig, 1896. 4th edn. Tübingen, 1921.

Rokeach, M. *The Open and the Closed Mind – Investigations into the Nature of Belief Systems and Personality Systems*. New York, 1960.

Rosenthal, E. I. J. *Political Thought in Medieval Islam*. Cambridge, 1958.

Rotenstreich, N. *Basic Problems of Marx's Philosophy*. Indianapolis, New York and Kansas City, 1965.

Roth, G. 'Critique and Adaptation', in R. Bendix and G. Roth, *Scholarship and Partisanship: Essays on Max Weber*. Berkeley, Los Angeles and London, 1971.

Rousseau, J.-J. *Du contrat social*, in *Oeuvres choisies*. Classiques Garnier. Paris, 1954.

Runciman, W. G. *Social Science and Political Theory*. Cambridge, 1963.

Schmoller, G. *Die soziale Frage: Klassenbildung, Arbeiterfrage, Klassenkampf*. München and Leipzig, 1918.

Schurmann, F. *Ideology and Organization in Communist China*. Berkeley and Los Angeles, 1966.

Seliger, M. 'The Conception of History of the French Historians of the Restoration (1815–1830) in their Treatment of French History.' Unpubl. doctoral thesis (in Hebrew). The Hebrew University of Jerusalem, 1956.

Seliger, M. 'Napoleonic Authoritarianism in French Liberal Thought', in A. Fuks and I. Halpern (eds.) *Studies in History, Scripta Hierosolymitana*, vII (1961).

Seliger, M. *The Liberal Politics of John Locke*. London and New York, 1968–9.

Seliger, M. 'Herbert Marcuse's One-dimensionality – The Old Style of the New Left', in K. von Beyme (ed.) *Theory and Politics: Festschrift zum 70. Geburtstag für Carl Joachim Friedrich*. Haag, 1971.

Seliger, M. 'Locke and Marcuse – Intermittent and Millennial Revolutionism', *Festschrift für Karl Loewenstein*. Tübingen, 1971.

Seliger, M. *Ideology and Politics*. London and New York, 1976.

Sombart, W. *Der proletarische Sozialismus* ('Marxismus'). 10th enlarged edn. 2 vols. Jena, 1924.

Stadler, P. *Karl Marx, Ideologie und Politik*. Göttingen, Frankfurt and Zürich, 1966.

Staël, Mme de. *Considérations sur les principaux événements de la Révolution Française (1818)*. New edn. Paris, 1842.

Stark, W. *The Sociology of Knowledge*. London, 1958.

Sternhell, Z. *Maurice Barrès et le nationalisme français*. Paris, 1972.

Strauss, L. *Persecution and the Art of Writing*. New York, 1952.

Thierry, A. *Considérations sur l'histoire de France*. Paris, 1840.

Tillich, P. *Der Mensch im Christentum und im Marxismus*. Düsseldorf, 1953.

Topitsch, E. *Vom Ursprung und Ende der Metaphysik. Eine Studie zur Weltanschauungskritik*. Wien, 1958.

Topitsch, E. *Sozialphilosophie zwischen Ideologie und Wissenschaft*. 2nd edn. Neuwied, 1966.

Touchard, J. *et al*. (eds.) *Histoire des idées politiques*. 2 vols. Paris, 1959.

Toynbee, A. J. *A Study of History – Abridgment of Volumes* i–vi, by D. C. Somervell. New York and London, 1947.

Trotsky, L. D. *Whither England?* New York, 1925.

Tucker, R. C. *Philosophy and Myth in Karl Marx*. Cambridge, 1961.

Watnick, M. 'Relativism and Class Consciousness: Georg Lukács', in Labedz (ed.) *Revisionism*.

Weber, M. *Gesammelte Aufsätze zur Religionssoziologie*. Tübingen, 1922–3.

Weber, M. 'Die "Objektivität" sozialwissenschaftlicher und sozialpolitischer Erkenntnis', in *Gesammelte Aufsätze zur Wissenschaftslehre*. Tübingen, 1922.

Weber, M. 'Der Sozialismus – Rede zur allgemeinen Orientierung von österreichischen Offizieren in Wien (1918)', in *Gesammelte Aufsätze zur Soziologie und Sozialpolitik*. Tübingen, 1924.

Weber, M. *Wirtschaft und Gesellschaft*. 2nd enlarged edn. Half-vols. i, ii. Tübingen, 1925.

Weber, M. *Politik als Beruf*. 2nd edn. München and Leipzig, 1926.

Wetter, G. *Dialectical Materialism: A Historical and Systematic Survey of Philosophy in the Soviet Union*. Trans. P. Heath. London, 1958.

Wiatr, J. J. 'Sociology – Marxism – Reality', *Social Research*, xxiv, 3 (1967).

INDEX